JAPAN'S FINANCIAL CRISIS AND ITS PARALLELS TO U.S. EXPERIENCE

RYOICHI MIKITANI
ADAM S. POSEN
EDITORS

JAPAN'S FINANCIAL CRISIS AND ITS PARALLELS TO U.S. EXPERIENCE

INSTITUTE FOR INTERNATIONAL ECONOMICS
Washington, DC
September 2000

Ryoichi Mikitani is professor of economics at Kobe Gaikuin University, Japan, and author of several books in Japanese. His area of specialization is monetary economics. He was trained at Harvard University and is a frequent visitor to the United States. He is member of the Research Group of International Comparative Financial Studies at Kobe University. He is coauthor of *Japan's New Central Banking Law: A Critical Review* (published by The Center on Japanese Economy and Business at Columbia University). He coedited *Monetary Policy and Financial Liberalization* (1993).

Adam S. Posen, senior fellow, is the author of the book *Restoring Japan's Economic Growth* (IIE, 1998; Japanese translation, Toyo Keizai, 1999), and a member of the Council on Foreign Relations Task Force on Japan. A monetary economist, he was on the research staff of the Federal Reserve Bank of New York (1994-97), and is the author of several publications on comparative monetary policymaking, inflation targeting, and central bank independence.

INSTITUTE FOR INTERNATIONAL ECONOMICS
11 Dupont Circle, NW
Washington, DC 20036-1207
(202) 328-9000 FAX: (202) 328-5432
http://www.iie.com

Typesetting by Automated Graphic Systems

Library of Congress Cataloging-in-Publication Data

Japan's financial crisis and it's parallels to US experience / Ryoichi Mikitani, Adam S. Posen, editors
p. cm.
Includes bibliographical references and index.
1. Monetary policy—Japan. 2. Financial crises—Japan. 3. Banks and banking—Japan. 4. Monetary policy—United States. 5. Financial crises—United States. 6. Banks and banking—United States. I. Mikitani, Ryoichi, 1992- II. Posen, Adam Simon. III. Institute for International Economics (U.S.)
HG1275.J385 2000
332'.0952—dc21 00-063287

ISBN 0-88132-289-X

Contents

Preface

The growth rates of the world's three major economies—the European Union, Japan, and the United States—are key determinants of the global economic outlook and the international policy agenda. Equally important is how these economies use economic policy to respond to common challenges. The performance and interaction of these economies and their policies have therefore been an ongoing focus of the research agenda of the Institute for International Economics. C. Fred Bergsten and William R. Cline's *The United States-Japan Economic Problem* (1985), Bela Balassa and Marcus Noland's *Japan in the World Economy* (1988), Bergsten and Noland's *Reconcilable Differences? US-Japan Economic Conflict* (1993), C. Randall Henning's *Currencies and Politics in the United States, Germany, and Japan* (1994) and Adam Posen's *Restoring Japan's Economic Growth* (1998) have all explored aspects of Japanese economic performance and its influence on—and lessons for—economic policy in the United States and other countries.

This *Special Report*, edited by Senior Fellow Adam Posen and Professor Ryoichi Mikitani of Kobe Gaikuin University in Japan, analyzes the causes and impact of the Japanese financial crisis of the last 10 years and compares it with the financial crisis in the United States from the mid-1980s to the early 1990s. Beyond assessing the prospects for Japan's recovery from its current straits, and the financial and monetary policy steps necessary to bring about that recovery, the authors also consider what lessons might be drawn to prevent and, failing that, to resolve such financial crises in the future.

By building bridges, both across the Pacific and from academia to policy, the editors have found a surprising degree of consensus among analysts of the American and Japanese financial crises. On the financial side, strong similarities emerge between the Japanese banking crisis of the 1990s and the American savings and loan crisis of the 1980s—both in source (mismanaged partial deregulation combined with too much regulatory forbearance) and in required means to resolution (injection of public funds, losses to shareholders, and liquidation of bad assets). On the monetary side, there is a common belief that the Bank of Japan has diverged from the norms of central banking best practice by allowing deflation to persist for so long.

There are some differences among the authors over tactics but all agree that the policy agenda for a recovering Japan should include promotion of a much smaller and more competitive banking sector, and a much more expansionary monetary policy. The authors also debate whether central banks should actively target asset price inflation and whether the well-known incentives for democratic politicians to delay responding to financial fragility can somehow be surmounted—issues which are of common concern to all of the major industrial economies. We hope these discussions will not only help move the Japanese financial crisis toward resolution but also improve policy in other countries before the next crisis.

The Institute for International Economics is a private nonprofit institution for the study and discussion of international economic policy. Its purpose is to analyze important issues in that area and develop and communicate practical new approaches for dealing with them. The Institute is completely nonpartisan.

The Institute is funded largely by philanthropic foundations. Major institutional grants are now being received from the William M. Keck, Jr. Foundation and the Starr Foundation. A number of other foundations and private corporations contribute to the highly diversified financial resources of the Institute. About 26 percent of the Institute's resources in our latest fiscal year were provided by contributors outside the United States, including about 11 percent from Japan.

Partial funding for this project was provided under our Akio Morita Studies Program, a program of studies in topics of central interest to the United States and Japan. The program was created in 1997 to honor our distinguished former director and honorary director, Akio Morita, the late cofounder and former CEO of Sony. The program is funded by the Sony Corporation, the New York Community Trust-The Peter G. Peterson Fund, and Mr. David Rockefeller.

The Board of Directors bears overall responsibility for the Institute and gives general guidance and approval to its research program—including the identification of topics that are likely to become important over the medium run (one to three years) and which should be addressed by the

Institute. The Director, working closely with the staff and outside Advisory Committee, is responsible for the development of particular projects and makes the final decision to publish an individual study.

The Institute hopes that its studies and other activities will contribute to building a stronger foundation for international economic policy around the world. We invite readers of these publications to let us know how they think we can best accomplish this objective.

C. Fred Bergsten
Director
September 2000

Acknowledgments

This volume grew out of a core of four papers presented at a panel on 9 January 2000 at the annual meeting of the American Economics Association. The panel was co-organized by Benjamin Friedman, who gathered the initial American participants, and Ryoichi Mikitani, who organized the Japanese counterparts. We are grateful to all participants, especially to those discussants who expanded their initial spoken remarks into standalone contributions to this volume. We are also grateful to Fred Bergsten, who made publication of this volume, with additional contributing authors, possible.

A special debt is owed to the publications team at the Institute for International Economics, headed by Brigitte Coulton, for their successful efforts to produce this transPacific multi-author work in a consistent and readable form. Adam Posen would particularly like to thank Production Coordinator Marla Banov and Copy Editor Alfred Imhoff for their contributions, without which this book would not have seen the light of day let alone lived up to its potential as a bridge between Japanese and American policy discussions. The authors of the individual chapters remain solely responsible for the opinions expressed and for any remaining errors in their respective contributions.

1

Introduction: Financial Similarities and Monetary Differences

Adam S. Posen

Japanese macroeconomic and financial policy in the past decade has failed to respond adequately to the largest financial crisis to occur in an industrial democracy in the past 60 years. The role of this inadequate policy response in deepening and lengthening Japan's stagnation since 1992—the costliest recession suffered by any advanced economy in the postwar period—has brought a wide consensus of frustration among economists internationally. Contrary to the popular picture of economists continually disagreeing with one another on macroeconomic issues, the analysis of financial crises (at least of those occurring in the industrial world) is an area where much agreement exists. Economists agree that such crises are the source of most of the costliest recorded interruptions in countries' economic growth, that they usually follow situations of partial deregulation and of asset price bubbles, that they require some combination of bank closures and public capital infusion to resolve, and that they both constrain and respond to monetary policy decisions.

None of this is to say that Japanese economic officials made unique mistakes—part of the reason for the consensus on just how bad financial crises are is that we have had so much experience with them. As Yoshinori Shimizu notes in his essay in this volume[1]: "The period 1980-96 witnessed widespread financial deregulation for many of the world's economies. As a result of this increasingly competitive environment, 133 out of 181

Adam S. Posen is a senior fellow at the Institute for International Economics.

1. In this introductory chapter, any quotations unaccompanied by a specific bibliographic citation are taken from the named author's contribution to this volume.

IMF member countries experienced significant banking-sector problems, which were often the worst seen since the Great Depression of the 1930s." This list of financial crisis victims besides Japan in just the past 15 years includes such other major economies as France, Sweden, the United Kingdom, and the United States.

As Benjamin Friedman reminds us in his essay: "A decade ago, it was US banks, and even more so the US savings and loan (S&L) industry, that were in crisis. These institutions too suffered major loan losses, experienced failure rates unprecedented since the depression of the 1930s (especially among S&Ls, but among banks as well), and saw the market capitalization of survivors fall to a small fraction of its precrisis level. Resolution of the crisis took significant government intervention, both in the provision of public funds to pay off the depositors of institutions that failed outright and in managing the process of consolidation among those that did not (at least not formally)."

There is even some fear that the shoe may be getting ready for a return to the US foot, given the huge run-up in US equity prices in the second half of the 1990s. In the words of Olivier Blanchard in his essay below, "How monetary policy should react to bubbles is clearly of more than historical interest. We now have one and a half experiments, the Japanese one, and the US one on the way up. What remains to be played out is the US one on the way down. It is an understatement that this may not be a bad time to assess the lessons from the Japanese full experiment."

This costly recurrence of financial crisis, despite hard-won knowledge, illustrates Alan Blinder's "Murphy's Law of economic policy": "Economists have the least influence on policy where they know the most and are most agreed; they have the most influence on policy where they know the least and disagree most vehemently."[2] In such a situation, it is all the more incumbent upon policy economists to understand the apparently overwhelming incentives for policymakers to act oppositely from the recommended course, and to redouble their efforts to communicate their recommendations in a form that will have influence. Rather than throwing up their hands in frustration as the incidents multiply, they need to show carefully and objectively that the mainstream analysis applies in the latest case as well, with the politically or ideologically driven policy missteps—and their economic costs—clearly delineated.

That is the uncynical intention and, we hope, useful purpose of this volume: to analyze the causes and impact of the Japanese financial crisis of the past 10 years; to put that crisis into perspective through comparison with the US financial crisis of the mid-1980s to the early 1990s; to assess the prospects for Japan's recovery from its current straits, and the financial and monetary policy steps necessary to bring about that recovery; to

2. Quoted in Paul Krugman, "Reckonings: A Rent Affair," *New York Times*, 7 June 2000, 31.

consider what lessons might be drawn to prevent and, failing that, resolve such financial crises in the future; and, finally, to identify for urgent consideration those remaining open policy issues of disagreement among economists raised by the experience of Japan in the past decade. The hope is both to have an influence on Japanese economic policy today, while so much remains to be done there, and also to reduce the likelihood and costliness of future financial crises elsewhere. Murphy's Law should not be taken for granted when so much is at stake.

In this pursuit, we have brought together leading Japanese and US economists, some with experience at the most senior policymaking levels, to discuss the Japanese financial crisis of the past decade. Although the degree of consensus among the contributing authors should not be exaggerated—for example, the desirability of central banks targeting asset prices to prevent bubbles (and perhaps thereby preempt crises) splits those writing here, pro and con—there is substantial agreement among the assembled analyses. On the financial side, there emerges a sense of extreme similarities between the Japanese banking crisis of the 1990s, and the US S&L crisis of the 1980s, both in source (mismanaged partial deregulation combined with too much regulatory forbearance) and in required means of resolution (injection of public funds, losses to shareholders, and liquidation of bad assets).

On the monetary side, there is a common belief that the Bank of Japan (BOJ) has diverged from the norms of central banking best practice, increasingly so since the Japanese economy fell back into recession in 1997, with a passive-aggressive acceptance of deflation. Although there are some differences over tactics, the authors here from both sides of the Pacific agree that a still recovering Japan requires a much smaller, more competitive, banking sector, along with a much more expansionary monetary policy, and that both are feasible goals. All these recommendations rest on more general lessons drawn about the nature of financial crises and the possibilities for monetary policy that make up the bulk of this volume.

The need for continued efforts in the financial and monetary arenas does not indicate that Japan remains in as precarious a position as it was in when its financial crisis was at its peak in 1997-98. At that time, especially between November 1997, when Yamaichi Securities and Hokkaido Takushoku Bank were closed, and October 1998, when the bank recapitalization legislation passed the Diet, Japan teetered on the brink of outright financial collapse.[3] Japanese savers were holding their money increasingly in cash or in postal savings accounts, and withdrawing funds from the private banking system; foreign banks were increasingly reluctant to engage in even overnight lending to Japanese banks, threatening basic liquidity in the payments system; cascading declines in land prices, stock

3. Posen (1998, chap. 4) gives an overview of the situation as of July 1998 before the reforms.

prices, and the yen were eroding banks' capital, inducing a spiral of debt deflation. The Bank of Japan was resorting to extreme purchases of corporate debt (at times, 50 percent of the commercial paper issued) just to keep the payments system going.

From September 1998 on, in a series of reversals of established Japanese government practices, fiscal policy became meaningfully expansionary, financial supervision was tightened, a pair of major failed banks were nationalized, and dispersion in performance among Japanese corporations (including the number of bankruptcies) was allowed to increase. A return to weakly positive economic growth has resulted, with continued expansion forecast for 2000-02; this has confounded many skeptics (including some Japanese government officials), who were convinced that Japan was on a trend toward permanent decline. At least as important, there has been some reintermediation in the Japanese banking system, with the "Japan premium" disappearing for the remaining number of banks active in international interbank markets, and the ratio of currency to deposits declining.

This partial and pragmatic program has put a floor under Japan's economic outlook, barring overt reversals in the stance of policy or in the enforcement of what financial reform has already been mandated. But the trend of Japanese economic growth remains well below potential output, with a cumulative output gap in excess of 12 percent of GDP, and financial reconstruction, let alone broader structural reform, remains far from complete. So the end of panic should not be a cause for satisfaction. The absence of an overt crisis does, however, provide the opportunity for reflection on how close Japan came to the brink, and what we can learn from this experience.

Financial Similarities

Despite the vast problems that remain, no area of Japanese economic life has undergone as radical a change as that of the financial system in the past 15 years. It is the mismanagement of this transformation that gave rise to financial fragility throughout the Japanese banking sector, and it is the delay in completing the transformation that has increased the cost of the financial crisis severalfold. The "Main Bank" system in Japan of cross-shareholdings and heavy corporate dependence upon bank loans for finance has been much studied and, although occasionally exaggerated in description, formed one of the central components of the Japanese economic framework before 1986.

The Ministry of Finance's postwar "convoy system" approach to bank supervision—allowing no banks to fail, having the large banks not only assist each other in time of need but rise and fall together, and keeping up heavy barriers to entry into corporate finance—reinforced the long-term lending relationships between the banks and corporations. Complementing the lending side of the banking system lay the savings side, where Japanese households kept the majority of their assets in low-yielding bank accounts that were perceived as riskless and that provided a pool of cheaply available, loanable funds. All the risk-averse constituents of Japanese economic life (e.g., bank managers, government bank supervisors, small savers, company salarymen from firms in *keiretsu* relationships) believed themselves to have an interest in the system.

Yet for all its embeddedness in a distinctive web of functional relationships, the breakdown of the Japanese Main Bank system, and the ensuing financial crisis, followed a sequence familiar to observers not only of the US S&L troubles but also of the French Crédit Lyonnais bailout, the Swedish banking crisis, and the UK property bubble, as well as others. This sequence fits very well with standard economic models of banks' and regulators' incentives, given modern theories of the imperfect information under which they both work. Without the existence of imperfect (i.e., costly to acquire and impossible to perfectly verify) information about corporate investment projects, there is no reason for banks to exist—all financing could be done in arm's-length securities transactions. Without the existence of imperfect information about bank balance sheets, there is no reason for deposit insurance or for regulatory supervision of deposit-taking institutions to prevent bank runs and payment system difficulties.

The standard path to financial crisis begins, unsurprisingly, with banks having grown in size, number, and complacency due to their initially protected status. As financial technology improves and deregulation starts, banking finds itself in a long-term sectoral decline as an industry, being squeezed by more efficient ways for corporations to raise funds and by demands for higher interest rates from savers who, at the margin, look for alternative investments. To make up for their declining margins on and quantity of loans to low-risk large corporations, banks begin lending to lower-quality borrowers and have to rely more heavily on collateral, including real estate. Partial deregulation limits the choices of new businesses into which banks can go, but a continued deposit insurance safety net encourages risk-taking behavior with readily available funds.

Given the years of protection from market discipline, most bank balance sheets remain beset by lax accounting practices and undercapitalization, even as the riskiness of their loan portfolios increases. When the rate of economic growth slows, and the prices of land and other assets decline, the banks suffer loan losses, and are forced to make these up by calling in other loans and (when enough losses accumulate) out of their capital. The contractionary process is frequently, though not inevitably, touched off by the collapse of an asset price bubble. When there has been a bubble, generally the volume of loans on banks' books, and the proportion of those loans likely to fail, is all the higher.

This begins a cycle of credit contraction and bank balance sheet erosion, and once this cycle starts, the size of the bad loan problem is likely to expand for some time. Any banks that for these reasons fall below the regulated capital standards, or worse below zero equity, have the incentive to "gamble on resurrection," that is, to roll over nonperforming loans or make additional risky loans in hopes of getting high enough returns to come back to solvency, because they have nothing more to lose. Because the majority of loans are backed by land as collateral, the accumulation of nonperforming loans also has a feedback effect on the quality of other borrowers' collateral through causing declines in real estate prices.

In combination with the usual effect on business failures of a recession, this decline in the value of borrowers' collateral increases the total number of nonperforming loans, further eroding banks' portfolios. It also increases the adverse selection of borrowers by banks, shifting their portfolios toward a worse balance of risk-return overall: Banks cut back new lending to low-risk, low-return projects because of the absence of potentially capital-rebuilding large gains there, but they continue to extend or roll over credit to outstanding questionable borrowers to put off, if not avoid, writing down the value of the loan losses.[4] Although banks hope that by waiting for greater economic growth they will see some of their nonperforming loans return to profitability, the banks actually work against macroeconomic recovery with their inefficient lending behavior, their accumulation of nonperforming loans, and their contribution to uncertainty in asset—particularly real estate—markets.

This is exactly what happened in Japan after deregulation. According to Ryoichi Mikitani in his essay below, "Toward the end of the 1970s, the Japanese economy caught up with the Western industrial countries. It was time to alter the economic regime from the old to the new one: from indicative industrial policy administered by the government to the guidance of the free market; from a bank-securities sector heavily regulated by the Ministry of Finance to a less regulated, more competitive, globally standardized financial sector; from Japanese corporatism to transparent management of corporations. . . . However, neither the financial institutions nor the big corporations were willing to take off their protective heavy coat and to work with their sleeves rolled up." Instead, Japanese banks repeated their old lending practices with their new customers, and they refused to shrink the industry even as demand for their services declined, given the vast body of deposits left in their hands by Japanese

---

4. Although some observers have made a major point of the distinctiveness of the Japanese Main Bank system in its having banks work out temporary liquidity problems for borrowers in relationships with the bank, the phenomenon of banks rolling over credits when under duress to avoid taking write-downs of bad loans is universal.

savers. Although it took time for the effects of increased competition to be felt, it was inevitable.

Shimizu demonstrates in his essay that increasing financial competition in Japan led to declining loan portfolio quality through exactly the channels predicted by the standard scenario. "The higher the initial share of large firms in [banks'] loan portfolios, the larger the shift of their lending patterns. The long-term-credit banks were forced to make the most drastic adjustments, given continued regulatory restrictions against banks entering the security busines. . .they clearly recognized the lower creditworthiness of these [newer, smaller] customers. In order to reduce their credit risks, banks made loans secured by real estate." This shift was seen in the United States following deregulation as well, and in both countries led to persistent biases in lending—Friedman notes that "in both Japan and the United States, lending on real estate rose sharply as a share of banks' credit creation in the years preceding the crisis—and, interestingly, continued to rise as the crisis unfolded. . . . The share of bank credit *indirectly* resting on real estate collateral was far greater."

When interest rates rose in Japan, the bubble burst, and growth slowed in 1990-92, the cycle of increasing financial fragility kicked in. Shimizu shows that "in the 1990s, risks in the Japanese economy markedly increased, and the banks' large share of the corporate loan market turned into a disadvantage. As stronger corporate borrowers turned to the bond market, banks were forced to make loans to less credible borrowers, and collateral was again an important criterion for loan approval. Naturally the drastic fall in land prices had an extremely serious effect on the stability of the financial system."

Land prices have fallen essentially continuously in Japan since that time, to one-third their peak value, and banks have been reluctant to liquidate the land collateral underlying the accumulating bad loans. There is evidence (some offered by Shimizu) that Japanese banks reduced their total lending as a result, prompting a credit crunch that exacerbated the recession.

What about the role of financial policy? In the standard financial crisis scenario, as noted, the grounds for crisis are laid with protection of the banking system from competition (e.g., Japan's convoy regulations), followed by partial gradual deregulation. Turning to policy response, banking supervisors allow a credit boom for lower-quality borrowers to occur in hopes of restoring bank profitability when the large, good borrowers go directly to capital markets. Of course, this just adds to the potential trouble on bank balance sheets when things go south. Regulators observe the bad loans, but keep quiet due to the banks' implicit or explicit offers of direct benefits and future employment, as well as bureaucratic disincentives to delivering bad news, and simple lack of experience with accurately evaluating risky loan portfolios.

When the bust comes, supervisors engage in forbearance, meaning that they allow banks time to carry nonperforming loans rather than demanding write-downs. This forbearance arises from the hope that a return to economic growth will come, and on its own will resolve many bad loan problems, without forcing the supervisors to blow the whistle. Having regulators from multiple competing agencies[5] adds to the incentive for forbearance, because there is the additional motivation of hoping the bad news happens on somebody else's watch, or at least that one's own agency should not be the first to admit to allowing problems to have accumulated. The interaction of moral hazard on the part of banks and regulatory forbearance on the part of supervisors is what causes the spiraling accumulation of bad loans.

This was the story in the United States in the 1980s. Friedman reminds us that "both the US government in general and the specific authorities responsible for dealing with the banking and S&L crisis acted, in some key respects, in ways that worsened the situation, and increased its ultimate cost to the economy and to the public treasury. The lessons to be drawn from that experience stem in part from observing what to do but also from what not to do." And despite this cautionary example, this was also the story in Japan in the 1990s. Bank regulators issued a litany of announcements meant to be reassuring about the extent of the bad loan problem and the adequacy of Japanese banks' capital, each of which was correctly disbelieved by other financial firms, foreign banks, and by Japanese savers as understating the problem. Each Pollyannish announcement by regulators, however, also meant another period of forbearance, during which not only were bad loans kept on the Japanese banks' books, but more bad loans and distressed real estate collateral were allowed to accumulate.

Nevertheless, the Japanese financial situation in the 1990s had at least five unique aspects. First is the issue of sheer size. The length of time during which the banks were allowed to remain undercapitalized and to accumulate bad loans, and the extent of the bad loans accumulated, were unprecedented for an industrial country. Conservative estimates put the total bad loans requiring write-downs at 9-10 percent of GDP; the high reasonable estimates are at 15 percent. For comparison, the United States S&L crisis cost the US taxpayer on the order of 3 percent of GDP. Second, the macroeconomic effects on the rest of the Japanese economy caused

---

5. In Japan, though all supervisors were under the Ministry of Finance, some were based out of the Bank of Japan, whereas others were part of the ministry's financial supervision arm proper, and there was bureaucratic competition. In the United States, the multitude of competing regulators—e.g., the Federal Reserve, the Comptroller of the Currency, the Federal Deposit Insurance Corporation, the Federal Savings and Loan Insurance Corporation, and various state agencies—contributed greatly to the problems of acknowledging and then responding to the S&L crisis and the ensuing banking problems.

by any given amount of bad loans were much greater than in most other countries that belong to the Organization for Economic Cooperation and Development (OECD). This higher impact was due to the higher relative dependence of Japanese businesses on bank lending than on alternative corporate finance sources, to the widespread use of land at inflated prices as loan collateral because of the enormous bubble that preceded the crisis, and to the holdings of nonfinancial corporate shares by banks as part of their capital (putting an additional negative feedback loop on lending). The more heavily securitized US financial system, without nonfinancial shareholdings by banks, had much smaller feedback effects from bank problems on growth.

The third difference between the Japanese and US financial crises, given the opacity of Japanese accounting and property markets, was the lack of dependable information on banks' foreclosed collateral. This impeded the identification and selling off of distressed assets, a critical step in any financial cleanup. As Robert Glauber notes in his essay, US accounting was hardly stellar itself in many of the S&Ls and their borrowers, but the US real estate market was far more liquid than Japan's. Fourth, the vestiges of belief in the convoy system, and the ability of Japanese savers to switch into government-guaranteed postal savings rather than demand change, further diminished official willingness to confront the issue. In contrast, in the United States, the winds of elected officials and even popular opinion in the 1980s were blowing in the direction of greater deregulation and greater risk taking by average US savers, so the political support for closing down the S&Ls was easier to assemble once the problem became clear (see Friedman's discussion).

Fifth, Japanese banks and bank regulators—more than those in any other OECD economy that faced a financial crisis—through much of the 1990s had an absence of macroeconomic assistance. The Japanese economy did not sustainably recover, and neither fiscal (up until 1998) nor monetary (throughout the decade) policy was of much help.[6] Even if regulatory forbearance on the bank-by-bank level is mistaken, growth of the economy as a whole is an aid to resolving financial crises. As Mikitani points out, "If this structural policy [of tightening supervision and closing banks] has a depressive or a stimulative effect on the economy, it must be accompanied by the appropriate macroeconomic policy to offset this effect." Whether and how best Japanese monetary policy can respond to this challenge is discussed in the second half of this book.

Most of these differences, however, imply no distinctions between the right course of financial policy to pursue in Japan, the United States, or elsewhere. They simply highlight what we know, that both the economic

---

6. Posen (1998) examines the fiscal and monetary policy failures in Japan up through mid-1998; the essays in this volume by Bernanke; Jinushi, Kuroki,and Miyao; and Posen detail the unresponsiveness of the Bank of Japan to slowing growth.

costs of inaction and the political opposition to action were higher in Japan's financial crisis. In fact, these two outcomes were interrelated. Friedman writes: "The message from this experience is that delaying action—in the hope that either a change in the economic environment or some independent development may turn matters around, or perhaps merely out of an inability to overcome political or administrative obstacles even after everyone recognizes what needs to be done—is a policy with a price." And this is likely only a difference in degree—Glauber believes that "in both countries, there is little doubt that the government's timidity in informing taxpayers of the full cost to resolve the crisis produced a large, unnecessary delay. The delay in both cases turned a relatively small cost into a staggeringly large one. Dealing with these crises takes political leadership, a quality often not in large supply."

It is the matter of what Japanese policy should do about falling land prices, and the illiquid market for distressed real estate assets, that splits this volume's contributors. Shimizu argues in his essay that, given the sheer size of the Japanese land price and collateral problem in the past decade (which he documents)—both in terms of the relative decline in land prices and the overwhelming share of financial commitments backed by land—it was understandable for financial authorities to be reluctant to engage in some interventions and force loan foreclosures. There simply is too much distressed real estate to allow for securitization and selling off. Moreover, trying to resolve the problem all at once might provoke a further free fall in the real estate market, if not a renewed crisis of financial confidence in Japan. While holding supervisors and the convoy scheme accountable for putting the Japanese financial system in this situation, Shimizu sees no clear path or policy option to resolution so long as land prices are depressed.

Glauber responds that "loans and mortgages on the balance sheets at US S&Ls were under water as well, and any sale through securitization or other means required recognizing losses" in the United States, just as it would in Japan. For the individual banks and their incentives, the situation is the same. More important, Friedman and Glauber agree, the dynamics of real estate markets relevant for policy are the same as well, and mandate rapid sales. Friedman notes that "it is easy to overstate concerns about the effect on real estate values due to sales of assumed loan collateral. . .[but] the medium- to longer-run effect of eliminating the overhang of real estate held for sale was often beneficial. Everybody knows this collateral will have to be sold sooner or later. Actually putting it on the block clears the air rather than spoiling the market." Glauber argues that holding off on liquidation actually makes things worse: "Markets do not recover when there is a large inventory overhanging them, waiting for sale."

Those Japanese banks that themselves remain under water after the sale of their collateral and the writing off of their bad loans must be closed. This is not merely a matter of policy to prevent the accumulation of more bad debt driven by moral hazard, and the wasting of public money (directly through squandered capital injections or indirectly through deposit insurance obligations). The long-term pressures on banking systems that began the move toward deregulation and the loss of high-quality corporate borrowers, and therefore that underlay the Japanese financial crisis, remain. "Even aside from the credit problems that reached the level of crisis, the banking industries in both the United States and Japan have for some time faced the need to downsize and restructure, but in neither country is the road to renewed profitability clear," notes Friedman. In his essay, Anil Kashyap "suggest[s] that any policy proposal to address the continuing problems of the banks first be evaluated by checking whether it is consistent with the view that the Japanese banking sector needs to shrink." Both Mikitani and Glauber discuss the positive but still shaky trend toward consolidation through mergers in the Japanese banking sector.

It must be acknowledged that Japanese financial policy changed significantly with the passage of legislation by the Obuchi government in October 1998,[7] although it has by no means resolved the financial problem. The legislation made available significant public funds for capital injections into viable banks (thereby reducing the extent of the moral hazard problem in lending), set out strict conditionality for the terms on which the banks could apply for this public capital (thereby removing the moral hazard problem in capital injections), and created a mechanism for nationalizing failed banks. This was implemented by the Financial Reconstruction Commission (FRC) founded in June 1998, which oversaw the new Financial Supervisory Agency (FSA) that had been split off from the Ministry of Finance. Japan has been very lucky in recent years to have, on the part of the bank supervisors who had left the ministry, a surprisingly strong spirit of zeal and commitment, as well as independence.

The Obuchi government's legislation gave the FRC and FSA real teeth with which to threaten the major banks. Not only were totally new intensive audits required before capital injections, but the banks had to give the FRC significant amounts of preferred shares in return for the capital. Under the terms of the agreements negotiated bank by bank, there was a sliding scale of when the preferred shares became options to convert into voting shares—for weaker banks asking for more capital, the share conversion became available earlier. If the bank's capital ratio fell below the mandated level (4 percent for domestic banks, and 8 percent for major banks engaging in international transactions) after the option date, the FRC could vote out management or even take over the bank. Meanwhile,

7. Eisuke Sakakibara's essay discusses this legislation as the culmination of a long process, notably influenced by the demands of the US government for conditionality in the injection of public funds.

if the banks chose not to take the public capital injections, they would be subject to nationalization anyway when their capital eroded (and all Japanese banks had weakened capital at this point). In all, by 1 April 1999, ¥7.5 trillion in new capital had been injected into all but one of the top 15 banks and all the important regional banks.[8]

As far as the new legislation was applied, the turnaround was extremely stark. Between October 1998 and April 1999, the Japan premium in interbank lending disappeared, savers shifted some deposits back into (selected) private banks and out of postal savings and cash at the margin, and the Japanese stock market rewarded bank stocks differentially. The FRC's nationalization of Long-Term Credit Bank on 23 October 1998 and (in a much quicker preemptive manner) of Nippon Credit Bank on 14 December 1998 clearly demonstrated that the law would be enforced. Savers, other banks, and purchasers of Japanese bank stocks (which had been rising steadily in the preceding year) all voted with their cash allocations that they found the cleanup credible as far as it went.

What is most important for our understanding, however, is that this partial financial cleanup provided the perfect natural experiment to verify that the dynamics of the Japanese financial crisis are indeed the same as those of its predecessor in the United States and in the standard sequence given above. For the large banks and their customers affected by the legislation, the policy-induced shift was right along the lines of an economic textbook—what had been an inefficient pooling equilibrium, wherein no banks could be distinguished from one another due to the convoy system and lack of transparency, was replaced by a more efficient sorting equilibrium, wherein the banks that could make themselves credibly solvent were rewarded by savers and markets rather than dragged down by the risks of their insolvent competitors.

The injection of new capital changed the incentives of the banks to stop rolling over bad loans or gambling on additional risky projects, as seen, for example, in the new policies of Shinsei Bank (formerly LTCB) toward Sogo's bankruptcy. Although this removal of moral hazard may have contributed to a minor credit crunch as banks with some equity newly at stake sought to rebuild their balance sheets, this was a necessary step, and the credit crunch was itself an indication that the policy was having the intended effect.

For comparison, those smaller, regional Japanese banks, on which the strictly conditional capital injections were not imposed, have continued largely with their business as before, including the rollover of nonper-

8. Five of what had been the top 20 banks had been forced by the FRC to move down a tier and out of the international markets. The politically sensitive smaller regional banks, with their loan portfolios to small and medium enterprises, have so far been spared such forced audits and conditional injections, despite their far worse condition than that of many of the major Japanese banks.

forming loans and the retention rather than sale of collateral. They also have not shown the same tendency toward mergers that the large banks have. Again, even the biggest recapitalized banks in Japan are not yet models of market efficiency, and the consolidation meant to result from their announced mergers remains to be seen—the October 1998 legislation has only dealt with a part of the Japanese financial problem. But the response to that legislation illustrates just how well economics does understand what needs to be done, even in Japan.

Monetary Differences

Developments in Japanese monetary policy in the past decade have displayed increasing divergence from Group of Seven (G-7) norms. As this book goes to press, deflation has been allowed to continue for more than 3 years of nearly monthly price declines on all major indices, and uncertainty about the justifications for the Bank of Japan monetary policy has mounted. Only three other OECD economies have experienced any deflation since the Depression, and in all three the central banks acted to reverse deflationary trends within a few months.

The BOJ has also resolutely refused to compensate, through looser monetary policy, for any contractionary effects of structural change, and has at times indicated that it wishes to tighten conditions despite the lack of sustained recovery.[9] In fact, on 10 August 2000, despite overt government opposition and widespread financial skepticism, the BOJ raised its overnight interest rate from zero to 0.25 percent, its first interest rate increase in 10 years. This increase ended the BOJ's "Zero-Interest-Rate Policy" (ZIRP), which had been in place since February 1999. Any one interest rate movement in a time of economic hardship, such as that in today's Japan, hardly ends the policy debate—in this instance, it only underlined the differences of opinion between BOJ insiders and the majority of outside monetary economists.

Monetary policymaking is never easy, and central banks' decisions are always subject to a wide range of conflicting opinions. The existence of even widespread criticism of a central bank does not necessarily indicate that the criticism is justified. Moreover, at times history has vindicated the central banks that pursued strategies that differed from those prevalent at the time among their brethren—certainly, the Bundesbank and the Swiss National Bank earned a great deal of credibility for maintaining relative price stability in the face of the 1970s oil shocks at equal or lower real cost than the at first overaccommodating, later disinflating central banks in the rest of the industrial economies.

9. Jinushi, Kuroki, and Miyao's and Posen's essays below document BOJ officials' own explanations of the Bank's strategies.

There are also times when the criticism of central banks is flying, both contemporaneously and retrospectively, but no consensus on the right monetary policy exists, even among thoughtful observers. Such an instance is the Bank of Japan's handling of the Japanese stock market and real estate bubbles of the 1980s. Some argue that the BOJ was too loose with policy for too long after the 1987 Louvre Accord, contributing to or even causing the bubble, whereas others argue that the BOJ was too tough in trying to "prick" the bubble, and that central banks only cause harm by attempting to do so (both camps are represented in the essays that follow in this volume).

This argument has echoes in the present US monetary policy situation, in which some believe that the Federal Reserve has been too threatening, if not too tight, toward stock market developments, while others believe that Chairman Alan Greenspan dropped the ball by speaking about "irrational exuberance" in December 1996 but not following up with a significantly tighter monetary policy—all this dispute in a context where the current central bank leadership is revered, and where economic growth and price stability have gone hand in hand for nearly a decade.

It is precisely because of the difficulty of monetary policymaking that practical analysis of difficult situations is necessary. And no situation in the past 15 years has appeared to be more difficult for a central bank and therefore more worthy of study than that of Japan. First, in the late 1980s, there was the rise of the asset price bubbles, unaccompanied by any signs of broader price inflation in the Japanese economy—a dilemma for any central bank, and one that repeats itself in the United States of the late 1990s. Following the stock and land market collapses, there came the challenge of recognizing and responding to debt deflation amid all the confusing signals given by a financial system undergoing deregulation and numerous distortions from efficiency (as discussed in the preceding section).

When the financial crisis became overt by 1997, and Japan's banking system was critically weakened, the specter was raised of a "liquidity trap" in Japan wherein expansionary monetary policy would be ineffectively "pushing on a string."[10] And throughout this period, Japanese economic policy was subject to pressure from the US government, sometimes directly affecting monetary policy in the form of either specific policy demands or movements in the yen-dollar exchange rate. But just as the existence of criticism does not always indicate that it is justified, by the same token, the appearance of challenging conditions does not necessarily imply that the choice of correct policy response is difficult. Even some of the apparent challenges might themselves be the result of, rather than a constraint upon, monetary policy decisions).

---

10. Most notably, see Krugman (1999)—although it should be noted the Krugman argued that a sufficiently expansionary monetary policy would have a real effect on the Japanese economy.

The second half of this volume is dedicated to such a study of the difficulties that have confronted the BOJ since the start of the bubble; the potential policy responses to them, both taken and ignored; and the motivations—economic, international, and political—for the strategies pursued. Underlying all these analyses is an implicit benchmark set by the Federal Reserve, which during this same period has been widely thought to have conducted an excellent monetary policy that contributed to the surprisingly strong peformance of the US economy in the 1990s. A critical question is how much the Bank of Japan simply faced far more difficult problems than the Fed due to the Japanese economic situation, and therefore had to pursue a different path—rather than the Bank itself deepening or even causing the problems through its choice of policies.

In this context, it is first worth recognizing that when the Japanese economy was growing strongly in the 1970s and 1980s, the Bank of Japan purused a monetary strategy much like that of the best central banks in the major economies. It is true that, until April 1998, the Bank of Japan was under the direction of the Ministry of Finance, rather than having independence like the Fed or the Bundesbank. Contrary to most presumptions about the response of central banks to political control, however, from the mid-1970s to the end of the 1980s the Bank of Japan delivered far more effective price stability than its lack of legal independence would have predicted.[11]

In its mouthing of monetary targets without actually following them, its intermittent response to the dollar-yen exchange rate as necessary, and its gradualism in responding to price shocks, the Bank of Japan behaved in every way like the typical OECD central bank of the period, if not better.[12] As was already noted, the lack of a preemptive response to the asset price bubble that emerged at the end of that period may indeed, upon reflection, turn out to be mistaken. But if it was a mistake, it was one that could hardly be considered atypical of central banks, either then or today—in Japan in the late 1980s, there was neither meaningful domestic price inflation nor excessive output movements nor an overt banking crisis, which together constitute the proximate targets to which central banks usually react.[13] Meanwhile, all central banks, including the Federal Reserve under Greenspan, seem to be reluctant to aggressively deflate potential asset price overvaluations.

In the 1990s, however, the Bank did take a course that diverged from usual practice. It spent most of the decade denying itself a role in reflating

11. Walsh (1996) discusses the Bank of Japan's outlier status in performance before independence.

12. A useful history of Bank of Japan monetary policy documenting this interpretation is Cargill, Hutchison, and Ito (1997).

13. See Bernanke and Mishkin (1992) and Mishkin and Posen (1997).

the Japanese economy, first by claiming that the situation was not serious, then by suggesting that its series of interest rate cuts would be sufficient, and then by asserting that domestic banking problems and international pressures constrained policy from a more aggressive response. All this took place with the approval, if not under the direction, of the Ministry of Finance, without much in the way of public accountability. In April 1998, the Bank of Japan gained independence from direct government control of monetary policy, and a new Monetary Policy Board of mostly outsiders was appointed to serve with Governor Masaru Hayami. This institutional change took place as part of a backlash against the failures of both the Ministry of Finance and the Bank itself in the area of financial supervision.

As with all central banks gaining independence in the 1990s, the Bank's mandate was set to maintain price stability, and the decisions about when to move interest rates how much (and whether to engage in open-market operations) were shifted to the Bank's control.[14] In keeping with the current fashion among most central banks, the new arrangement was accompanied by increased transparency, which included formal commitments to promptly issue minutes of board meetings and public explanations accompanying interest rate changes. Unfortunately, the Bank of Japan has remained opaque in the most significant way, by failing to publicly specify either the medium-term goal of its policy or its intermediate target.

Thus, it is up to economic researchers to determine ex post what strategy actually guided the Bank of Japan's policymaking from the late 1980s to the present. In their essay for this volume, Toshiki Jinushi, Yoshihiro Kuroki, and Ryuzo Miyao estimate a "good policy rule" for the Bank of Japan, based on a Taylor rule fit to the BOJ's reaction function during the 1975-85 period. As with most previous research applying Taylor rules to other countries' monetary policies, a policy reaction function that takes both inflation and output into account (roughly equally) does a very good job of predicting interest rate movements for the BOJ.

Extending this rule through the end of 1998, Jinushi, Kuroki, and Miyao find that "there seem to be four major deviations [of the BOJ from the estimated good policy rule]: 1. The delay in policy restraint, 1987-88; 2. Insufficient policy restraint, 1990-91; 3. The delay in easing policy restraint, 1992 to early 1995; 4. The delay in easing policy restraint, 1997 to early 1998." In short, their analysis indicates that the BOJ was behind the curve in responding to the Japanese bubble, and has been too tight for most of the time since.

In keeping with most observers' assessments, the BOJ's initial deviation from the rule toward looseness in 1987-88 is ascribed to the Japanese

14. Exchange rate policy, including sterilized intervention, remained under the direction of the Ministry of Finance in consultation with the Bank, which also is typical of independent central banks (including the Federal Reserve).

government's commitment to expanding domestic demand as part of the Louvre Accord. Jinushi, Kuroki, and Miyao note that "the international coordination was reasonable in the sense that the attainment of economic prosperity should not involve sacrifices by other countries. However, we have to keep in mind that the policy coordination brought a change in the domestic policy stance." That change in policy stance, however justified, led to a diversion from what Jinushi, Kuroki, and Miyao see as a growing concern by the BOJ about the rising bubble—something that some might argue was mirrored in the Federal Reserve holding off on interest rate hikes in 1997-98 due to the Asian financial crisis.

What is interesting about Jinushi, Kuroki, and Miyao's evaluation is that they base it on their Taylor rule, which does not include an asset price value or inflation term along with regular consumer price index (CPI) inflation and the output gap. In other words, the BOJ was too loose in the late 1980s, even without taking stocks and land into account. This would be a happy result if it also meant the converse: that simply targeting inflation with sufficient responses to above-target inflation forecasts would be enough to prevent bubbles along the way.

Jinushi, Kuroki, and Miyao, and Blanchard, however, do think that the BOJ should have taken the Japanese asset price bubble directly into account. Blanchard shows in a simple model that targeting inflation without targeting the bubble "keeps output stable as the bubble grows. But it may imply a very unpleasant aftermath once the bubble has crashed: a lot of useless capital, serious collateral problems for firms, and thus a potentially low natural level of output for some time after the crash." This image is, of course, familiar to anyone who has seen the Japanese economy since its 1992 stock market crash. Assuming that a stock market bubble biases firms toward overinvestment, it may be worth even some sacrifice of growth through a tighter policy to prevent this kind of capital boom-bust cycle.

The problem is one of timing: A central bank should not prevent every run-up in stock prices, so it must allow the bubble to get under way before it can recognize one (it hopes) and then react. Blanchard states, "What is proposed [in his essay] is a policy designed, if not to prevent bubbles, at least to prevent them from becoming too big." But if the bubble is growing without transmitting price pressures to the rest of the economy, as was the case in Japan, and if the country is already at a low level of inflation, the real economic cost of pricking the bubble can be quite high, perhaps even in comparison with the aftermath of overcapacity. Given the long and uncertain lags between monetary policy decisions and their effect on the real economy, one can have the worst of both worlds: a bubble burst so late as to have a large negative impact, and a monetary contraction so late in affecting the real economy that it amplifies the harm done by the bubble. These concerns are part of the motivation for Ben Bernanke's belief, stated in his essay below, that a central bank that targets inflation but does not try to prick asset bubbles will on balance do better.

Conversely, if the bursting of a bubble once begun is inevitable, and if central banks ignoring asset price movements just allows the bubble to grow bigger, preemption may indeed save money. Blanchard states, "Admittedly, the choice facing the central bank [between ignoring the bubble or not] is not pleasant. But this is not the point. The point is that the right strategy is likely to be somewhere in between the two pure strategies, that is, to tighten money more in the presence of a bubble than is implied by inflation targeting [alone]."

Of course, this depends on the central bank having some idea of when a bubble is occurring. The ability of the Federal Reserve to ascertain that positive structural change was underlying US growth in the 1990s, and therefore that stocks were not dreadfully overvalued, may turn out to be remarkably prescient. But—given the endogeneity of the value of investments to the growth of the economy—one cannot yet be sure. Japan in the 1990s is a cautionary example of how investments whose high returns once seemed structural turned out to feed a cyclical downturn when the bubble burst. Blanchard is right to point out that "one natural objection at this point is that the central bank knows little about the 'natural P/E ratio.' The point is well taken, but it applies to at least two other components of the Taylor rule: How much does the central bank know about the natural interest rate, and about the natural level of output?" The Japanese experience alone does not settle this issue, especially because the central bank's and private estimates of Japan's potential output varied in line with stock market expectations.

In looking at the past decade, it rapidly becomes clear that the BOJ's policy stance has gone from too accommodative to insufficiently so. As Blanchard reminds us in his comments on Jinushi, Kuroki, and Miyao's essay, "The Phillips curve wisdom remains largely true in modern treatments of the determination of prices, wages, and output: If output is above its natural level, then we are likely to see inflation increase. If it is below, inflation is likely to decrease. As inflation is slowly decreasing today in Japan, this strongly suggests that output is below its natural level."[15] Despite this obvious indicator of deficient demand, discussed as well in the opening of Bernanke's essay below, Jinushi, Kuroki, and Miyao observe: "The problem [from 1992-95] was that the BOJ might have misjudged how serious the economic situation was, so that the pace of monetary loosening lagged events. Of course, the BOJ knew that the large amount of debt prevented the economy from recovering and that the

15. For a more detailed econometric assessment of Japan's growing output gap in the 1990s, see Posen (1998, chap. 1 and appendix).

economy was still in a severe condition. . . . However, as far as we can tell, the BOJ did not use the expression of 'deflationary gap' or 'debt-deflation' in the early 1990s. . .it therefore can be interpreted as a delay in judgment by the BOJ during that time."

It turns out, however, that the BOJ's tight money policy was not solely a matter of misjudgment of the situation, it was also a reflection of a shift in priorities. Using two different econometric methods, Jinushi, Kuroki, and Miyao establish that the weight the BOJ put on inflation goals relative to real output concerns rose significantly in both statistical and economic terms after 1987—and two other recent studies independently confirm this result.[16] This is a clear divergence from the relative balance between output and inflation goals, and the tendency to respond to whatever macroeconomic variable under the most stress at that time (which in Japan would have been real output), that characterizes most central bank behavior, including that of the BOJ before 1987.

There is strong economic justification behind the central bank consensus in practice that output goals should be taken into account, and that price stability should not be pursued too aggressively when the economy is already at low inflation. In a world of sticky nominal contracts, especially debt contracts, with resistance to price and wage cuts, sharp increases in interest rates near zero inflation have a depressing and destabilizing effect on the real economy. In macroeconomic terms, the Phillips curve becomes flatter as one approaches zero inflation, with a larger movement in real output required for a given change in inflation. A wealth of theoretical and econometric evidence supports the claim of Jinushi, Kuroki, and Miyao that "imposing a larger weight on inflation under a low and stable inflation environment implies that the central bank is simply content with the fact of low and stable inflation and does little to stabilize the real economy. Consequently, with [a flattening Phillips curve and a greater relative weight on inflation goals] combined, the business fluctuations could actually become unprecedentedly large, as we observed they did in the late 1980s and early 1990s [in Japan]." This is why most central banks in the industrial economies target an inflation rate of 2 percent or more, whether or not they announce that target, and why they expand in response to weakness in aggregate demand. This is why I maintain in my essay for this volume that "the BOJ's policy was not neutral or at its limit [with its rate cuts in the 1990s], and the Japanese economy was not going its own bad way, despite monetary efforts. In fact, . . . the deflation and real volatility [seen] were exactly what any monetary economist would have predicted to be the result of pursuing tight monetary policy at zero or negative inflation in an advanced economy."

16. See Bernanke and Gertler (2000) and Kuttner and Posen (2000), who also identify a structural break in the BOJ's reaction function, toward the more counterinflationary, in 1987.

Leaving aside the question of how it got there, once the independent BOJ found itself in 1998 facing a deflationary situation, with a fragile banking system, and little room (after February 1999, no room) to cut the nominal interest rates under its control, what could be done? In a widely cited working paper (strongly promoted by the BOJ), Okina (1999) argued that once interest rates had been cut to zero, there was nothing else the BOJ could do to stimulate the economy. Money creation would be ineffective because banks (rebuilding their balance sheets by holding onto Japanese Government Bonds, or JGBs) would be unwilling to lend, and announcement of an inflation target would be ineffective if not further destabilizing because it could not credibly be attained. Governor Hayami and other senior BOJ officials made this argument in public with their reaffirmation that the ZIRP was not only as far as they could go but actually was an expansionary monetary policy. This BOJ stance was at odds with the norms of central banks, as seen not only in the types of estimations of policy reaction functions done by Jinushi, Kuroki, and Miyao, but in the criticism leveled at the BOJ by economists in other central banks. For the most part, this criticism came in veiled academic form, in a circuit of conferences about the conduct of monetary policy in a low-inflation environment, and about the possibility and implications of a liquidity trap, held at various central banks and research institutions during 1999.

As Bernanke argues in his essay, "Contrary to the claims of at least some Japanese central bankers, monetary policy is far from impotent today in Japan. . . . First—despite the apparent liquidity trap—monetary policymakers retain the power to increase nominal aggregate demand and the price level. Second, increased nominal spending and rising prices will lead to increases in real economic activity." This is because loose policy is not a matter of just the nominal interest rate, but of inflation expectations. He further writes: "One only need recall that nominal interest rates remained close to zero in many countries throughout the Great Depression, a period of massive monetary contraction and deflationary pressure. In short, low interest rates may just as well be a sign of expected deflation and monetary tightness as of monetary ease." The key is to turn around those deflationary expectations.

Bernanke proposes, and Blanchard seconds, the idea that the BOJ use a positive publicly announced inflation target combined with the expansion of the money supply and/or depreciation of the yen (both through the printing of yen by the BOJ). On the basis of simple arbitrage arguments (modeled in Blanchard's essay), Bernanke shows that the idea that BOJ purchases of JGBs or dollars would be ineffective comes to a reductio ad absurdum—the Bank could simply keep issuing yen, and keep purchasing assets, until it owned an unlimited amount of either the Japanese or the US economy's capital stock, if those receiving the printed yen did not spend them. But if they spent the yen, Japanese nominal income and the price level would indeed rise.

The inflation target announcement speeds the process and reduces the public's uncertainty about the BOJ's plans. Bernanke explains, "On the issue of announcement effects, theory and practice suggest that 'cheap talk' can in fact sometimes affect expectations, particularly when there is no conflict between what a 'player' announces and that player's incentives. In technical language, announcements can serve as equilibrium selection devices." If the Bank wishes to raise the Japanese price level, it has nothing to fear from telling the public what it intends, and it may find its job eased by so doing. As Blanchard observes, "This use of monetary policy [to create promised inflation] has often been presented as rather exotic, perhaps too exotic to be relied on. . . . In fact, this use of monetary policy is far from exotic. Indeed, one can argue that monetary policy works mostly—entirely?—through its effects on expectations." That is not to say the announcement alone is enough, because the money must actually be printed until the announcement is believed, and there are ways of distributing the printed money that are more likely than others to have the desired effect. Blanchard, for example, prefers drawing attention to the effect on the yen-dollar rate because "the decrease in real interest rates [due to monetary expansion] will not be directly visible. But the increase in the nominal exchange rate will. This will allow both the central bank and the financial markets to assess the credibility of the new policy."

The practical aspects of implementing a more expansionary policy under the present circumstances of financial fragility have been of great concern to the Bank of Japan. Even when BOJ officials began to admit that they could create inflation, despite being at zero nominal interest rates, they raised issues with the likely side effects of so doing. What would happen if an inflation target were announced, only to be missed, given the uncertainties of money creation with a damaged banking system? What would be the effect on fiscal policy and the banking system if inflation were to suddenly spike upward? In my contribution to this volume, I agree that "it is, no doubt, true that the BOJ at present would not be able to move inflation as predictably as in the precrisis era. . . . And it would be difficult to predict the necessary size and lags of such [open-market] purchases to have the desired effect [in the absence of the normal instrument]. But, so what? Just because a policy is difficult to implement precisely does not mean that it carries enormous risks. . .or that the policy cannot be the best of available alternatives."

The alternative to the BOJ conducting a more expansionary policy, and anchoring expectations with an inflation (or other nominal) target, is the costly course it is already on, as discussed by Jinushi, Kuroki, and Miyao: deflation, volatility in the real economy, and uncertainty in financial markets. And whatever one thinks of Japanese politicians' proclivities for public works spending, the BOJ's pursuit of positive inflation through the limited monetization of JGBs need not open the floodgates. In the words of Bernanke, "Cooperation with the fiscal authorities in pursuit of a common goal is not the same as subservience." This is just as true for an independent central bank as for a dependent one—consider the interaction of the Federal Reserve and the Clinton administration in the 1990s. In general, Bernanke suggests, "It is better for the public to know that the BOJ is doing all it can to reflate the economy, and that it understand why the Bank is taking the actions it does. The alternative is for the private sector to be left to its doubts about the willingness or competence of the BOJ to help the macroeconomic situation."

Given the economic arguments and the obviously outlier behavior of the BOJ, as well as the persistence of deflation, it is not only the Japanese public that is left wondering why the Bank of Japan has chosen this course of deflationary policy. It is also a matter of profound significance to political economy. As I note below, "For the past 20 years, both academic and practical discussions of monetary policy mostly have been about how to keep central banks from allowing *too much* inflation. . . . Then one comes to the Bank of Japan in the past decade. Suddenly, the problem is not keeping inflation from rising, but how to keep the price level from falling." An answer is not easy to come by, even when one takes political factors into account. Most independent central banks, including new ones eager to establish their credibility, do not so publicly challenge the prevailing opinion of both elected officials and mainstream economists as did the Bank of Japan in the past 2 years.

Between a process of elimination, and careful reading of the statements of BOJ policy board members, I am led to the conclusion that a desire by the BOJ to promote structural change in the Japanese economy is a primary motivation for the Bank's passive-aggressive acceptance of deflation. Leaving aside the doubts about whether a tight monetary stance on net does the Japanese economy good, or even in partial equilibrium enhances structural reform, the ability of this justification for the BOJ's policies to survive extended public scrutiny seems dubious. It is only because the BOJ is not held accountable for attaining a publicly announced policy goal, as most independent central banks are, that it can pursue this course—with a requirement to publish a target, the BOJ would have to acknowledge that it is actually targeting zero inflation by pursuing its current policies, and then defend that goal. Jinushi, Kuroki, and Miyao argue in their essay that a public inflation target in Japan today would be interpreted too strictly, which would induce real instability. My interpretation is the opposite, that the lack of an explicit inflation target allows the BOJ to pursue price stability at all costs.

An alternative explanation for the Bank of Japan's monetary policy in the past decade, and in fact for the fluctuations in the Japanese real economy, is put forward by Eisuke Sakakibara in his contribution to this volume. Sakakibara, a former Japanese vice minister of finance for international affairs, argues that US policy demands upon Japan, at times motivated by mercantilist or populist pressures for trade relief, drove both the yen-dollar exchange rate and financial developments in Japan. "These three periods [recession, 1992-94; recovery, 1995-96; and deflation from financial crisis, 1997-98] describe the evolution of the Japanese economy, and correspond somewhat with changes in US economic policy toward Japan. This is no coincidence. Throughout these three periods, Japan-United States relations and foreign exchange and equity markets played a very important role." This argument dovetails with the academic work of Ronald McKinnon, who maintains that mercantile trade pressures from the United States have created ongoing expectations of yen appreciation against the dollar (because that is the only way seen to reduce the US bilateral trade deficit with Japan), and that expected yen appreciation is the driving force behind Japan's recession of the 1990s.[17]

For example, rather than attributing the Japanese recession of 1993-94 to the effects of the bubble on the financial system described by Shimizu, and to the tight monetary policy that Jinushi, Kuroki, and Miyao discern, Sakakibara writes: "Prospects for a Japanese recovery that existed during 1993-94 were dashed as the strong yen canceled out the initially favorable signs of an upturn in domestic demand. . . . The Japanese recovery thus was delayed by as much as a year or a year and a half because the yen was too strong, which was the result, to a significant degree, of tough, populist, election-conscious US policies."

According to Sakakibara, even the timing and extent of public capital injection into the Japanese banking system were determined by US pressures. "Up to [September 1998], the US Treasury was emphasizing the liquidation of insolvent banks and expeditious downsizing and restructuring of viable banks. . . . However, in September, in the midst of suffering from the Long-Term Capital Management problem themselves, the US authorities. . .demanded that the Japanese government increase [the public funds], . . .and that the funds be infused as quickly as possible. . . . This was a boon to the Japanese government because US ambivalence about the infusion of public money had been a big factor in making Japanese public opinion largely antagonistic toward such infusion."

Jeffrey Shafer, Sakakibara's onetime counterpart as US undersecretary of the treasury for international affairs, views the same period quite differently. In his essay below, Shafer argues that "whatever the [Clinton] administration's goals with respect to economic relations with Japan, their pursuit had nowhere near the impact on the exchange rate or on the Japanese economy more broadly as did the fundamental economic forces

17. See, e.g., McKinnon and Ohno (1997).

at work. . . . If US pressure had been more successful in stimulating structural reforms or in encouraging growth policies, it would have had a stronger impact." He attributes the 1993-94 appreciation of the yen against the dollar to a combination of budget tightening in the United States (reducing interest rates), capital outflows, and markets acting to limit the US trade deficit, not to trade negotiations. According to Shafer, "The yen. . . began to recover [in late 1998] when new fundamentals did emerge: a change of policy in Tokyo that brought meaningful fiscal stimulus, an effective response to the banking crisis, and a resumption of growth." These policies certainly were welcomed in Washington, but it was the Obuchi government's decisions that led to the change in exchange rates, not an increase in US "pragmatism" (as Sakakibara characterizes it) with regard to the Japanese bank bailout.

The contrast between Sakakibara's and Shafer's interpretations of events during the past decade not only sheds light on the differing perceptions on opposite sides of the trans-Pacific table—it also emphasizes how potentially important international factors can be to monetary policy decisions and outcomes. Unquestionably, the United States was exerting pressure on Japan for specific policies during the past decade, first for trade opening, and later for macroeconomic stimulus and financial reform. Also, unquestionably, the US government felt quite frustrated by the lack of response of the Japanese government to its own domestic recession, let alone the US requests.

If Sakakibara is right that the United States effectively used exchange rate markets as a means of commercial policy, then whether or not the United States chooses to participate in joint intervention efforts is a critical signal to the markets, and has a direct influence on the Japanese economy. Such a world also renders questions of what the BOJ should or should not be doing largely irrelevant. Yet the United States pursued a "strong dollar" policy for most of the period in question, and, as Sakakibara himself notes, on many occasions joint interventions had no or the opposite effect on the yen-dollar rate from that intended. In the words of Shafer, "The record strongly suggests that the fundamentals drove the exchange rate and these exchange rate movements drove the perception of statements. It was not the statements or the sterilized intervention that created the durable movements in the markets." If that is a fair characterization, the Bank of Japan's own policy choices are indeed significant.

References

Bernanke, Ben S., and Mark Gertler. 1999. Monetary Policy and Asset Price Volatility. In *1999 Symposium: New Challenges for Monetary Policy*. Kansas City: Federal Reserve Bank of Kansas City.

Bernanke, Ben, and Frederic Mishkin. 1992. Central Bank Behavior and the Strategy of Monetary Policy: Observations from Six Industrial Countries. In *NBER Macroeconomics Annual*, ed. Olivier Blanchard and Stanley Fischer. Cambridge, MA: MIT Press.

Cargill, Thomas, Michael Hutchison, and Takatoshi Ito. 1997. *The Political Economy of Japanese Monetary Policy*. Cambridge, MA: MIT Press.

Krugman, Paul. 1999. It's Baaack: Japanese Monetary Policy and the Liquidity Trap. *Brookings Papers on Economic Activity* 2: 137-205. Washington: Brookings Institution.

Kuttner, Kenneth N., and Adam S. Posen. 2000. Inflation, Monetary Transparency, and G3 Exchange Rate Volatility. Working Paper 00-6 (July). Photocopy. Washington: Institute for International Economics.

McKinnon, Ronald, and Kenichi Ohno. 1997. *Dollar and Yen: Resolving Economic Conflict Between the United States and Japan*. Cambridge, MA: MIT Press.

Mishkin, Frederic, and Adam Posen. 1997. Inflation Targeting: Lessons from Four Countries. *Federal Reserve Bank of New York Economic Policy Review*, August: 9-110.

Okina, Kunio. 1999. *Monetary Policy under Zero Inflation—A Response to Criticisms and Questions Regarding Monetary Policy*. Discussion Paper 99-E-20. Tokyo: Institute for International Monetary and Economic Studies, Bank of Japan.

Posen, Adam S. 1998. *Restoring Japan's Economic Growth*. Washington: Institute for International Economics.

Walsh, Carl. 1996. Inflation and Central Bank Independence: Is Japan Really an Outlier? *IMES BOJ Monetary and Economic Studies* 15 (May): 1.

2

The Facts of the Japanese Financial Crisis

RYOICHI MIKITANI

There would be no objection among economists to the view that the two most serious economic problems of the 20th century were the Great Depression of the 1930s and the financial crises of the late 1980s to early 1990s in the United States, Europe, Japan, and newly industrialized East Asian countries. Of course, the former was really *the* great depression—the deepest worldwide depression, which inflicted immense damage not only upon the United States but also the entire world. However, the current depression in Japan is not the type of recession that is part of ordinary business cycles, which Japan has experienced several times since the end of World War I.

Ordinary and Extraordinary Business Cycles and Economic Crises

The extraordinary nature of the present Heisei depression is revealed in the prolonged, 10-year stagnation of Japan's economy, the huge socioeconomic losses, and the lack of evidence for a vigorous recovery. A common feature of the recent financial crises and the Great Depression, however, is that during the period before each, a long boom created a euphoric atmosphere that originated in the financial and real estate sectors and finally turned into the "bubble" state of speculation. Almost everyone expected profit, which depended upon future price rises, in which one

---

Ryoichi Mikitani is professor in the Faculty of Economics, Kobe Gakuin University.

believed almost with certainty. Yet this euphoria could not sustain itself in the long run. Sooner or later, this bubble would be pricked. Everyone's expectations would be turned around 180 degrees, and the real sectors of the economy would be damaged severely.

The immediate question is whether the difference between an ordinary business cycle and an extraordinary boom, crash, and depression cycle (EBC) is just a matter of degree or whether it depends on the nature of the regime. If there is a difference in nature between them, should the appropriate policies to address them be different?

There are three basic types of ordinary business cycles—the inventory cycle, the typical main business cycle, and the construction cycle. These cycles are caused by the gap between demand and supply in the investment components of national products—inventory investment, plant and equipment investment, and construction investment. Business cycle theory is one of the most contentious fields in economics. The causes and processes of business cycles have been argued over by many economists. Economists are divided into two broad schools—the monetary business cycle school and the real business cycle school. However, in the past, not enough attention has been paid to the institutional aspect.[1]

Tentatively, we can call an institutional policy framework a "regime." In some business cycles, this "regime" factor will not play an important role, but in others it will be the critical factor. We define an ordinary business cycle as one in which the gap between aggregate demand and aggregate supply is the main problem and the existing regime is not critical. In an ordinary business cycle, stabilization policy seeks to adjust either aggregate demand or aggregate supply, or both, to full employment equilibrium. And even without such a policy, there would be self-adjustment toward equilibrium as part of the ordinary business cycle. No policy would be better than another, in some cases, if the self-healing is fast and efficient. In this case, the business cycle might be interpreted as an automatic adjustment process of the economy to maintain the existing regime.

However, as noted above, there exists another type of violent economic fluctuation, the EBC—such as the Great Depression during the 1930s and Japan's current Heisei depression. In these EBC cases, a euphoric socioeconomic atmosphere is generated during a long-lasting boom, which leads to excessive speculation in the market, particularly of assets such as stocks and real estate. Sooner or later, this excessive speculation is ended by a policy or some inherent economic constraint. This is the life cycle of the economic "bubble." If no appropriate macroeconomic

---

1. By "institutional" we mean the institutional framework, particularly channels of savings and investment, structures of corporations, rules of markets and transactions, and economic and business conventions.

policy response is taken, there will be danger of a deflationary spiral and economic stagnation.

This kind of EBC crisis, because it is so different from an ordinary business cycle, will not have a self-correcting force to recover under the existing regime, and to maintain the economic system itself will be very difficult. It is in this respect that there seems to be a considerable qualitative difference between an ordinary business cycle and an EBC. We might interpret an EBC as evidence that economic progress and development are becoming less effective or even impossible under the existing regime. For example, was the Great Depression simply a gigantic ordinary business cycle depression, or a symptom of maladjustment between a source of power for economic development and the regime within which that innovative economic power must work?

It is clear that the decade after World War I was the transitional period from the international gold standard of the pound sterling to the dollar key-currency system. Domestically in the United States, this was the beginning of corporate finance by the masses through the stock market, the mass consumption of durable goods, and weaker banking supervision and no provision of safety nets for bank depositors (despite the rapid development of the banking business, including stock brokerages).

In Japan, after World War II, the government implemented an industrial policy of giving subsidies and various kinds of administrative guidance to industries and banks. This was successful until Japan caught up with the Western industrial nations toward the late 1970s, by which time the ability of the government to target appropriate industries had greatly weakened. Since Japan has now caught up economically with the industrial countries, it needs to target industries in coordination with market forces and the insights of entrepreneurs. To fulfill this goal, the industry-government complex and the cross holding of stock among corporations and banks must be transformed. Corporate governance by stockholders must be established, and the adoption of global standards must be promoted. These changes have become imperative for potential Japanese innovative power to develop fully. Answering the question of why this power and the existing regime came into conflict is fundamental to understanding the country's economic difficulties.

We can conceptually distinguish an ordinary business cycle from an EBC. But it is very difficult to identify each of them in advance, particularly during the boom phase. This raises the difficult question for policymakers of how to adopt and implement macroeconomic countercyclical policy and structural policy to change regimes. When it is necessary to change regimes, it is right to reform through structural policy and wrong not to reform the regime. We may call this the Type One error. In contrast, when it is not necessary to reform, it is right not to do so. In fact, it is wrong to reform when it is not necessary to do so. We may call this the Type Two error.

In the prosperity phase of the business cycle, a precautionary restrictive stabilization policy stance might be taken, if the time lag of the policy's effect on the economy is large and if prosperity is of the ordinary business cycle type. However, our knowledge of economies and economic policy is not so reliable as to enable us to engage in activist policymaking. At this stage, it is extremely difficult to identify whether the necessity of reforming the existing regime exists.

As the economy approaches its peak, inflationary pressure gradually becomes evident. If a restrictive policy is not applied, the boom may turn out to be excessive, inflation will set in, and the cost of reducing inflationary expectations afterward will be large. Furthermore, the boom will continue and become euphoric. This might happen if the regime is mismatched with innovative economic power. If this is the case, we then have to take prompt and somewhat drastic corrective measures toward the regime.

If this structural policy has a depressive or a stimulative effect on the economy, it must be accompanied by the appropriate macroeconomic policy to offset this effect. A mix of structural policy and macrostabilization policy must be undertaken quickly and simultaneously. This promptness is required to minimize the cumulative loss due to the gap between the economic potential and the deterring regime. The regime reform must be somewhat drastic, because it is necessary to alter people's expectations. However, the complete offsetting of industrial policy by aggregate demand policy might not be best, because the motivation to reform would then be lessened. At this stage of the business cycle, the loss from the Type One error might be larger than that from the Type Two error.

When the EBC enters the crash phase and economic activity spirals down, competition-oriented structural reform might be harmful and endanger the economic system itself. Policies to prevent the downward spiral should be undertaken as emergency measures, but the reform of the regime must not be forgotten as the goal of medium- and long-term policy. It is very important to maintain the will and incentive for structural reform.

If there are two types of economic fluctuation—the ordinary business cycle and the extraordinary boom-crisis type of economic fluctuation—we must distinguish them and take appropriate measures. To do that, we have to increase our knowledge by identifying the difference between them, and determine the correct policies for each case. For this purpose, studies of different countries and various times are important.

As a study over time, comparison of the Great Depression of the 1930s with the present Japanese Heisei depression would be interesting. As a study across countries, research on the financial debacle of the United States, Japan, and other East Asian countries might contribute to our knowledge in this field. This research must clarify several important questions, such as why the mismatch of innovative economic growth power and the economic regime arises, how we should reform the regime, and when we should implement reform plans.

The Japanese Heisei Depression

We now take a retrospective look at the Japanese Heisei depression. Toward the end of the 1970s, the Japanese economy caught up with the Western industrial countries. It was time to alter the economic regime from the old to the new one—from indicative industrial policy administered by the government to the guidance of the free market; from a banking-securities sector heavily regulated by the Ministry of Finance to a less regulated, more competitive, globally standardized financial sector; from Japanese corporatism to transparent management of corporations—in short, from the Japanese standard to the global standard. However, neither the financial institutions nor the big corporations were willing to take off their protective heavy coat and work with their sleeves rolled up. Instead, deregulation has been conducted in a Japanese way by the Japanese government, with "gradualism" that preserves the interests of the beneficiaries of the old regime. Deregulation in Japan therefore has not brought about freer entry, new enterprises, and vigorous innovative activity, as it did in the United States.

To carry out the Plaza Accord in 1985, the Japanese government and the Bank of Japan (BOJ) implemented an easy monetary policy to mitigate the depressive effect of implementing the international agreement on the yen's appreciation against the dollar. Japan—surprised by the downfall of New York stock prices on Black Monday in 1987—continued its easy monetary policy for more than 2 years, unlike Germany. The prices of land and stocks soared to more than triple their 1985 level.

We have to investigate how this mistaken monetary policy was formulated and implemented. Was it the sole independent decision of the BOJ or the political decision of the government and politicians? (See Sakakibara's essay in this volume for a discussion of this topic.) It is deplorable that there is no serious official report on this apparently mistaken policy. This is the chronic Japanese disease. The transparency of monetary policymaking is as important as the result of the policy, both because of the need for policymakers to be accountable and also in order to advance the economics of central banking.

In retrospect, the BOJ officials and serious economists should not have permitted pseudo-economics to explain the high prices of land and stocks with various false assumptions. We should have put questions to ourselves, such as "is there any balance between the monetary-financial sector and the real sector of economy?" and "if asset prices in Japan are far from equilibrium, what would happen to the Japanese economy if these prices fell drastically?" It would be too simplistic for central bankers to stick to a single policy goal, the stability of "flow" prices, without paying appropriate attention to others, such as stock prices and the associated overswing of the real economy (documented in the essay by Jinushi, Kuroki, and Miyao in this volume).

The bank loan with collateral, mainly real estate, has been a "regime" in Japanese bank-lending practice (documented in Shimizu's essay in this volume). If the price of real estate keeps rising, this is a very safe business convention for banks. If the price falls, it becomes a very risky practice. In a euphoric economic environment, it is very difficult for an individual to resist the social atmosphere and to build his own expectation differently from others.

Toward the end of the 1980s, it became evident to everyone that the soaring prices of land and stocks were having adverse effects not only on the economy but also on society itself. So, belatedly, BOJ began to raise its discount rate and to restrict the money supply, while the government undertook selective measures to control land prices. Finally, stock prices began to fall, and then urban land prices followed suit.

At this point in time, it was very difficult for policymakers to select the appropriate policies. However, after having confirmed the decline of prices to a normal level, we should have implemented an accommodative monetary policy and income-supportive fiscal policy. Nevertheless, the restrictive monetary policy actually continued, and the consumption tax rate was even raised. The Japanese economy has since plunged further into stagnation.

Unfortunately, Japanese banks have not wanted to dispose of their bad loan portfolios swiftly, and have been awaiting a recovery of asset prices that has yet to occur. Meanwhile, three big banks and one of the four largest security companies have failed. This has been the worst aspect of dealing with the economic crisis. Now, a huge amount of public money, amounting to about ¥60 trillion ($550 billion), has been poured into the reconstruction of the Japanese banking system. The gap between potential and actual GDP during the crisis period from 1992 through 1998 amounted to a huge sum (¥340 trillion, 68 percent of current GDP, under an assumption of the 4 percent average growth rate from 1976 through 1991; ¥180 trillion, 36 percent of current GDP, assuming a 3 percent growth rate).[2]

Toward Financial-Sector Reform

The Obuchi administration strongly emphasized macroeconomic recovery as its first priority and hardly paid attention to other aspects of the econ-

2. In Posen (1998, chapter 1 and appendix), Japanese potential output growth is estimated to decline 3 percent from 1988 to 1992, to an annual rate of 1.75 percent. This implies a cumulative output gap of 15 percent of current GDP.

omy (public debt, deregulation of industries, transparent banking supervision, etc.). If the restructuring of the Japanese economy should fail, why and for what are we paying this huge cost? When we think of the speedy, drastic solutions of financial crises in the United States, Sweden, and some other countries, we have to conclude that the distinction must be accounted for by the difference in the character of Japanese society and in the way the nation is governed. Is there a unique Japanese way to reform the regime? Is Japan special?

In November 1996, the Hashimoto cabinet published the Japanese Financial Big Bang plan and promised to attain its goals by the year 2001. The plan's two most important objectives were to complete the disposition of the banks' bad debt and establish the Tokyo financial market as a competitive international market of the caliber of New York and London. In other words, the set goals of financial reform were (1) for Japan to harvest the fruits of the ongoing information technology (IT) revolution and globalization of the world economy and (2) for the country to raise the efficiency of not only its financial sector but also its economy to levels as high as other advanced countries.

The harsh fact is that neither the elimination of the bad debt nor the internationalization of the Tokyo market has been realized. To attain these goals, fundamental reform of the financial sector of Japan is vital; however, the incumbent financial institutions will not change without competitive circumstances brought on by new entrants from abroad and the domestic nonbank sectors.

Generally speaking, the economic functions of the monetary and financial sectors are to provide the payments system for the economy, to serve as a financial intermediary between savers and investors (including transactions of existing assets and debts), and to create credit for new investments. These three are closely interrelated, but separable. However, historically, and especially in Japan, these functions were conducted mainly by banks until World War II. Recently in the United States and Europe, and even in Japan, financial intermediation for big corporations has been increasingly carried out through the capital markets.

Over the past two decades, information technology has been developing tremendously, immensely increasing capacities to communicate, process, and analyze information. This IT revolution has had an enormous impact upon the financial sector. First, it has decreased the cost of monetary transactions in the payments system and raised the level of convenience for the public (e.g., 24-hour automated teller machines). In the fields of financial intermediation and credit creation, transaction costs have greatly decreased, risk has become more diversified, and the scope of financial assets and debts has broadened.

A little more than 5 years ago, there were 21 "big" banks in Japan (city, long-term-credit, and trust banks). Now the country has three gigantic (megasized) banking groups (as of July 2000)—Tokyo Mitsubishi-Mitsubishi Trust group, Mizuho group (Fuji, Dai-Ichi Kangyo, IBJ), and Mitsui-Sumitomo group (Sakura and Sumitomo); two large regional banking groups—Asahi and Daiwa; and two restructured banks—Shinsei (the former Long-Term Credit Bank of Japan, taken over by the Ripplewood Holdings Co. of the United States) and a new bank (the former Nippon Saiken Bank, taken over by the Softbank group in Japan). The Hokkaido Takushoku Bank was the only big bank in 1997 to go bankrupt (not big enough not to fail!). At present the mergers and acquisitions movement of banks in Japan seems to have not yet finished. The remaining independent banks will sooner or later merge or be absorbed, and in the near future only five or so megabanks from the previous 21 will remain.

Since the end of 1998, three conspicuous changes have been developing in Japanese banking. The first was the merger of the big banks. The combined assets of the four gigantic banking groups now are about ¥100 trillion, which constitutes more than 50 percent of the total assets of all banks in Japan. However, the strategy for their future management is not clear. The four groups appear to want to be engaged in all three fields of banking (investment, retail, and regional banking), although each group has its own field of emphasis.

The second unprecedented event was the purchase of failed banks by foreign financial concerns and domestic nonbank businesses. The third event is the proposal to establish new banks by nonbank businesses (e.g., the 7-11 convenience store company, with 8,000 stores) and by high-technology companies in Internet businesses (e.g., Sony). The market for banking would be divided into three submarkets: retail, regional, and wholesale banking (wholesale banking is usually called investment banking).

In wholesale banking, transactions are large, the playing field is the global market, and customers are big corporations, governments, and billionaires. A wholesale bank's main resources are in its capability to evaluate future investment risks and returns. The customers of retail banks are the multitude of consumers and income earners. These banks' main business is to facilitate the payment of countless small transactions, take care of small savers, and perhaps make loans to common consumers. In between are the regional banks, whose main activity is to provide services to small and medium-sized businesses.

Until recently, almost all big Japanese banks engaged in all three kinds of banking services; however, nonprice competition was common, and sometimes they cooperated with each other under the guidance of the Ministry of Finance. If there are economies of scope (i.e., synergy effects) gained by conducting activities in two or three markets under a single roof, universal banking (in this sense) is rational and productive not only for the banking sector but also for the economy as a whole. The issue now is whether the ongoing IT revolution is amplifying this synergy or not. We must wait for rigorous empirical research for complete understanding, but recent developments in the United States and Europe suggest that the IT revolution is decreasing rather than increasing synergy. Therefore, the segmentation of banking activity into three areas—each with separate management—will raise the productivity of each submarket and also make the whole banking industry stronger.

There is a hopeful sign in Japan for this direction. But there is also a danger. If the gigantic banking groups collude to form a monopoly in the money transfer system and also in the market for small savers, they may reap the rent from this monopoly and use the excess profit as a kind of internal subsidy to support their investment banking departments' competition with nonbank entities. This unfair competition will not produce the optimum results of financial reform, but rather create a loss for the economy. To prevent this loss, it is very important that new requirements for entry into the financial sector create free-market conditions, and also that banks disclose as much information about their management as possible.

At present, thanks to the entry of new foreign banks and domestic nonbank firms, retail banking in Japan is becoming considerably more competitive. But we must be vigilant against any monopoly in this field. In investment banking, the competition from overseas and domestic securities firms will be as keen as ever. The problem is the middle market of regional banking. In this area, Schumpeterian bankers can play an active role as fund suppliers for innovative small and medium-sized firms. This is very important for the dynamic development of the Japanese economy. Unfortunately, it seems to me that we cannot expect much from the incumbent regional banks in Japan, because they are too accustomed to the outmoded Japanese bank-management system. Here again, we need competitive incentives from outsiders and nonbank firms in the form of venture capital. One of the basic challenges left for economists is how to separate Japan's banking and commerce.

Reference

Posen, Adam S. 1998. *Restoring Japan's Economic Growth.* Washington: Institute for International Economics.

3

Japan Now and the United States Then: Lessons from the Parallels

BENJAMIN M. FRIEDMAN

For much of the last decade, Japan's banking crisis has been at the center of attention in the ongoing discussion of that country's broader economic difficulties and of what public policy actions could alleviate them. The enormous loan losses and balance sheet erosion that nearly all Japanese banks have sustained during this period, and the resulting impairment of their ability to carry out ordinary credit creation activities, have been both a consequence and a cause of Japan's prolonged economic stagnation. Of the 21 institutions that made up the standard list of Japanese "large banks" in 1990, by the decade's end two had disappeared through failure and nationalization, and four others were consolidated into two by merger. At the time of writing, five of the remaining 17 are in the process of merging into two new entities, thus reducing the list to 14. But few observers think the shrinkage is over, or that the banks that remain are now healthy institutions. Questions about what further steps the Japanese authorities should take to foster the banks' recovery—and to ensure their soundness once they have recovered—therefore continue to be pertinent.

A decade ago, it was US banks, and even more so the US savings and loan (S&L) industry, that were in crisis. These institutions too suffered major loan losses, experienced failure rates unprecedented since the depression of the 1930s (especially among S&Ls, but among banks as

---

Benjamin M. Friedman is professor of economics at Harvard University. *He is grateful to Robert Glauber, Toshiki Jinushi, Anil Kashyap, Richard Mattione, Ryoichi Mikitani, Adam Posen, Hal Scott, and Yoshinori Shimizu for helpful discussions and comments on an earlier draft, and to the Harvard Program for Financial Research for research support.*

well), and saw the market capitalization of survivors fall to a small fraction of its precrisis level. Resolution of the crisis took significant government intervention, both in the provision of public funds to pay off the depositors of institutions that failed outright and in managing the process of consolidation among those that did not (at least not formally). And although the 1990-91 business recession in the United States was neither severe nor protracted, growth during the initial years of the recovery was unusually sluggish, and many observers cited continuing problems at credit-creating institutions as one of the chief obstacles—"headwinds," as Alan Greenspan called them—that the economy had to overcome.

This essay reviews the parallels between Japan's banking crisis of the 1990s and the US banking and S&L crisis of a decade ago, with the object of drawing lessons from US experience to bear on the public policy decisions that Japan still faces today. In so doing, it is important at the outset to highlight two caveats. First, these two situations are not identical, and the story told here is not merely one of parallels. As the discussion below makes clear, in some respects the two are not parallel at all. There are significant differences, some of which bear directly on matters of appropriate public policy. Second, it is most surely not the case that the lessons to be drawn for Japan today consist entirely of applying what the United States did a decade ago. To the contrary, both the US government in general and the specific authorities responsible for dealing with the banking and S&L crisis acted, in some key respects, in ways that worsened the situation and increased its ultimate cost to the economy and to the public treasury. The lessons to be drawn from that experience stem in part from observing what to do but also from observing what not to do.

Some of the most interesting questions that one would most want to put to these two experiences, either in parallel or considered entirely separately, remain largely outside the scope of this essay: Most basically, to what extent have Japan's banking problems been a cause, rather than merely a consequence, of the subpar growth that began in 1992 and continues today? And, looking forward, will these problems in the banking system prevent Japan from achieving full economic recovery once other ingredients for renewed expansion, such as appropriate fiscal and monetary policies, are in place?

The fundamental difficulty in addressing such questions is that of distinguishing supply shocks from demand shocks in a market—namely, the market for credit—in which important elements of the relevant price vector, as well as key determinants of both supply and demand, are unobservable. Growth in Japanese banks' outstanding volume of loans slowed sharply during the course of 1991, but so did growth of nonfinancial economic activity. Similarly, by 1993 both loan growth and real economic growth hit approximately zero. As the economy staged a short-lived recovery in 1995 and 1996, so too did loan growth. By 1998, both loan volume and the gross domestic product were shrinking. Moreover, all the while a variety of other factors that might plausibly have affected credit creation or nonfinancial activity or both—changes in fiscal and monetary policies, in asset values, in the regulatory environment, in the pace of economic activity outside Japan, and so on—were at work. No doubt the roughly congruent co-movements of Japanese banks' loans and Japanese GDP during the 1990s will provide fodder for econometric tests of what was causing what for years to come.

For the purposes of policymakers trying to look forward, this more fundamental uncertainty surrounding the importance of Japan's banking crisis in accounting for the country's persistent economic difficulties is compounded by the effect of falling asset values. There is no need to dwell on the well-known role of falling prices of equities, and especially real estate, both in undermining the Japanese banks' loan portfolios and in depressing Japanese economic activity more generally. (The discussion below lists this factor, of course, but the entire subject has been voluminously documented elsewhere.) But falling asset prices also render confusing what are ordinarily reliable market signals, and therefore cloud policymakers' ability to assess even the contemporary situation. Most obviously, when prices in general are falling, low nominal interest rates do not necessarily mean low real rates. In addition, when either low or falling asset prices erode nonfinancial firms' net worth, even low real interest rates on government securities and on obligations of other highly rated borrowers do not necessarily mean a low cost of credit to other would-be borrowers. Similarly, even highly liquid bank balance sheets do not mean "easy money" if banks are unwilling or unable to lend because of concerns about the quality of their own assets or those of would-be borrowers.

These ambiguities notwithstanding, the central theme argued in this essay is that there *are* important parallels between Japan's banking crisis and that experienced not long ago in the United States, and, further, that these parallels are instructive with respect to actions that Japan should or should not take in its current situation. Moreover, in drawing the lessons of these parallels, it is useful to distinguish between the approach the United States took to addressing the problems in its commercial banking industry, which involved a variety of regulatory actions but no direct use of public funds, and the quite different approach taken in the S&L industry, which at last tally had cost US taxpayers $126 billion.

The first section begins by acknowledging some significant ways in which Japan's banking crisis and what happened in the United States are *not* similar. The second section takes up the main theme of the essay by listing some of the most important parallels between the two situations. The third section suggests implications for Japanese policymakers. The fourth section concludes by raising several questions from the perspective of the political economy of Japan's banking crisis and the public policy response to it.

Some Dissimilarities

Nobody would argue that two countries as different as Japan and the United States, or two financial systems as dissimilar as these two countries', would undergo precisely parallel experiences of banking-sector crisis. Any view that is not so naïve as to be useless must be more nuanced. It is helpful at the outset, therefore, to take note of some significant differences that bear quite directly on the extent to which what happened in the United States can yield eight lessons for Japan in this area.

1. The banking system is more important in Japan than in the United States, both as an intermediator of savings and as a creator of credit. In Japan, approximately a third of all household savings goes into bank deposits of one form or other. In the United States, only 13 percent of household savings consists of accounts in banks and other depository institutions. (Direct holdings of equities plus holdings of mutual fund shares represent 33 percent of US household savings, 36 percent is in life insurance and pension reserves, and another 7 percent is in nonbank credit market instruments. In Japan, equity and mutual fund holdings represent only 7 percent of household savings, and 28 percent is in insurance reserves.) Analogous comparisons are not available for the importance of banks' lending because of noncomparability of Japanese and US financial statistics, but the share of their total credit that Japanese nonfinancial business corporations draw from banks is surely greater than the 11 percent for US nonfinancial firms.[1]

2. The Japanese banking system has traditionally been a concentrated industry with high barriers to entry and, until only recently, barriers to exit almost as high. As of the beginning of the 1990s, the 21 "large banks"—11 city banks, 7 trust banks, and 3 long-term-credit banks—held 73 percent of Japan's banking assets. Moreover, new institutions, like the *jusen* (home mortgage lending companies) established in the early 1970s, have often been funded and principally controlled by the same group of large banks. As might be expected in a system with so few distinct players and little movement in or out, the extent of public disclosure of banks' loan portfolios, balance sheets, and profitability was traditionally limited. Indeed, from the end of World War II until

1. Hoshi and Kashyap (forthcoming) provide data that, while not fully comparable to US statistics, illustrate the importance of bank lending to business in Japan; see especially tables 7.8, 7.9, and 7.10.

1995, no Japanese bank ever publicly reported an annual loss, presumably not because no bank ever actually ran an operating loss but because the banks that did would have found it disadvantageous to reveal their losses, and weak disclosure requirements allowed them not to do so.

By contrast, as of 1985 the United States had more than 14,000 banks and more than 3,000 savings and loan associations. New institutions were frequently chartered (420 new banks, and even more S&Ls, were started between 1980 and 1990), and some quickly acquired significant market share. At the same time, many institutions disappeared (more through merger than failure, although there were some large failures, such as Franklin National in 1978 and Continental Illinois in 1984). Also, bank regulators and, in the case of publicly traded companies, the Securities and Exchange Commission and the national stock exchanges impose disclosure requirements far more stringent than in Japan.

3. In addition to the 34 percent of Japanese household savings held in bank deposits, another 19 percent is in the Postal Savings System, so that more than half of all Japanese household savings is government insured. But at least for bank deposits, deposit insurance has always been much more informal in Japan than in the United States. Japan did not have any formal deposit insurance until 1971, and the Deposit Insurance Corporation (DIC) created then has never been used directly to pay off depositors of a failed institution. Indeed, until 1992 the DIC was never used at all, and even then it merely provided funds to aid in a rescue merger. Instead of closing and liquidating a failed bank, the Japanese authorities typically relied on informal intervention to arrange a purchase-and-assumption by a viable institution.

   By contrast, in the United States the Federal Deposit Insurance Corporation (FDIC) (and, when it was in existence, the Federal Savings and Loan Insurance Corporation, or FSLIC) sometimes handles failures through purchase-and-assumption transactions but also sometimes liquidates the institution and pays off the insured depositors. As Milhaupt (1999) has pointed out, in addition to the frequently suggested cultural origins of this different approach to dealing with problems more generally, part of the reason for the difference was probably that until 1998 Japanese law treated the outright failure of a bank as if it were the bankruptcy of a nonfinancial operating company. By contrast, US law—recognizing the potential for cascading collateral damage if *all* of a *bank's* creditors have to wait while the mess is sorted out before receiving what they are due—explicitly exempts banks from the commercial bankruptcy code.

4. Japanese banks can and do own equity securities on their own account, and the value of the equities they hold is included in their capital for

regulatory purposes. By contrast, under the 1933 Glass-Steagall Act, US banks could not normally hold equities. Even now, after Congress has repealed Glass-Steagall, any equities that a bank owns must be in a separate account distinct from the bank's primary balance sheet.

This difference has had two important implications in Japan. First, a declining stock market directly affects not just banks' customers but the banks themselves. Second, the valuation of equity holdings for purposes of calculating banks' capital—for example, how to treat unrealized capital gains and losses—is a significant regulatory issue in Japan but not in the United States. For example, because of the different treatment of realized versus unrealized gains, Japanese banks sold long-held (and therefore low cost-basis) equities, even into a declining market, in order to record gains with which to offset pretax losses from nonperforming loans.

5. The Japanese banking crisis has had no equivalent to the extraordinary regional disparity at the core of US banking problems, and especially the S&L problems, of a decade ago. Of the 1,617 US *banks* that failed during 1980-94, 599 were in Texas and another 122 in neighboring Oklahoma. Although the banks that failed in Oklahoma were mostly small, the Texas failures collectively had $60 billion in assets (vs. $146 billion for all 49 other states combined). The problem in the savings and loan industry was even more geographically concentrated. Of the 747 S&L failures formally resolved by the Resolution Trust Corporation (RTC), 137 were in Texas and another 52 in neighboring Louisiana, while 73 were in California.

   The heavy concentration of these problems in Texas highlights the role of a price decline for a single commodity—namely, oil—in triggering what happened in the United States. And the point is relevant not just economically but politically. California's is the largest US congressional delegation, Texas' the second-largest. During the mid- and late 1980s, when the crisis was building but the government systematically delayed action, Californian Ronald Reagan was president and Texan Jim Wright was speaker of the House of Representatives. Because it was in the interest of the owners and managers of underwater banks and S&Ls to keep these institutions operating, the ability to bring political pressure to bear at top levels of the executive and legislative branches of government delayed action that it would have been in the public interest to take earlier.

6. In the end, however, in the United States' social and political culture it did prove possible substantially to wipe out an entire financial industry—the S&Ls. Savings and loan associations had existed in the United States for more than half a century. At their peak, S&Ls accounted for 9 percent of US household savings and held 48 percent of US home

mortgages. Historically, the industry had played a significant part in achieving the popular postwar goal of making individual home ownership more widespread. The S&Ls had their own government-sponsored insurance system, the FSLIC, and several highly effective lobbying organizations, including the US League of Savings Associations and the National Council of Savings Associations. As of the beginning of the 1990s, S&Ls also provided jobs for nearly 350,000 employees.

Even so, as Kaufman observed, commenting not just on the S&L crisis but on the banking industry more generally, "At the height of the crisis, neither bankers nor bank regulators had sufficient public credibility and stature to effectively fight the reforms" (1997, 16). Once the mounting costs of keeping the industry going became clear, most Americans either supported shutting it down or were at least indifferent, and the country's political structure responded accordingly. It is not at all clear that Japan would, or could, act similarly under analogous circumstances. Indeed, despite the widely discussed antipathy toward the banks exhibited by much of the Japanese public, the public authorities have taken few actions likely to result in closing banks or putting bank managers out of work.

7. A big part of the story of how a large number of US banks survived and then recovered in the first half of the 1990s was the persistence of high interest rates by historical standards, and in particular wide spreads between lending rates and deposit rates, during much of the first half of the 1990s. On average, during 1992-95 (the recession ended in 1991), the US *prime* commercial lending rate was 7.06 percent, versus 4.07 percent for *Treasury bills* and substantially less for most forms of bank deposits. (In earlier US recovery periods, the prime vs. Treasury spread had averaged 1.97 percent during 1976-79 and 2.35 percent during 1983-85.) By contrast, Japanese banks' *average* loan-to-deposit spread has mostly hovered in the 1.60-1.75 percent range since mid-1993.

8. As many observers have emphasized, Japanese monetary policy has literally hit the constraint at zero nominal interest rates. This unusual phenomenon matters in two ways for purposes of the banking crisis. At the macroeconomic level, as has been widely discussed, hitting the zero constraint limits what the Bank of Japan can do to pursue a more expansionary monetary policy.[2] More narrowly with respect to Japan's banks, hitting the zero constraint almost surely implies a compression

2. Contrary to repeated assertions by the Bank and some members of its Policy Committee, this does *not* mean that there is *nothing* further that monetary policy can do to stimulate economic expansion; see, e.g., Bernanke's essay in this volume.

of the interest rate structure, including a narrowing of spreads of lending rates over deposit rates. In contrast to this aspect of Japan's current situation, the United States in modern times has never approached zero nominal interest rates. The monthly average low point for 3-month US Treasury bills in the aftermath of the 1990-91 recession was 2.86 percent in October 1992.

Parallels: Origins of the Crises and Responses to Them

These differences notwithstanding, the central argument of this essay is that the banking crisis in Japan now and in the United States then have reflected important parallels, enough so that what happened in the United States is capable of providing helpful lessons for Japanese policymakers. Some of these parallels are widely recognized, others less so. To gain a sense of the overall congruence between the two countries' experiences, it is useful to review them together, looking first at aspects of what caused the respective crisis and second at policymakers' responses.

Origins of the Two Crises

1. Almost all observers of both these situations have emphasized the role of falling asset prices as a major trigger of the crisis. In Japan, the average price of metropolitan residential land approximately doubled in the first half of the 1980s, then approximately tripled in the second half. Residential land then lost roughly 50 percent of that peak value in the first half of the 1990s. The fluctuation in the price of commercial land was apparently more extreme, although commercial real estate values are typically harder to measure because of the paucity of sufficiently comparable transactions. The Nikkei average stock price rose from barely ¥7,000 in 1982 to nearly ¥39,000 at year-end 1989, and then fell to below ¥13,000 in 1998.

   In the United States, at least at the national level, fluctuations in vacancy rates and new construction can take the place of hard-to-measure price levels in conveying a sense of the scale of this dimension of the banking problems that ensued. The vacancy rate for commercial office space in major metropolitan markets rose from 4 percent in 1980 to 18 percent in 1986, despite the fact that 1980 was a recession year and 1986 was the fourth year of a robust economic expansion. Completions of new office space in those same markets, which had totaled 99 million square feet during the first half of the 1980s and another 101 million during the latter half of the decade, collapsed to just 28 million during the first half of the 1990s. Similar patterns of boom and bust, although less severe, also characterized the retail and industrial real estate markets. In Texas, where the 1986 break in oil prices had devastating effects on much of the local economy, all of these fluctuations were far more extreme.

2. In both Japan and the United States, lending on real estate rose sharply as a share of banks' credit creation in the years preceding the crisis—and, interestingly, continued to rise as the crisis unfolded. The share of Japanese banks' total loans extended directly to the real estate industry rose from less than 6 percent in 1980 to nearly 12 percent in 1990, and rose modestly further by the mid-1990s. The share of bank credit *indirectly* resting on real estate collateral was far greater, however, because as prices rose so much of the tangible wealth of both corporate and household borrowers consisted of land values.

   Among US commercial banks, real estate loans rose from 32 percent of all bank loans and leases in 1980 to 43 percent in 1990, and from 18 to 27 percent of total bank assets. While all categories of real estate loans increased as a share of banks' portfolios during the 1980s, by far the largest percentage increases were in loans for construction and land development and in loans on nonfarm nonresidential properties—both of which almost doubled as a share of the aggregate portfolio. Not surprisingly, banks that subsequently failed started off the decade on average with a distinctly larger share of their overall real estate loan portfolios devoted to loans on commercial property than did banks that did not fail (43 vs. 32 percent), and the average difference widened steadily thereafter (by 1990, 51 percent vs. the same 32 percent as before).

3. In both countries, the increase in banks' lending activity directed toward real estate partly reflected the decline of their traditional core business of lending to established nonfinancial operating companies. In the United States, this is a story of very long standing, one that has advanced apparently inexorably throughout the postwar period. Major elements underlying this structural shift include the development of the commercial paper market and the increasing importance of the corporate bond market, both of which have primarily worked to the advantage of the larger, better-known borrowers, and the rise of nonbank finance companies (for example, G.E. Credit), which now aggressively compete for the business of smaller borrowers. Although the share of US banks' total assets held in commercial and industrial loans has fluctuated fairly narrowly in recent decades (it is usually in the 18-20 percent range), the borrower base has progressively shifted to smaller, less secure firms. The share of nonfinancial business corporations' liabilities owed to banks has mostly declined over the years, from 16 percent in 1960 to 11 percent today.

Many of these same developments—for example, the emergence of a commercial paper market—have occurred in Japan as well, albeit with later timing. Even so, the dominant trend over time in both countries is for the banks to lose what used to be their core commercial lending business from which they once were reliably able to make a competitive market return while assuming only limited levels of risk. As a result of this structural change in their competitive environment, banks in the United States have repeatedly been led to seek profitability from new and greater forms of risk taking. (Recall the real estate investment trust problem of the 1970s, the developing-country debt crisis of the early 1980s, and the high-leverage exposure of the mid- to late 1980s, not to mention commercial real estate once again in the late 1980s and on into the early 1990s.) It appears that Japanese banks, facing a similar structural challenge, have taken some of the same missteps in response.

4. Banks, and in the United States especially savings and loan associations, have been better able to strike out in these new directions before the crisis occurred because both the US and Japanese governments progressively relaxed important regulatory restrictions. In the United States, the 1971 Hunt Commission Report and the House Banking Committee's 1975 report *Financial Institutions in the Nation's Economy* called for removing deposit interest rate ceilings, giving banks and S&Ls new lending and investment powers, eliminating restrictions on statewide branching, and taking other mostly expansive steps. The two pieces of legislation that incorporated most of these actions were the Depository Institutions Deregulation and Monetary Control Act of 1980 and the Garn-St. Germain Act of 1982. Garn-St. Germain also removed all existing statutory limits (such as aggregate percentage limits, maximum loan-to-value ratios, and minimum amortization terms) on real estate lending by nationally chartered banks, increased banks' loan limits for a single borrower from 10 to 15 percent of a bank's capital (25 percent if the loan is collateralized), and permitted S&Ls to invest up to 5 percent of their assets in commercial loans and up to 30 percent in consumer loans. Although the Office of the Comptroller of the Currency (OCC) was given authority to set restrictions on national banks' real estate lending, however, in keeping with the antiregulatory attitudes of the Reagan administration, the OCC opted to impose no limits.

   In Japan, as Hoshi and Kashyap (1999) have emphasized, a parallel wave of deregulation has likewise fostered the transformation of banks' portfolios. On the borrowers' side, beginning in 1975 deregulation allowed the creation of Japanese bond and commercial paper markets, thereby freeing many nonfinancial operating companies from their traditional dependence on bank credit. Also, beginning in 1979 the Japanese authorities progressively relaxed restrictions on the banks' activities. Key steps in this latter process included permission for banks to issue and deal in certificates of deposit (1979), to lend in yen outside Japan (1982), to affiliate with mortgage securities companies (1983), to issue mortgage bonds on their own account (1986), and to underwrite and deal in commercial paper (1987).

5. In both countries, this progressive deregulation combined with deposit insurance (and limited shareholder liability) to create a classic moral hazard problem. In Japan, as noted above, the Deposit Insurance Corporation (DIC) was established in 1971. Membership was (and is) compulsory for virtually all depository institutions. Even more important, however, was the informal but strong presumption that the controlling authorities, principally the Ministry of Finance and the Bank of Japan, would arrange affairs so that no bank would fail in such a way as to cause depositors to suffer losses. In the event, that presumption proved correct. In the United States, deposit insurance had existed since the 1930s, but with a maximum coverage per account that left large deposits uninsured. Moreover, uninsured depositors occasionally did sustain losses in bank failures, so that the possibility of loss was well understood. In 1982, however, the Garn-St. Germain Act raised the insurance limit from $40,000 to $100,000.[3]

6. As numerous observers have emphasized, the ability of banks (and, in the United States, especially S&Ls) to exploit this moral hazard situation was enhanced by lax prudential supervision. In Japan, the close relationships between lending institutions and their supposed unit-level regulators and examiners has by now become the stuff of high-level national scandal. In the United States, the problem was less a matter of individual regulators' malfeasance or conflict of interest than a reflection of the antiregulatory mood of the Reagan era. At the same time that new legislation was expanding banks' scope of activities, the most severe business recession of the postwar period was creating record-level bankruptcies, and the developing-country debt crisis was breaking abroad, the number of bank examiners employed by the FDIC *fell* from 1,713 in 1979 to 1,389 in 1984, and the number employed by the OCC likewise *fell* from 2,151 to 1,722. Not surprisingly, the average interval between examinations increased significantly, even for banks with the lowest ratings. Although the matter is hard to describe except anecdotally, in both countries out-and-out criminal corruption and self-dealing also seem to have been a significant part of what happened.

---

3. In the original legislative discussion, the proposal was a more routine increase to $50,000, to allow for then-recent inflation. As Davison relates the relevant history, "The lower figure remained in the bill, however, until it was replaced by the $100,000 limit at a late-night House-Senate conference. The decision, scarcely remarked at the time, would come to be viewed by many as having weighty consequences" (1997, 93).

7. Even aside from credit problems that reached the level of crisis, the banking industries in both the United States and Japan have for some time faced the need to downsize and restructure, but in neither country is the road to renewed profitability clear. At least before Glass-Steagall was repealed, most US banks had apparently recognized the difficulty of finding new sources of revenue and had therefore turned to expense reduction as the most promising way of enhancing profits. Success at these efforts has been mixed, to say the least. No doubt banks' investment in technology will save expenses over some horizon, but in the short run (and, for many banks, the medium run as well) this investment has proved very costly. The banks that have invested the most also run the greatest risk of being leapfrogged as yet newer technology emerges.

   The other principal route US banks have taken in the effort to achieve expense reduction is consolidation. Although here too the motivating logic is clear enough, in practice to date the cost savings achieved by many US bank mergers have been disappointing. Meanwhile, Japanese banks are only just beginning to go down a similar path characterized by consolidation, investment in technology, and staff reductions. It is too soon to know whether they will be more successful in this regard than their US counterparts. It is also too soon to know how the repeal of Glass-Steagall will affect the situation in the United States. But the point remains that the industry in both countries needs to restructure.

Responses to the Crises

1. Once the crises were recognized, in neither country did the central bank resort to price inflation as a solution to the banks' problems. The recent high for US inflation, as measured by the chained GDP price index, was 3.9 percent in 1990. Since then, inflation has slowed almost without interruption. Inflation in 1999 was 1.4 percent, up only modestly from 1.2 percent in 1998. In Japan, the recent high for inflation, measured by the implicit GDP deflator, was 2.3 percent in 1989. By 1994, Japanese prices were falling. Since then, inflation has hovered near zero.

2. The main response of the banking authorities in both countries was, in the first instance, regulatory "forbearance"—in other words, either redefining the rules to make them less restrictive or simply looking the other way when restrictions were violated. In the United States, the most extreme form of regulatory forbearance was that practiced by the FSLIC, under which (as both Kane 1989 and White 1991 have emphasized in great detail) large numbers of insolvent and marginally solvent S&Ls were permitted to remain in operation for periods that

ran to several years. US bank regulators also, however, permitted some large banks (including some that subsequently failed) to operate for long periods with minimal capital. In some cases—for example, mutual savings banks in the Northeast and banks with troubled loans in the energy and agriculture sectors—this forbearance was even explicitly mandated by legislation.

In Japan, regulatory forbearance began when the first Ministry of Finance inspection of the *jusen*, in 1991, showed 40 percent of all loans on the books to be nonperforming and the response was a 10-year regulatory restructuring window. (By 1995, 75 percent of all *jusen* assets were nonperforming, and this part of the industry had to be shut down.) Since then, the equivalent of regulatory forbearance in Japan has largely taken the form of weak supervision standards, which continually allowed banks to resist classifying as nonperforming their dubious or even underwater credits. As a result, most observers of the Japanese banking industry in time came to dismiss each successive private or official announcement of the scale of the "bad loan" problem as a gross understatement, and correspondingly to regard all banks' capital positions as overstated. By the late 1990s, it had become commonplace for private analysts to conclude that in aggregate the entire Japanese banking industry was insolvent, or even that each of the 21 large banks was individually insolvent.

3. The policy of regulatory forbearance in both countries was in part a reflection of the hope that in time a changed economic environment would take care of the problem (a hope that in the United States was eventually realized for most banks, but not for the S&Ls). But it was also a direct consequence of the delay in provision of public funds. After all, the alternative to regulatory forbearance often means closing an institution down. If the institution's liabilities exceed its assets, this takes an infusion of money. In both the United States and Japan, that money was slow to be provided, even after it became clear that the US FDIC and FSLIC, and the Japanese DIC, were out of money.

   In the United States, the first break came in 1987, when the Competitive Equality Banking Act (CEBA) provided just under $11 billion to recapitalize the FSLIC. (CEBA also mandated a forbearance program for weak but "well-managed" S&Ls.) Subsequent legislation created the Resolution Trust Corporation and its financing arm, the Resolution Finance Corporation, with the ability to issue securities directly against not only assets acquired but also a US government guarantee. The total amount of public funds that Congress authorized for the S&L rescue operation, in various pieces of legislation, was $159 billion. The eventual direct cost to taxpayers included $42 billion in costs reimbursed to the FSLIC for cases handled during 1986-89 and another $79 billion in costs borne through the RTC on cases handled from 1989 on.[4] In

4. These costs are net of the proceeds of asset liquidations, and they exclude author $6 billion in tax benefits awarded to private acquirers of failed S&Ls.

Japan, the first formal provision of public funds did not come until 1995, when the government put ¥7 trillion into a subsidiary of the DIC to allow it to acquire the remaining assets of the failed *jusen*. Two pieces of legislation passed in 1998 put up another ¥60 trillion—of which ¥17 trillion went into a special DIC account to bolster the protection of banks' deposits; ¥18 trillion went into an account to be used for bank liquidations, temporary nationalizations, and the creation of "bridge banks" to receive the assets of failed banks; and ¥25 trillion went for injections of funds to recapitalize surviving institutions. As of year-end 1999, 15 of the surviving large banks had drawn down ¥7.5 trillion from this third amount in exchange for issuing to the DIC new convertible preferred shares. (Soon after these capital infusions, the "Japan premium" in the interbank lending market mostly disappeared, and the prices of Japanese bank stocks rose sharply.) In far smaller amounts, the government has similarly injected capital into the most important regional banks. Hence, in both countries the government eventually did commit serious amounts of public funds, but delay in doing so—a delay due to a combination of reluctance to impose on taxpayers, reluctance to accept the consequences for individual institutions and reluctance to acknowledge bad news, all together with hopes that changing economic conditions would resolve the problem without needing any public funds—was a major part of the story.

4. In both countries, the banks themselves—in other words, the banks' shareholders—have borne part of the cost of the crisis. In the United States, the S&L industry directly bore $22 billion in FSLIC costs for 1985-89 resolutions (vs. $42 billion from taxpayers) and $6 billion in RTC costs for 1989-95 resolutions (versus $79 billion from taxpayers). Banks' deposit insurance premiums rose to cover costs of FDIC assistance to banks that failed. More important, many banks cut their dividends, in some cases to zero, and the shareholders of many banks saw the market value of their equity reduced to a fraction of what it had been before the crisis.

   In Japan, the market price of many bank stocks fell to only 10 percent or so of their previous peak value, before recovering sharply—but still only to levels far below their previous peaks—in 1999. As of the September 1999 reporting date, the cumulative loss taken on disposal of bad loans by all Japanese banks was ¥61 trillion (compared with 1998 GDP of ¥497 trillion). Moreover, the charge to Japanese bank shareholders is still ongoing. In 1999, 16 of the 17 surviving large banks (all but the recently merged Bank of Tokyo Mitsubishi) cut their dividends. Two of these, both trust banks, eliminated their dividends altogether.

Policy Implications for Japan

Six potentially important lessons, some narrowly focused on the banking industry's problems and others pertinent to the Japanese economy more generally, emerge from a consideration of these parallels (and differences) between Japan's banking crisis and that in the United States a decade or so ago.

1. *Act more promptly.* Careful studies of the US savings and loan cleanup have shown that a crucial factor influencing the cost of resolving individual institutions' insolvencies was delay by the responsible authorities. In short, delay is expensive. Ely and Varaiya (1997), for example, showed that delays in RTC resolutions significantly raised resolution costs and reduced the premiums received on auction sales of institutions taken into receivership. According to their estimates, each additional *1-month* delay reduced the auction premium by $118,000, compared with a mean premium received of $5.8 million and a median premium of just $712,000. The message from this experience is that delaying action—in the hope that either a change in the economic environment or some independent development may turn matters around, or perhaps merely out of an inability to overcome political or administrative obstacles even after everyone recognizes what needs to be done—is a policy with a price. Moreover, in the US experience, the price was high enough to make most such delays objects of regret after the fact.

2. *Avoid regulatory forbearance.* The US experience shows that regulatory forbearance sometimes paid off but was mostly a bad idea. Further, the uses of forbearance that had more positive results—for example, the Net Worth Certificate Program, mandated under the Garn-St. Germain Act to enable insolvent mutual savings banks to hold out until what had been an extraordinary level of interest rates as well as an extraordinary yield curve reverted more nearly to normal (which both did)—were narrowly targeted in scope and applied in circumstances that minimized the resulting moral hazard problems. Hanc (1997) found that of the more than 1,650 commercial banks that failed during 1980-92, nearly 350 would have faced earlier closure if the "prompt corrective action" rules later put in place under the 1991 FDICIA legislation had been in effect all along. He concluded that, although these delays due to regulatory forbearance were mostly not costly, some were.

   In the case of S&Ls, it is clear that FSLIC forbearance in enforcing capital requirements provided support to many highly risky institutions and even some that in effect ran as Ponzi schemes. As Kane and Yu (1996) have shown, under any of several sets of assumptions it would have been far less expensive to taxpayers to close undercapitalized S&Ls more promptly. The main conclusion from this experience is that both kinds of delays are costly: delays in resolving failures once they have occurred, as well as delays in declaring that insolvent or undercapitalized institutions have failed and closing them. Japan's "Prompt Corrective Action" legislation (enacted in 1997, and loosely based on the US model), and the establishment of the Financial Supervisory Agency (FSA) as an independent regulatory body in 1998, were clearly useful steps. Closing the Hokkaido Takushoku Bank (in 1997) and temporarily nationalizing Long-Term Credit Bank and Nippon Credit Bank (both in 1998) just as clearly represented the end of, or at least a major change in, Japan's traditional "convoy" system of bank regulation. But undercapitalized or even insolvent banks remain a concern. Similarly, while the FSA's aggressive posture is certainly welcome—examples include the agency's more proactive stance on declaring loan losses and its role in seeking restructuring conditions as part of the injection of new capital into the 15 banks that took advantage of this opportunity—as of the time of writing, it is too early to conclude with confidence that this apparently new regime will mark a lasting break with the past. Hence regulatory forbearance remains a temptation to be avoided.

3. *Force consolidations.* Yet another reason for seeking to eliminate insolvent or undercapitalized lenders is to improve the competitive environment for the survivors. Because insolvency greatly magnifies the usual moral hazard problems, insolvent banks can and often do undercut solvent ones in competition for credit business, thus making it more difficult for the solvent banks to be profitable without bearing excessive risk. As of the time of writing, when little new bank lending is occurring in Japan anyway, it is hard to argue that this further aspect of regulatory forbearance is a currently active problem. But the object of Japanese policy in this area should be to recreate a banking system capable of supporting an economic expansion once other factors—most important, fiscal and monetary policies—produce one. Attempting to create that support by allowing insolvent institutions to provide the credit only ensures that neither the banking system nor the economic expansion will prove robust. A central lesson to remember from the US experience is that, despite years of excessive regulatory forbearance, in the end the principal use of public funds was *to put institutions out of business.* The new prevalence in Japan of mergers completed and mergers in progress, among not only regional banks but also the large "city" and "trust" banks—all presumably with approval from the Financial Reconstruction Commission (or FRC, established in 1998 to oversee the bank restructuring process)—suggests progress along just these lines. Even so, it remains to be seen whether this strategy repre-

sents the kind of effort to eliminate bank offices and duplicative functions that has motivated many large bank mergers in the United States (admittedly, with limited concrete payoff to date) or merely an attempt to "change the name over the door" while keeping in place an "overbanked" financial system.

Similarly, the potential role of foreign competitors remains, as always in Japan, an unresolved question. In 1999, the FRC approved the sale of Long-Term Credit Bank, which the DIC had nationalized the year before, to Ripplewood Holdings, a US investment firm. (Similar foreign acquisitions of failed Japanese firms have taken place outside the banking sector—e.g., Merrill Lynch's purchase of Yamaichi Securities and G.E. Capital's purchase of Japan Leasing.) But more recently the FRC, apparently under some political pressure, declined to approve an analogous sale of Nippon Credit Bank to a foreign buyer. More generally, the FRC has chosen thus far to conduct such negotiations mostly in secret, in contrast to the transparency achieved by the RTC's use of competitive auction procedures in the United States.

4. *Sell the collateral.* The Japanese authorities have already moved, in a limited way through the Cooperative Credit Purchasing Company (CCPC), to acquire nonperforming bank assets. Set up in 1993 and funded mostly during the following 2 years, the CCPC used ¥5.8 trillion to purchase more than 11,000 loans against more than 20,000 properties, consisting mostly of real estate. As of March 1999, the CCPC had sold roughly half of these properties and had realized ¥2.5 trillion from the sales. But the CCPC is a limited vehicle, not least because its purchase of a nonperforming loan is typically financed by its own borrowing from the selling bank (so that the bank removes a bad asset from its balance sheet and replaces it with a presumably good asset: the obligation of the CCPC). The US experience suggests that more of this kind of activity (however financed)—importantly including both the loan purchases and the collateral sales—would be helpful. It is easy to overstate concerns about the effect on real estate values due to sales of assumed loan collateral. In most cases, in the United States, the negative short-run impact from sales of government-assumed collateral was less than the market had anticipated. Moreover, the medium- to longer-run effect of eliminating the overhang of real estate held for sale was often beneficial. Everybody knows that this collateral will have to be sold sooner or later. Actually putting it on the block clears the air rather than spoiling the market.

5. *Penalize shareholders, not depositors.* There is no need for depositors, especially holders of small and medium-sized deposits, to bear losses in a banking crisis. Especially in the wake of the US S&L industry collapse, some economists have called for an end to deposit insurance.

But the answer to the moral hazard problem is not to eliminate deposit insurance altogether but rather to limit it by size of deposit and, even more important, to exercise effective prudential regulation and supervision. (Japan's plan to limit deposit insurance to ¥10 million per account, originally scheduled to take effect in March 2001 but now delayed until 2002, is a good idea; but the sooner the better.)

By contrast, when banks suffer losses, it is important for bank shareholders to lose their equity, and sometimes for bank managers to lose their jobs. Yes, there are limits on the appropriate reliance on market discipline. But as the US experience shows, the natural instinct of public authorities is to err by relying too little on market discipline, not too much. Nothing draws investors' attention to a problem more effectively than for shareholders of an insolvent firm to be told the truth: that the value of their investment is zero. Similarly, nothing teaches the value of good job performance better than seeing those who have performed poorly face directly the consequences of their institution's corporate failure, rather than continue to reap the usual personal rewards.

6. *Apply expansionary fiscal and monetary policies.* The record of the banking crises in both Japan and the United States makes clear that, while banking-sector problems can be a cause of poor economic growth, they are also a consequence. Conversely, the banks' (but not S&Ls') experience in the United States showed how fast a banking system can restore its capital position and rebuild profitability once insolvent institutions have been cleared away *and* the economy has staged a significant recovery. For this reason, it is all the more important to do what Japan should have been doing all along on other grounds—namely, using expansionary fiscal and monetary policy to foster economic expansion. Recently, both fiscal and monetary policies in Japan have taken important steps in the right direction. But much still remains to be done. In the fiscal area, as Posen (1998) has argued, the main policy thrust should center on tax cuts. In the monetary area, as Bernanke's essay in this volume forcefully makes clear, the Bank of Japan should first realize the error of its belief that hitting the zero bound on nominal interest rates precludes its doing anything more to ease monetary policy, and then go ahead and carry out yet further expansionary open market operations. Both fiscal policy and monetary policy lie beyond the scope of this essay, which focuses more directly on the banking sector, but the appropriate use of these macroeconomic instruments to spur a business recovery nonetheless is an important part of coping with Japan's banking crisis.

Some Questions of Political Economy

There is no need to summarize the six suggestions for Japanese policymakers offered immediately above on the basis of parallels between Japan's and the United States' respective banking crises. Instead, it is useful to conclude by posing several questions about the Japanese crisis from the perspective of political economy.

First, where did all the money go? It is important to keep in mind that what is at issue when banks and other lenders fail is not just numbers on balance sheets but transfers of real resources. In the US banking and S&L crises, it was clear after the fact that much of the money lost represented dissipation of the US economy's real resources in constructing office buildings, energy extraction facilities, and other physical projects that in the end the market did not value. (It was also probably true, though less straightforward to document, that much of the rest represented the transfer of resources to corrupt and self-dealing operators of depository institutions.) Such a judgment is harder to draw for Japan, because so much of the problem there centered on loans not for construction, although that was also important, but for what amounted to speculation in land or equities. To be sure, those who bought these assets at inflated prices lost their investment, and the lenders that backed them also lost. But for every investor who bought at the top there was also a seller. Did the Japanese banking crisis mostly amount to a huge transfer mechanism—*from* banks, taxpayers, and investors *to* yet other investors? In short, where did the money go?

Second, is it fair to treat Japanese banks as strictly private firms, whose shareholders and managers should appropriately be subject to market discipline when their institutions' affairs go badly? Under Japan's traditional system of administrative guidance of the entire financial sector—and, more broadly, in light of the consensual nature of Japanese society as a whole—perhaps the banks, in lending so aggressively against rapidly inflating real estate and equity values, were merely acting as agents of public policy. If so, then the conventional rationale underlying the argument for exposing these institutions and their managers to market discipline would not apply. At the same time, however, drawing that judgment would also then imply that these institutions were not truly private competitors and therefore that their earning a competitive market rate of return on average over time would not be warranted.

Finally, why the failure to address these costly problems—either the banking crisis or Japan's economic malaise more generally—for so many years? Normally, when a country is paralyzed in the face of costly problems like these, its inaction stems from some kind of internal structural conflict that prevents the society from reaching a consensus on what is to be done. But at least as most Westerners see Japan, its society is not particularly subject to such conflicts. Nor, at least with regard to the banking crisis, does there appear to be a real lack of consensus on what to do. Are Western observers missing some fundamental aspect of Japan's social makeup? Whatever the answer, one hopes that the progress made in addressing these problems in just the past year or two continues.

References

Davison, Lee. 1997. Banking Legislation and Regulation. In *History of the 1980s: Lessons for the Future*, vol. 1. Washington: Federal Deposit Insurance Corporation.

Ely, David P., and Nikhil P. Varaiya. 1997. Assessing the Resolution of Insolvent Thrift Institutions Post FIRREA: The Impact of Resolution Delays. *Journal of Financial Services Research* 11 (June): 255-82.

Hanc, George. 1997. The Banking Crises of the 1980s and Early 1990s: Summary and Implications. In *History of the 1980s: Lessons for the Future*, vol. 1. Washington: Federal Deposit Insurance Corporation.

Hoshi, Takeo, and Anil K. Kashyap. 1999. The Japanese Banking Crisis: Where Did It Come From and How Will It End? *NBER 1999 Macroeconomics Annual*. Cambridge, MA: MIT Press.

Hoshi, Takeo, and Anil K. Kashyap. Forthcoming. *Keiretsu Financing*. Cambridge, MA: MIT Press.

Kane, Edward J. 1989. *The S&L Insurance Mess: How Did It Happen?* Washington: Urban Institute.

Kane, Edward J., and Min-Teh Yu. 1996. Opportunity Cost of Capital Forbearance During the Final Years of the FSLIC Mess. *Quarterly Review of Economics and Finance* 36 (Fall): 271-90.

Kaufman, George G. 1997. Preventing Banking Crises in the Future: Lessons from Past Mistakes. *Review of Monetary and Financial Studies* 13-14 (November): 7-25.

Milhaupt, Curtis J. 1999. Japan's Experience with Deposit Insurance and Failing Banks: Implications for Financial Regulatory Design? *Monetary and Economic Studies* (Bank of Japan) 17 (August): 21-46.

White, Lawrence J. 1991. *The S&L Debacle: Public Policy Lessons for Bank and Thrift Regulation*. New York: Oxford University Press.

4

Convoy Regulation, Bank Management, and the Financial Crisis in Japan

YOSHINORI SHIMIZU

Introduction

The 1990s were a lost decade for the Japanese economy. This prolonged depression was rooted in the troubled financial system, which brought about a credit crunch and a resulting pessimism about growth opportunities. In 1999, the Japanese government decided to spend ¥67 trillion (13.2 percent of GDP) of public funds to try to overcome the country's financial crisis.

The period 1980-96 witnessed widespread financial deregulation for many of the world's economies. As a result of this increasingly competitive environment, 133 out of 181 IMF member countries experienced significant banking-sector problems, which were the worst seen since the Great Depression of the 1930s.[1] The problems experienced by the Japanese banking sector have many common characteristics with those in other IMF member countries. Financial market deregulation also appears to add to

Yoshinori Shimizu is professor in the Graduate School of Commerce, Hitotsubashi University. *The author is grateful to Ronald Masulis for valuable suggestions and Sohn Young Hwan for research assistance. He benefited from the participants in our session of the AEA meeting, especially Benjamin Friedman, Robert Glauber, Anil Kashyap, Adam Posen, and Ryuzo Miyao. Any errors that remain are the author's.*

1. Lindgren, Garcia, and Saal (1996).

the market's fragility.[2] In magnitude, the problems of Japan's banking industry rank among the most serious.

There are clear reasons why Japan experienced a financial crisis of this magnitude following financial deregulation. After World War II, regulations were implemented to try to safeguard the financial system. Unfortunately, they worked perniciously to induce banks to take excessive risks when the financial environment changed. Asset inflation in the late 1980s played a crucial role in this process. The financial structure of the Japanese economy and key policies—such as the collateral principle used in the bank loan approval process, and the importance of land prices as a source of collateral—also were important elements in explaining what happened.

In this essay, we first examine fundamental characteristics of the Japanese financial system under the government's convoy regulations, banks' reaction to deregulation, and how that reaction was related to the asset bubbles in the late 1980s. Then we present a theory of bank lending and collateral to explain the banks' lending behavior and the important role played by rising land prices. We go on to analyze empirically the relationship among land prices, bank loans, and funds raised in the capital market to assess what happened in the Japanese financial market during this period. The conclusion summarizes the main arguments.

Convoy Regulation and the Financial System

Convoy regulations were devised to safeguard the soundness of the Japanese financial system after World War II. Among the many regulations that suppressed competition among banks, regulation of deposit interest rates had the most profound impact. In order to ensure the effectiveness of regulation without reducing bank deposits, interest rates were regulated in all other markets as well. Restraints on interest rates and on corporate bond issuance in the capital market were implemented. The permitted size of corporate bond issues was strictly allocated among large firms by the Committee on Security Issues (Kisaikai), which was under control of the monetary authorities.

This system of funds allocation contributed to the high growth of the Japanese economy in the 1960s. On the basis of the collateral principle, permission for corporate bond issues was preferentially allocated to heavy industries and chemicals, which had large amounts of collateral, in the form of large factories, land, and production facilities. The "income-doubling policy" in the 1960s fostered the growth of heavy industries and chemicals, which had high income elasticities of demand in the export market at that time. Approval of a bond issue under the existing regulated

2. Demirgüc-Kunt and Detragiache (1998).

Figure 4.1 The composition of financial assets of individuals in Japan (percent)

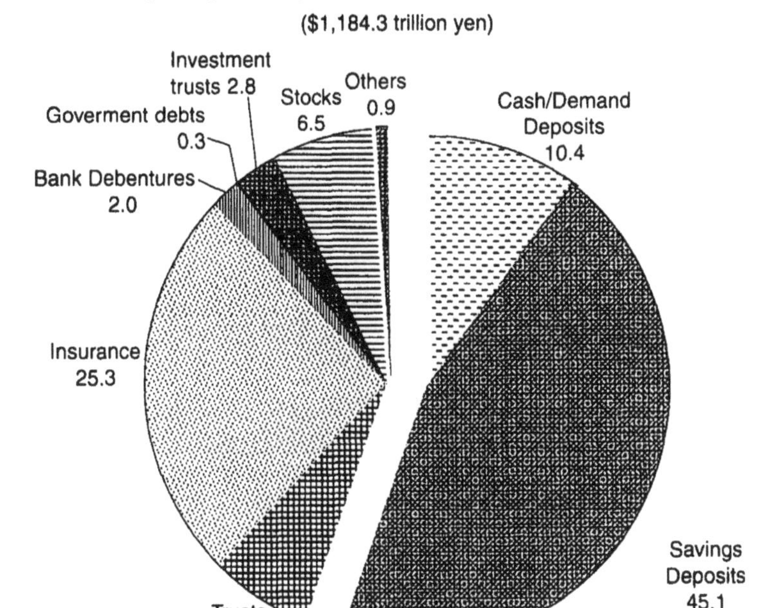

Note: As of the end of 1995.

Source: Nomura Investment Trust.

interest rate regime implied an allocation of a low-cost and long-term source of funds to these firms.

Since all defaulted corporate bonds were bought back by trustee banks, there were no defaults in which individual investors suffered losses. In practice, collateral was required to obtain bank guarantees on the corporate bonds. Thus, through the guarantee process, the collateral principle used in the bank loan market also affected the corporate bond market. The regulation of the primary market for corporate bonds and constraints on interest rates deprived the capital market of the opportunity to evaluate and price credit risk. This limited the growth of the capital market. Corporate bonds with higher risks, which required higher-risk premiums, were prohibited. As a result, "investor protection" regulation worked to protect the dominant share of banks in the Japanese financial market.

Figures 4.1 and 4.2 show the composition of financial assets of individuals in Japan and in the United States, respectively, as of the mid-1990s. The share of bank deposits was 55.5 percent in Japan, but only 16 percent in the United States. In the 1980s, the funds of the banking system increased dramatically due to the creation of new large deposit accounts that gave

Figure 4.2 The composition of financial assets of individuals in the United States (percent)

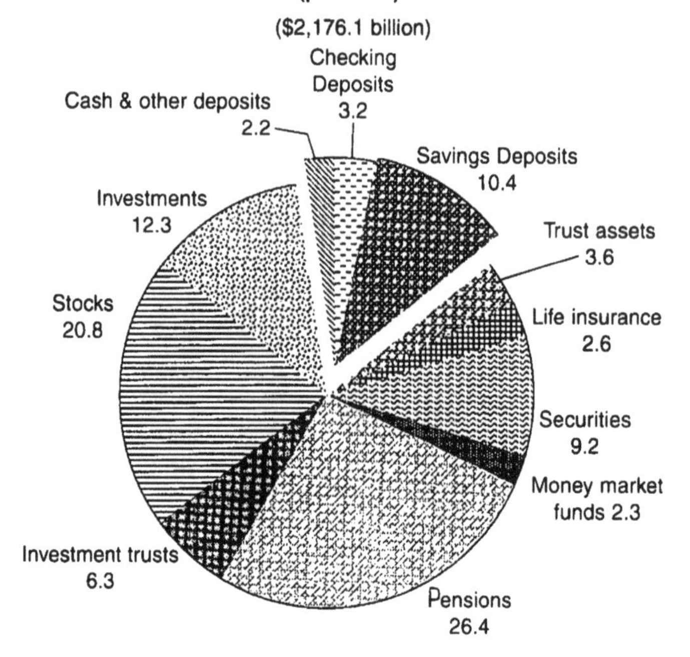

Note: As of March 1996.

Source: Nomura Investment Trust.

higher interest rates. These increased deposits in the banks became a principal cause of the bubble economy, because banks had to find borrowers while large corporations went increasingly to capital markets directly after deregulation. There was a mismatch between deregulation of corporate capital practices and ongoing limits on bank activities.

Thus, banks were the primary gatekeepers responsible for supplying long-term funds to Japanese corporations. In order to obtain long-term loans or bond guarantees, collateral was a critical ingredient. The dominant source of collateral for Japanese corporations was real estate, especially land, and having this collateral then gave access to the financial market.

With regulated interest rates, the banks' dominant capital market position is a major source of their profits, which also insured their soundness during the period of high growth, when the overall risk of the economy was low. Since a bank's profits were proportional to the size of its outstanding loans, all banks competed with each other to obtain larger deposit balances, which could then be lent out as loans. This pattern of competition

Figure 4.3 Funds raised in the capital market

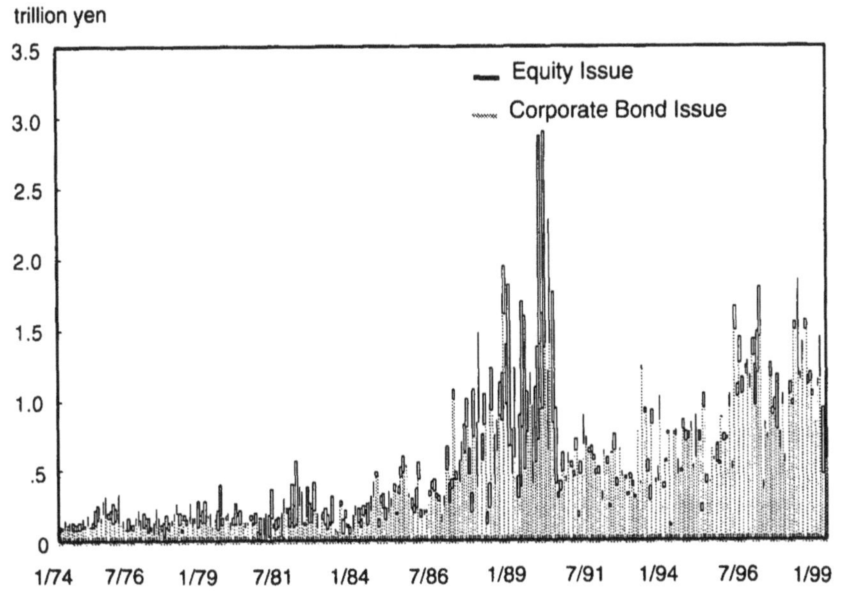

Sources: Monthly Report on Public and Corporate Debts, Monthly Statistics of Tokyo Stock Exchange.

among Japanese banks has a long tradition under the convoy regulations, which have been outstanding for several decades.

In the 1990s, risks in the Japanese economy markedly increased, and the banks' large share of the corporate loan market turned into a disadvantage. As stronger corporate borrowers turned to the bond market, banks were forced to make loans to less credible borrowers, and collateral was again an important criterion for loan approval. Naturally, the drastic fall in land prices had an extremely serious effect on the stability of the financial system. Thus, the crisis of the Japanese financial system in the 1990s was a result of the convoy regulations, which effectively safeguarded the financial system prior to deregulation.

Fund-Raising by Large Firms

The Japanese financial market in the second half of the 1980s was most evidently characterized by a rapid increase in capital market fund-raising by corporations in the face of progressive financial deregulation. Figure 4.3 shows the movement of fund-raising in the Japanese capital market and its growth rate relative to the same month of the previous year.

This enormous increase in capital-market fund-raising was brought about partly by equity issues at a time when stock prices were rapidly rising and partly by the emergence of new financial instruments, such as commercial paper, foreign debt issues, and unsecured corporate debentures.

Under the convoy regulations, only large firms were allowed access to the capital market. These large firms raised more funds than they needed for capital investments from newly liberalized capital markets. Supported by soaring stock prices, large corporations issued equity, convertible bonds, and bonds with warrants at historically high prices and extremely low interest rates. They invested the new funds in assets that promised higher rates of return. These assets included certificates of deposit and foreign currency deposits, unregulated interest-rate accounts for large deposits, and financial instruments that benefited from soaring stock prices, such as special money trusts and trust funds.

Among all assets, real estate had the highest long-run rate of return up to 1990. The average annual rate of growth in land prices in the six largest Japanese cities was 12.7 percent from 1955 to 1990, and 23.1 percent from 1985 to 1990 (see figure 4.18 below). Large firms' investments in the domestic real estate and stock markets boosted the soaring prices in these markets, which were later labeled "asset bubbles." The increased land prices had a significant impact on the behavior of banks, as will be discussed below.

Large firms began to raise funds exclusively through security issues in the capital markets and reduced their borrowing from banks. They even used the funds they raised to repay outstanding bank loans. The declining growth rate of bank loans to large firms is shown in figures 4.4 and 4.5. This trend has been continuing since the early 1970s, when the Japanese economy shifted from a high-growth to a slower-growth period. The declining shares of long-term corporate loans held by long-term-credit banks and trust banks (whose customers were large firms) are shown in figure 4.6. Figure 4.7 shows the shares of loans secured by real estate across different groups of banks. It illustrates an accelerated fall in loan shares by long-term-credit banks and a steady increase in the share for regional banks (whose main customers were medium-sized and small firms). This contrast is clearer in figure 4.8, which shows the shares of secured loans using real estate as collateral.

The figures highlight the fact that reduced demand by large firms for bank loans most seriously affected long-term-credit banks, which ultimately resulted in the nationalization in 1998 of two long-term-credit banks, Japan Credit Bank and Japan Long-Term Credit Bank. The long-term-credit banks were also adversely affected by the deregulation of interest rates in the capital market, which preceded the deregulation of deposit interest rates. Under the convoy regulations, long-term-credit banks could issue corporate bonds to raise low-cost long-term sources of

Figure 4.4 Bank loans by size of borrowers

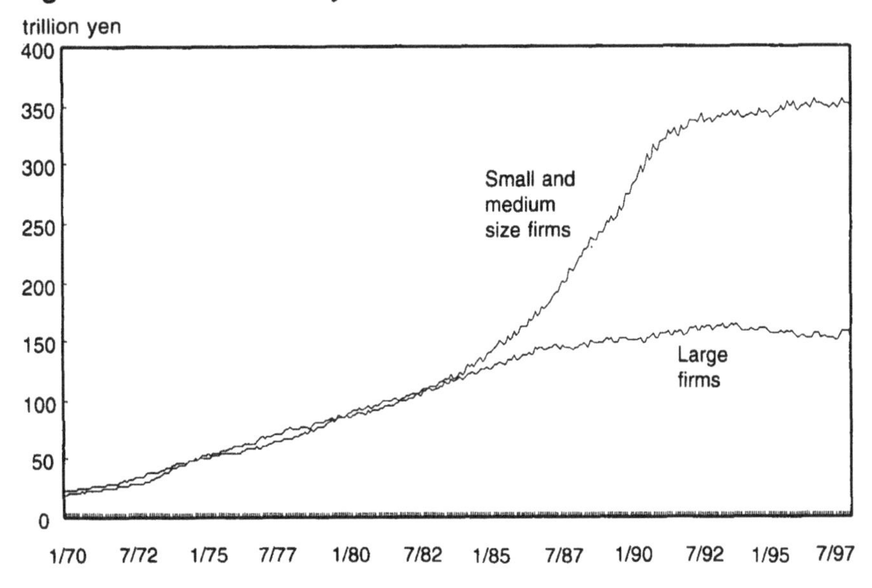

Source: Economic Statistics Monthly. Converted into a continuous data by the author.

Figure 4.5 Growth rates of bank loans

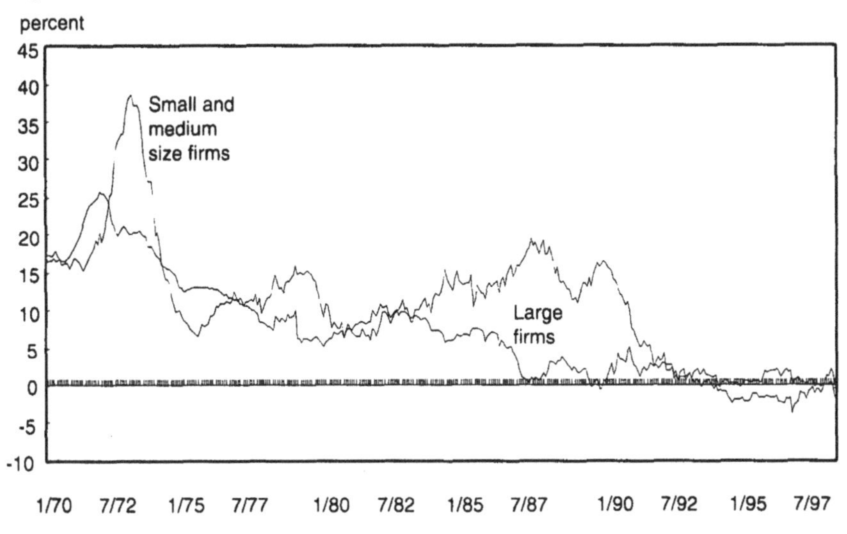

Source: Economic Statistics Monthly. Converted into continuous data by the author.

Figure 4.6 Share of long-term loans

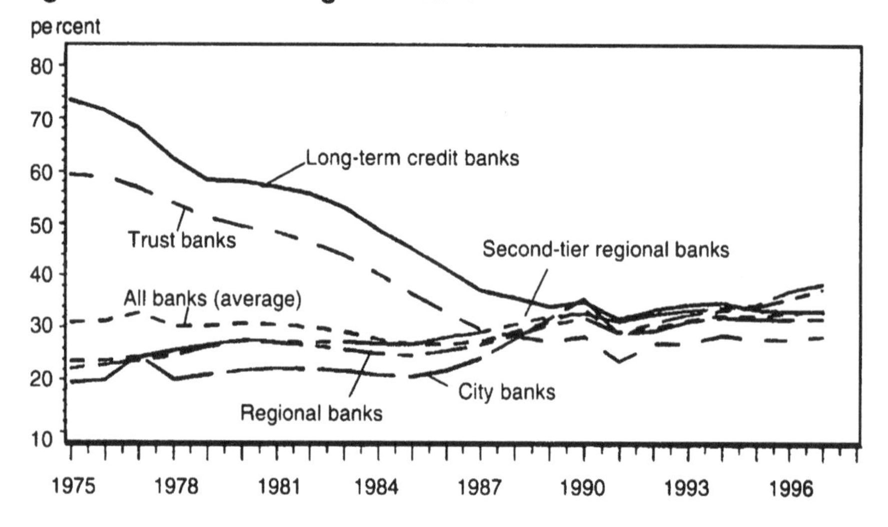

Source: Calculated by the author based on *Bank Financial Data, Nikkei Electronic Economic Database System.*

Figure 4.7 Share of loans secured by real estate

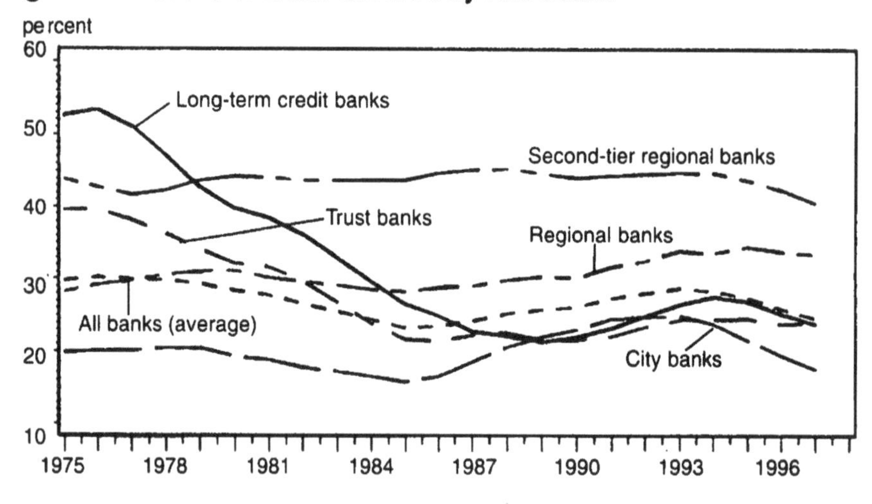

Source: Calculated by the author based on *Bank Financial Data, Nikkei Electronic Economic Database System.*

Figure 4.8 Share of loans secured by real estate in secured loans

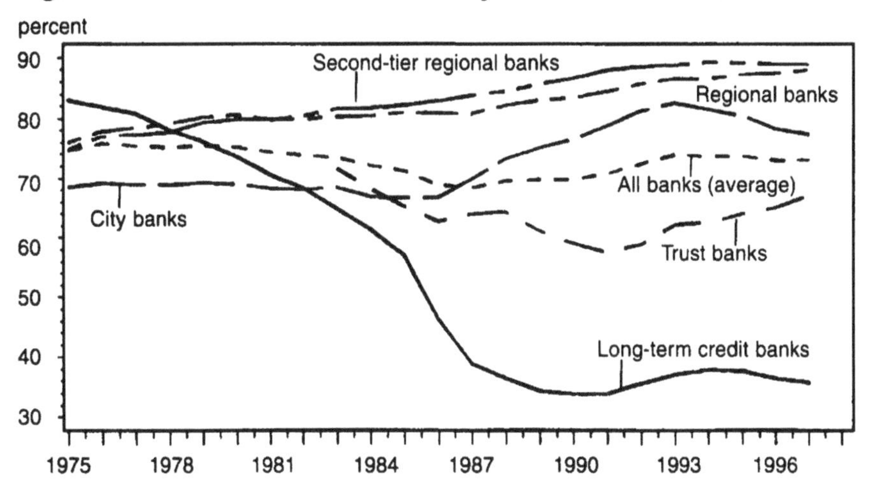

Source: Calculated by the author based on *Bank Financial Data, Nikkei Electronic Economic Database System.*

funds, while other banks could not. On the other hand, long-term-credit banks were not allowed to take deposit accounts, and only had relationships with large firms. This is the reason why they had little or no access to small and medium-sized firms and individual customers, which were the province of the regional banks.

Once the liberalization of interest rates began in the capital market, however, the cost of funds of long-term-credit banks rose, before the rise in the cost of deposits of other banks. Since their main customers were large firms, the fall in loan demand was more serious. Long-term-credit banks eagerly hoped to enter the securities business to meet large firms' increased demand for funds from security offerings. Unfortunately, the process of deregulation was slow, because it was based on the policy of "measures to mitigate drastic changes" in the financial markets. Banks have been allowed to establish subsidiaries to enter the security business only since 1993. Even at that time, bank subsidiaries were not allowed to have a stock-trading business. Therefore, long-term-credit banks were very seriously affected by deregulation and were forced to find new borrowers while facing higher costs of funds. Although the situation is more or less the same for all groups of banks, the long-term-credit banks, which were most privileged under the convoy regulations, experienced the most damaging impacts of the slowly implemented financial deregulation process.

Figure 4.9 Deposits of domestically licensed banks

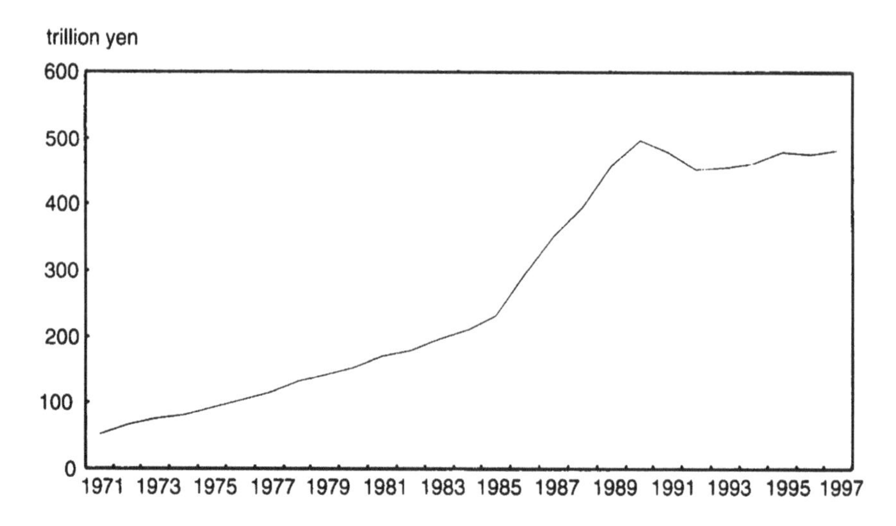

Source: Economic Statistics Annual, Bank of Japan.

Increased Bank Lending to Small and Medium-Sized Firms

When deposit interest rates were liberalized, starting with large deposits in 1985, bank deposit levels increased rapidly, as shown in figure 4.9. Bank fund-raising through newly allowed sources increased as well. From a naïve viewpoint, it was a wonderful opportunity for banks to increase their profit by making larger loans. On the other hand, loans demand by large firms declined sharply, squeezing banks' profit margins on loans to these customers. In the late 1980s, nearly all Japanese banks were feeling competitive pressures to find new loan customers.

There were five kinds of loans with which most banks expanded their portfolios: (1) to small and medium-sized firms, (2) to the real estate industry, (3) to the finance industry, (4) to individuals, and (5) to overseas investors. Figures 4.10 through 4.14 show the shares of loans going to each category. As shown in figures 4.15 and 4.16, the shift in loans from the manufacturing sector to the service sector also is a common trend among all these banks. The higher the initial share of large firms in their loan portfolios, the larger the shift of their lending patterns. The long-term-credit banks were forced to make the most drastic adjustments, given

Figure 4.10 Share of loans to small and medium firms

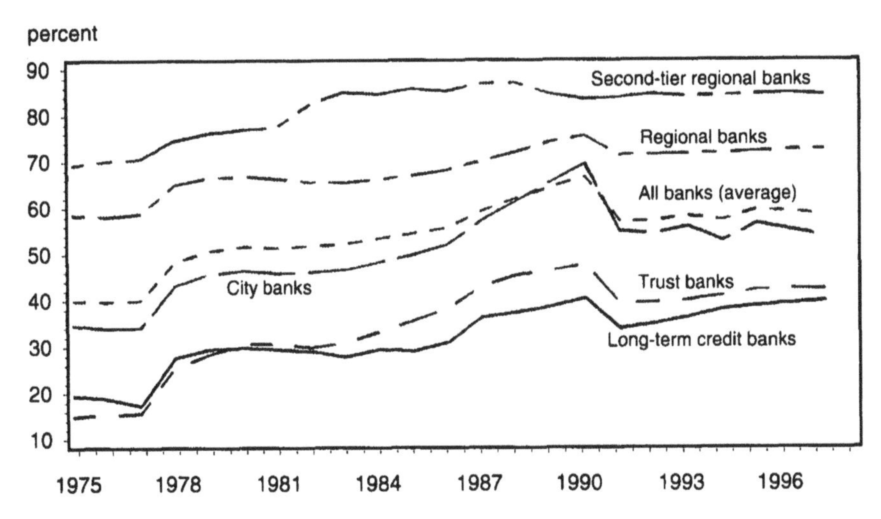

Note: From September 1977, the definition of small and medium firms was enlarged.

Source: Calculated by the author on the basis of *Bank Financial Data, Nikkei Electronic Economic Database System.*

Figure 4.11 Share of loans to real estate industry

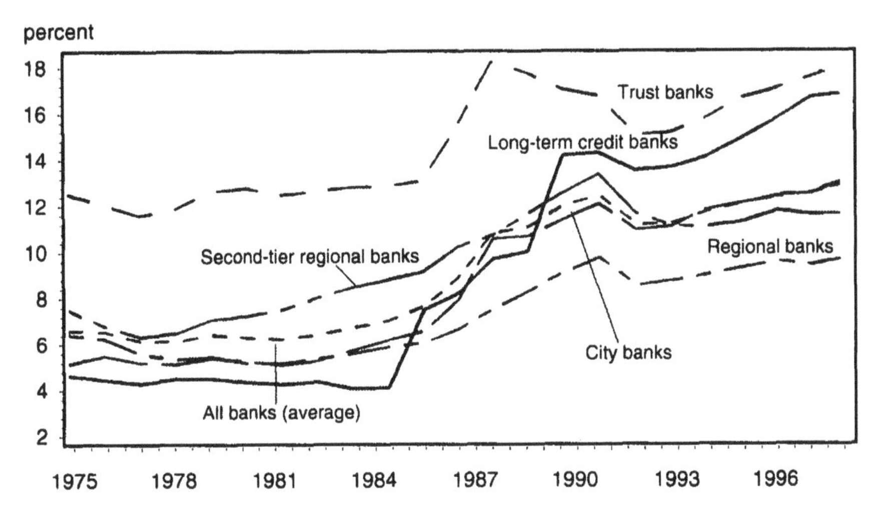

Source: Calculated by the author on the basis of *Bank Financial Data, Nikkei Electronic Economic Database System.*

Figure 4.12 Share of loans to finance and insurance industries

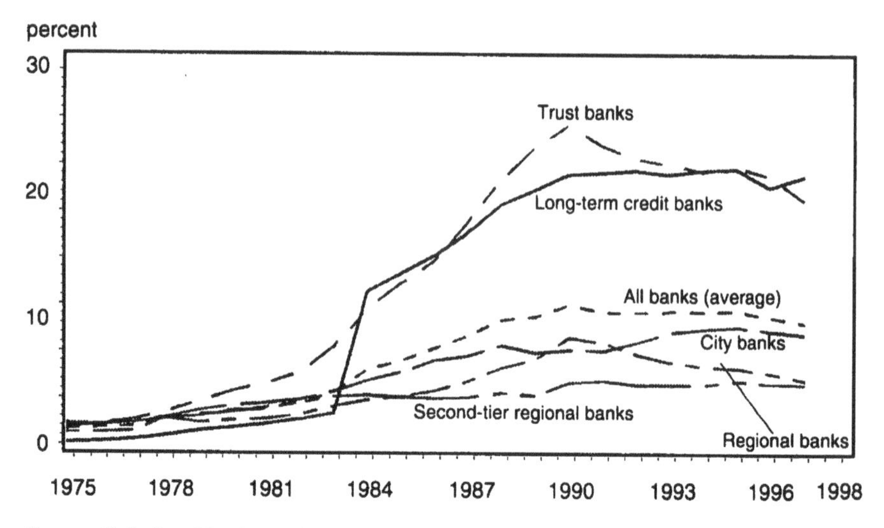

Source: Calculated by the author on the basis of *Bank Financial Data, Nikkei Electronic Economic Database System.*

Figure 4.13 Share of mortgage loans to individuals

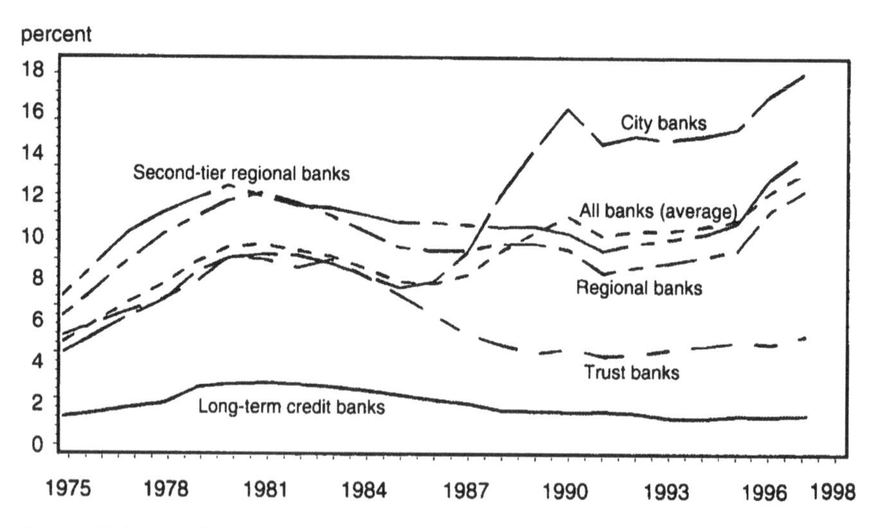

Source: Calculated by the author based on *Bank Financial Data, Nikkei Electronic Economic Database System.*

Figure 4.14 Shares of overseas loans

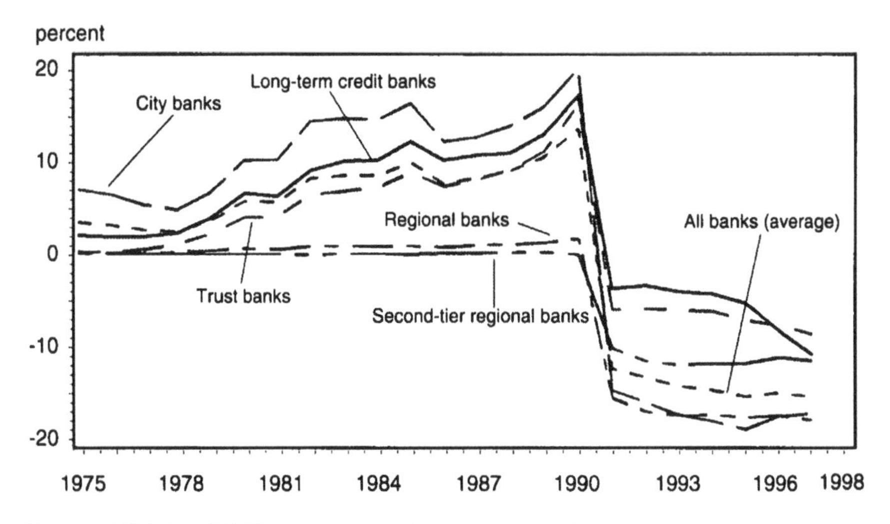

Note: In 1991, the definition of overseas loans was revised.

Source: Calculated by the author based on *Bank Financial Data, Nikkei Electronic Economic Database System.*

Figure 4.15 Share of loans to manufacturing industry

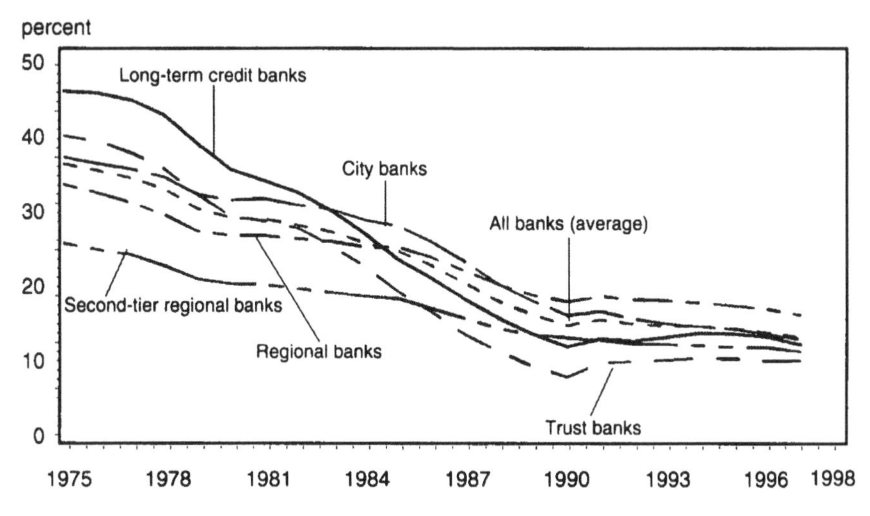

Source: Calculated by the author on the basis of *Bank Financial Data, Nikkei Electronic Economic Database System.*

Figure 4.16 Share of loans to service industry

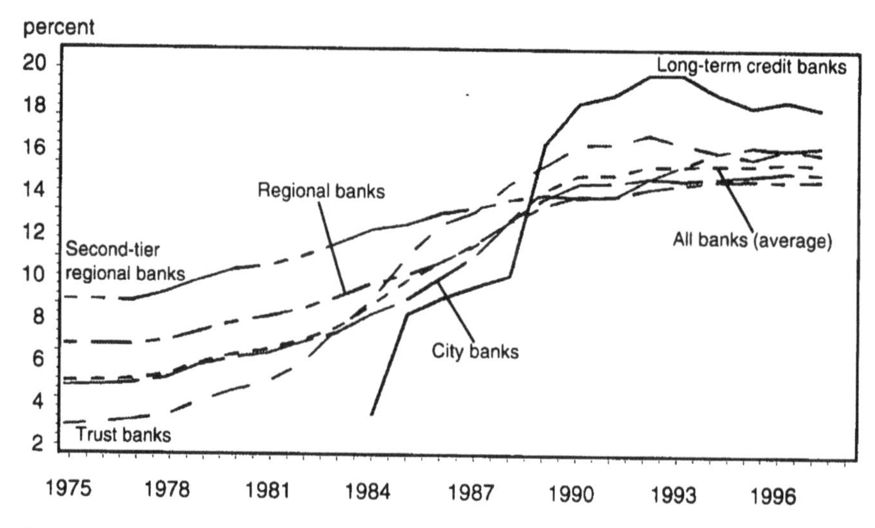

Source: Calculated by the author on the basis of *Bank Financial Data, Nikkei Electronic Economic Database System.*

continued regulatory restrictions against banks entering the security business.

Banks could enjoy higher profit margins for these new loans, but they clearly recognized the lower creditworthiness of these customers. In order to reduce their credit risks, banks made loans secured by real estate. Land had been the most profitable asset to hold for more than four decades following World War II. Securing loans by land had been a long tradition among Japanese banks for over a century, since the establishment of the modern banking system in the Meiji era.[3]

The soaring land and stock prices enhanced the creditworthiness of small and medium-sized firms, individuals with mortgages, the real estate industry, and nonbank financial institutions. Nonbank financial institutions expanded their own loans to the real estate industry and to residential mortgage borrowers. Long-term-credit banks did not have deposit accounts and consequently lacked easy access to small and medium-sized corporate customers. They increased loans to their 100-percent-owned financial subsidiaries, through which loans to the real estate industry increased drastically. This was a major cause of the financial failure of the two long-term-credit banks in 1998.

Until the early 1980s, it was a standard practice of banks to make loans for less than 60-70 percent of the market value of the land serving as collateral. In the late 1980s, when most people were convinced that a

3. See Asakura (1978).

Figure 4.17 Nikkei stock averages

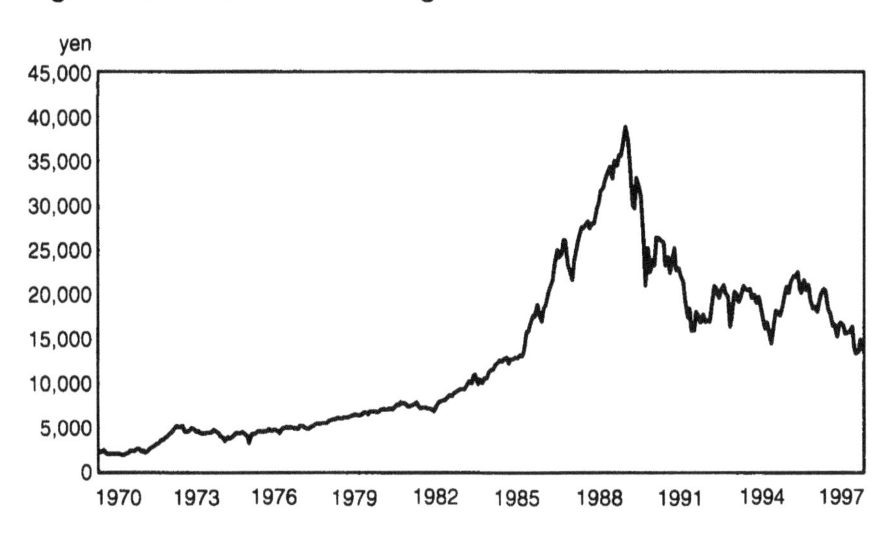

Source: Economic Statistics Monthly, Bank of Japan.

further rise in land prices was inevitable, it became common practice to lend up to the full market value of the land. A critical problem for the banks was a lack of diversification across sources of collateral. As long as most loans were secured by the borrower's landholdings, diversification across different industries had little meaning. Soaring land prices, the collateral principle, and bank competition for larger market shares as an extension of traditional bank behavior under the convoy regulations—together, these factors were the seeds for the financial crisis that occurred a decade later.

The Credit Crunch and the Financial Crisis

The bursting of the stock and real estate bubbles in 1990 fundamentally changed the Japanese financial market environment. Figures 4.17, 4.18, and 4.19 show stock prices, land prices for the six largest cities, and land prices for all of Japan, respectively.

The plunge in stock prices reduced the value of stocks held by banks, which was counted as a part of banks' equity capital on the basis of the Bank for International Settlements (BIS) equity capital regulation. Banks were forced to reduce the size of their loans to meet BIS capital regulation of 8 percent for internationally operating banks, and 4 percent for domestically operating banks, which caused a serious credit crunch in Japan. In addition to the stock market collapse, the credit crunch had a strong

Figure 4.18a Land prices of 6 largest cities

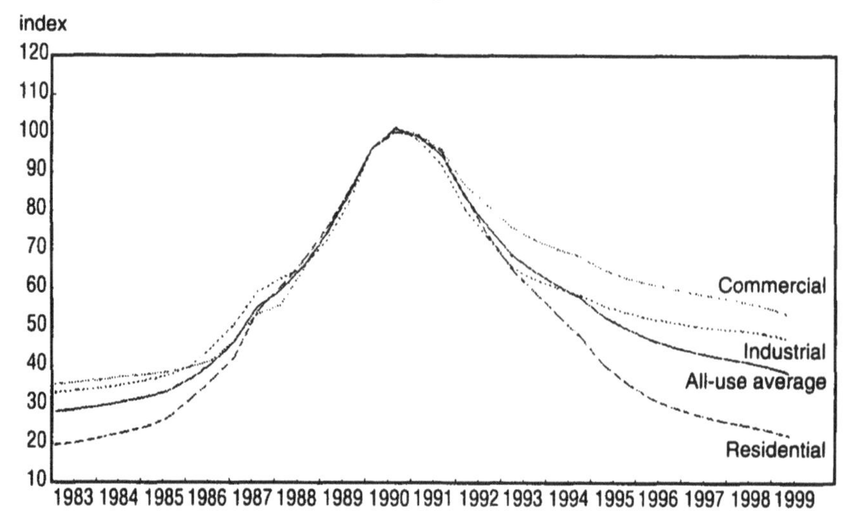

Note: The period for each year is noted as of March.

Source: Price Indexes of Urban Areas, Nippon Institute of Real Estate Research.

Figure 4.18b Change of prices relative to 6 months earlier

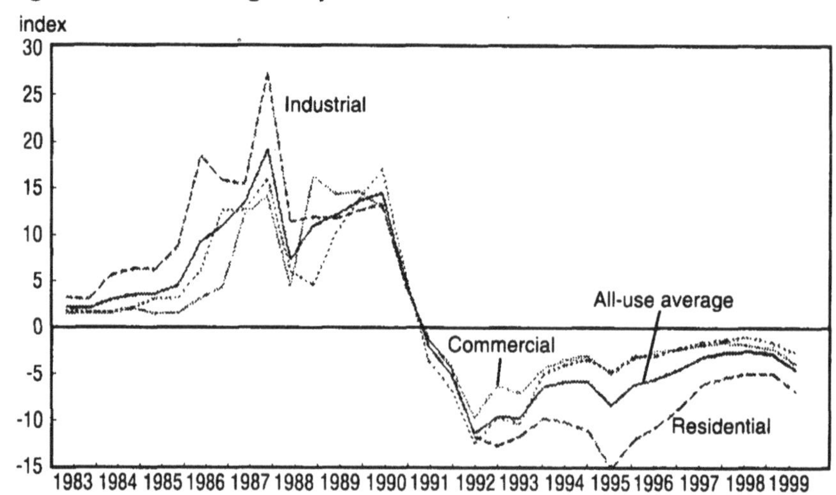

Note: The period for each year is noted as of March.

Source: Price Indexes of Urban Areas, Nippon Institute of Real Estate Research.

negative impact on the whole industrial backbone of Japan. Fear of financial crisis further depressed expectations for the growth rate of the economy, which put further downward pressure on domestic asset prices.

As shown in figure 4.5 above, the fall in the loan growth rate after 1990 was especially drastic for small and medium-sized firms. The growth rate

Figure 4.19a Land prices for all of Japan

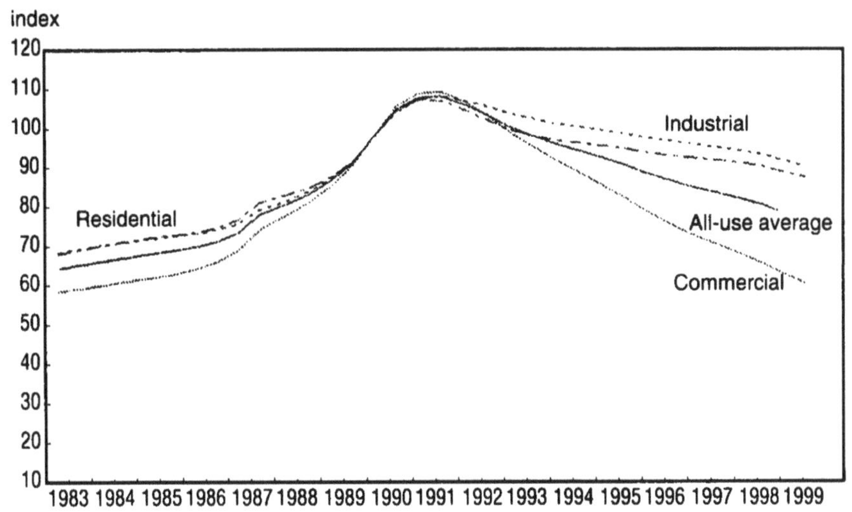

Source: Price Indexes of Urban Areas, Nippon Institute of Real Estate Research.

Figure 4.19b Land prices relative to 6 months earlier

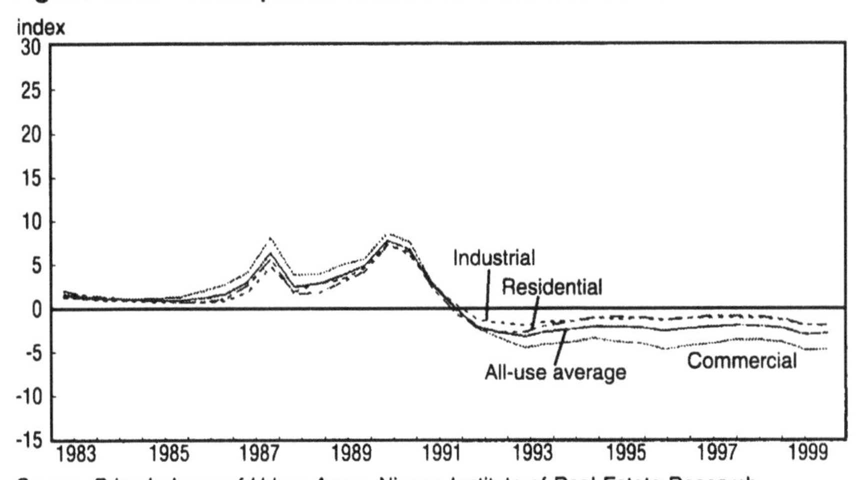

Source: Price Indexes of Urban Areas, Nippon Institute of Real Estate Research.

of loans to large firms was negative in the mid-1990s. Due to the land price plunge, small and medium-sized firms lost their main source of collateral, substantially reducing their creditworthiness and loan access in the early 1990s.

As far as the credit crunch is concerned, the fall in stock prices is the prime cause. There is no question that the negative impact of the fall in stock prices to a level less than half its prior high-water mark had an extremely serious effect on the economy. With respect to the stability of

Figure 4.20 Share of loans secured by securities in secured loans

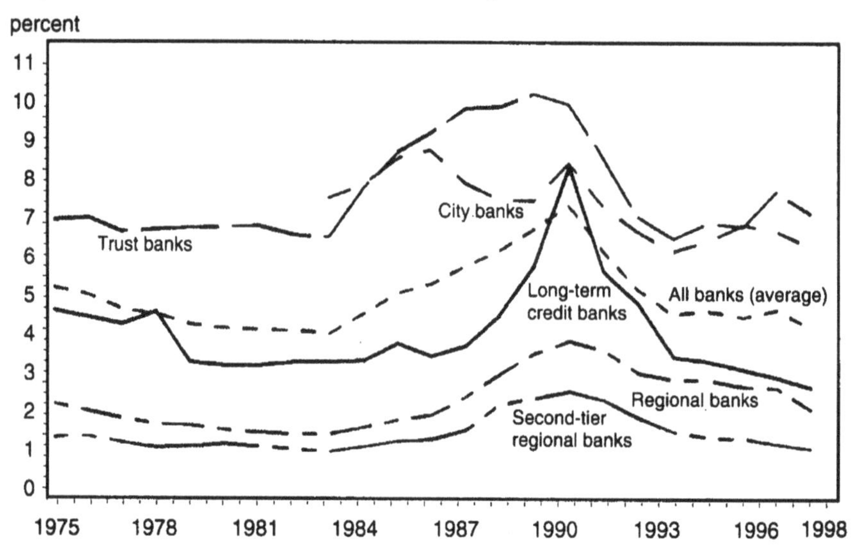

Source: Calculated by the author on the basis of *Bank Financial Data, Nikkei Electronic Economic Database System.*

Japan's financial system, however, the stock price crash had a much less serious impact than the fall in land prices.

The shares of loans secured by securities are shown in figure 4.20. It is far smaller than the share of loans secured by real estate, as shown in figure 4.8 above. Stocks are only a part of the securities used as collateral for bank loans. In this sense, a fall in land prices to a level one-third of their peak reduced the quality of a bank's loan portfolio tremendously. As of the end of 1999, land prices continued to fall. Worse than that, the land serving as collateral on defaulted loans could not be liquidated in this extremely depressed real estate market. Bad loans increased, and the underlying collateral could not be liquidated. Thus, banks were forced to further reduce their loan originations.

Since land served as an anchor of the Japanese credit system, the collapse of the real estate market brought about a crisis for the whole financial system. As a natural course of deregulation, less efficient banks were forced out of business. When everybody believes that the financial system itself is sound, failures of individual banks do not threaten the system. Since the collapse in land prices is a factor that affects the foundation of the credit system, this financial crisis is unlikely to end until the price of land stabilizes at some lower level. To facilitate Japan's economic recovery, policies to bring liquidity to the real estate market are needed, such as tax reform, securitization of real estate, and lifting building restrictions to make more efficient use of land and higher rates of return on real estate possible.

Land has historically had the highest rate of return in Japan's postwar regulated interest rate environment. It is also tax-attractive in that, when it is held by corporations, it is exempt from the inheritance tax, which is quite high in Japan. With deregulation of the financial market, the rates of return of all types of assets will be readjusted. The current fall in land prices may be part of a general realignment of asset rates of return in a globally deregulated economy.

The fundamental cause of the Japanese financial crisis is the excessive share of the financial market controlled by the banking sector, which requires collateral before loans can be originated. In a deregulated world with higher economic risks, the social system of risk taking has to be changed to a system of risk sharing among investors capable of evaluating and underwriting these risks. A deeper capital market and a reduced role for the banking system will be needed.

Comparison with US Experience

The important role of collateral in bank loans is universal.[4] Whenever and wherever, plunges in asset prices in the real estate market and the stock market seriously damage the financial system. Since the share of real estate in secured loans in Japan is higher than in the United States, the fall in real estate prices has a more profound impact on the Japanese financial system than in the United States. The US financial system may be more susceptible to changes in stock market conditions. This could explain why the Federal Reserve System intervened in the recent case of Long-Term Capital Management, despite the unpopular bailout policy.

In the late 1980s, nevertheless, the US financial market had the same experience with the fall of real estate prices, and many banks suffered from it. Fortunately, however, the real estate market recovered in the early 1990s, helping banks, savings and loans, and the Resolution Trust Corporation as well. The stable demand for multifamily housing; the securitization of real estate, especially the innovations in financial technology such as pass-through securities; the economic recovery; increasing stock prices—all favored the stability of the US financial system. Also in the United States, the recovery of the real estate market was a key element in ending the turmoil in the financial system in the 1980s.

A problem in the real estate market in Japan is that land prices have been determined not only by the present value of the expected yields

4. The analysis of this section should not be misinterpreted. It is intended to explore the reason for Japan's delayed policy action to fix the problem, and not intended to endorse the policy actually taken.

but also by an expected capital gain. This overpricing makes securitization at the current price levels more difficult. Since buildings depreciate quickly in Japan, land without buildings has been most remunerative to hold. With falling land prices, the supply of land increased in the 1990s, which facilitated a further fall in prices.[5]

Before World War II, the large banks were not used to accepting land as collateral. For regional banks, land was a popular collateral, because there was no other eligible collateral in local areas. In the course of Japanese history, financial crises occurred each time land prices plunged, as in 1885, 1920, and 1927. In those days, agricultural land was an asset with a high rate of return due to the tenancy system. After agricultural land reform abolished the tenancy system (mandated by the occupation army after World War II), land without buildings became an important collateral for all groups of banks, because land prices increased in line with the high growth of the economy. The regulation of deposit interest rates encouraged a higher rate of return of landholdings. Land, more than equities, had been believed to be the safest collateral for bank loans.

The fall in land prices in the 1990s was the first large-scale adjustment of asset prices since World War II. Given the history of bank lending policy in Japan, it is not surprising that the drastic fall in land prices caused a financial crisis on a large scale. It is easy to blame the delay in policy response for the lack of restructuring of the financial system. However, the delay might partly be attributable as well to the recognition by the bank supervisory authority of the extraordinary scale of outstanding bad loans—a magnitude of debt whose rapid write-off would surely endanger the whole Japanese financial system. If the supervisors correctly recognized in the early 1990s the fact "that in aggregate the entire Japanese banking industry or even that each of the 21 large banks were insolvent, which became common knowledge for private analysts in the late 1990s,"[6] what more could the supervisory authority have done at that time?

---

5. Western observers may think that the situation was the same in the United States and accuse bank managers of not deciding to sell real estate at lower prices. Because of an expectation of a further fall in prices, however, the real estate market was frozen, and sales were not possible even at lower prices. Legal procedures related to the collateral right were another factor that delayed the liquidation process of real estate. Accounting rules were relevant as well. Once banks sold their real estate at lower prices, it revealed the losses that did not show up on their balance sheet as long as they held the assets and valued them at the purchase price. Moreover, sales of assets at very low prices could be interpreted by the market as a signal of a bank's financial difficulty and lead to a bank run, unless all other banks did the same thing. Therefore, the weaker a bank's financial position, the harder for it to sell assets at lower prices. This pattern of bank behavior, known as *Yokonarabi* (parallel behavior), is a result of the convoy regulation.

6. See chapter 3 of this volume, by Friedman.

In order to fix the financial system, even at the early stage of the early 1990s, a huge quantity of public funds was needed. This policy had been proposed by Kiichi Miyazawa, the prime minister at that time. But public opinion, and thus politicians, strongly opposed a policy that could render the impression of helping troubled banks by using public money. His proposal was simply ignored. It was evident that even the proposed amount of the public money was far less than needed, unless land prices stopped falling.

The policy of spending public money to fix the troubled financial system could not obtain political support unless the seriousness of the problem was well understood by the public. For this purpose, a full disclosure of the magnitude of bad loans was needed; this, however, could easily have triggered a financial panic. This dilemma was the prime cause of the supervisory authorities' forbearance policy, which eventually led to even more public money being needed to end the financial crisis.[7]

In retrospect, there is no question that the government should have acted at an earlier stage. In practice, however, a decision to spend an amount of public money equivalent to one year's total national budget could not be made without wide public support. The savings and loan association problem in the United States was far smaller in magnitude than the Japanese banking problem and did not directly endanger the payment system. Yet it took more than a decade as well to fix the problem. When the size of the problem is too big to handle, it is not easy to act quickly. If we attribute Japan's forbearance policy only to the poor performance of the politicians and the bureaucrats or some unique characteristics of Japan, it dwarfs the problem. The lesson we should learn is that the problem is common all over the world, and the social cost of the problem that stems from crises in a fractional reserve banking system can be huge, especially when that industry is protected over a long period of time. We need to work on the framing of a new type of banking system.

This course of events is a result of the convoy regulations, which lasted nearly a half-century in Japan and necessarily created vested interests among involved parties, which are consistent with the capture theory of regulation put forth by Stigler.[8] In order to change the long-established vested interests, it took time. As pointed out by Miller, a change in the political system is needed, promoting effective political competition that

7. For example, Mr. Yoshimasa Nishimura, former chief of the banking bureau of the Ministry of Finance, wrote in 1999 that the MoF's fear of a possible financial panic was why a bailout was delayed for 5 years. See Yoshimasa Nishimura, Kinyugyosei no haiin (The Cause of the Failed Banking Policy), Tokyo, Bungeishunzyu, 1999, 112-15.

8. See Stigler (1964; 1971).

can make the public choice of alternative policies possible.[9] Japan needs to establish a financial system that is effectively motivated and regulated by the undistorted market mechanism.

A Theory of Bank Lending and Collateral

The Model

The above-mentioned behavior of banks in the late 1980s can be explained as simple profit-maximizing behavior according to the theory of bank lending, which explicitly takes the role of collateral into account.

A bank's expected profit (π^e) is defined by

$$\pi^e = (1 - p)(r - i)A + p\{(r - i) - (1 - \tau)\}A, \tag{1}$$

where p is the default loan probability, which is subjectively determined by the bank, r is the lending interest rate, i is the bank's cost of funds, and A is the loan amount. The loan demand (A) function is

$$D = A(r,\tau) \qquad \frac{\partial A}{\partial r} < 0, \ \frac{\partial A}{\partial \tau} < 0 \tag{2}$$

and is a decreasing function of both lending rate (r) and the collateral rate (τ) defined as the proportion of a loan that the bank believes to be recoverable by disposing of the collateral in case of a default. So

$$\tau = \frac{\alpha W}{A}, \tag{3}$$

where a ($a < 1$) is the lender's discount rate on the market value of the collateral (W) to calculate the secured amount of a loan.

The variables τ, r, i, p all have to satisfy the following conditions:

$$\tau \geq 0 \tag{4}$$

$$r, i > 0 \tag{5}$$

$$r - i > 0 \tag{6}$$

$$1 > p \geq 0 \tag{7}$$

9. See Miller (1993).

There are four different ways to solve this model, depending on the specification of which variables are under the lender's control. If both r and τ are control variables, then we can get the results that can explain the different lending patterns of different types of financial institutions.[10] In the following version of the model, we assume that the lending rate is fixed at a competitive level in the bank loan market.[11] An individual bank controls the collateral rate (τ), taking the borrower's default probability into account and indirectly determining the amount of loan (A) in order to maximize its profit. For simplicity, the cost of funds (i) is presumed to be given.

The first-order condition for profit maximization[12] is

$$\tau(1 - r)p = \eta\{(r - i) - p\}, \tag{8}$$

or

$$\tau = \frac{(r - i) - p}{(1 - \eta)p}, \tag{9}$$

where η is the elasticity of demand for loans with respect to τ and is defined as follows:

$$\eta = -\frac{\partial A}{\partial \tau}\frac{\tau}{A} > 0. \tag{10}$$

Since $\tau \geq 0$ from equations (4) and (8), the following relationship has to be satisfied:

$$\eta \gtreqless 1 \text{ depending on } p \gtreqless r - i. \tag{11}$$

Figure 4.21 illustrates the situation. $D(r, \tau)$ is a borrower's loan demand curve with respect to the collateral rate (τ). If it is a straight line, $\eta > 1$

---

10. In this case, the optimum values are $r = \frac{(p + i)\epsilon}{\eta + \epsilon - 1}$, $\tau = \frac{(p + i)\eta}{p(\eta + \epsilon - 1)}$, where $\epsilon = -\frac{\partial A}{\partial r}\frac{r}{A} > 0$, and at the optimum point $\epsilon > 1$ always holds. This version of the model explains a variety of lending patterns by the types of borrowers for different financial institutions in terms of the parameters. See Shimizu (1997a, 38-57).

11. When r is a control variable with a given ∂, the optimum condition for r is $r = \frac{\epsilon\{i + (1 - \tau)p\}}{\epsilon - 1}$.

12. The second-order condition is $-\frac{2\frac{\partial A}{\partial r}}{D''} < \frac{\partial^2 A}{\partial r^2} < -\frac{2\frac{\partial A}{\partial r}}{D'}$, where $D' = (r - i) - (1 - \tau)p > 0$, and $D'' = (r - i) - (1 - \tau)p < 0$. Since $\frac{\partial^2 A}{\partial r^2}$ is not far from zero, this condition is satisfied under normal conditions.

Figure 4.21 The collateral rate and the demand elasticity

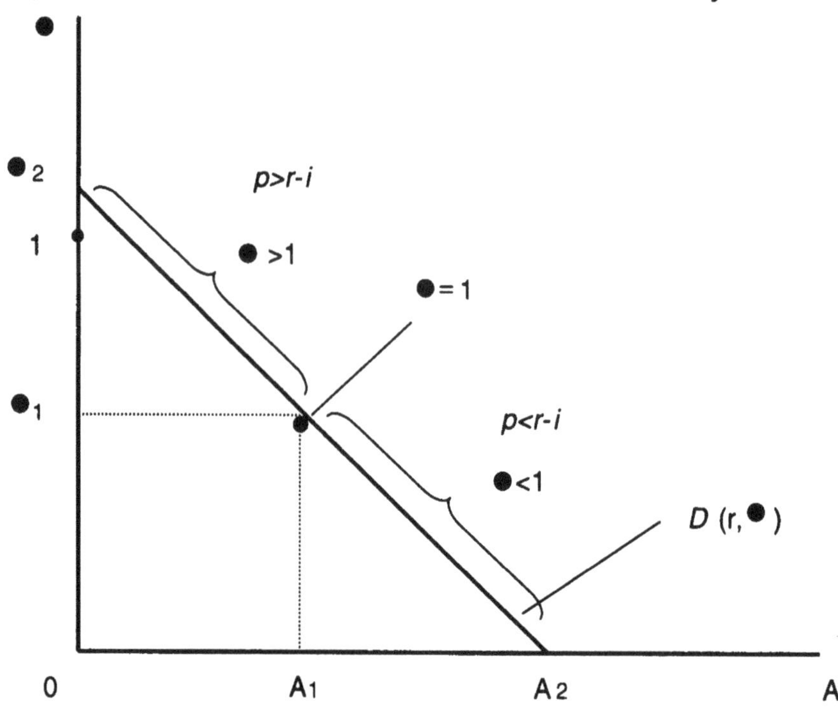

represents the upper half and $\eta < 1$ represents the lower half of the line. For borrowers whose default probability is higher than the bank's profit margin, a bank sets τ so that $\tau_1 < \tau < \tau_2$, and the amount of the loan is determined between 0 and A_1. On the other hand, for borrowers whose default probability is less than the bank's profit margin, τ is set between 0 and τ so that the amount of the loan is determined between A_1 and A_2. Even with the same demand curve and the same loan interest rate, a borrower with a lower default probability can get larger loans than a borrower with a higher default probability.

For a highly credible borrower whose default probability is zero ($p = 0$), $\eta = 0$ from equation (8). The only point that satisfies this condition is A_2. At this point, the maximum loan amount is at $\tau = 0$, and the collateral rate ceases to function as another price in the loan market. Standard models of bank lending that do not explicitly take the role of collateral into account are special cases of our model, in which all borrowers have a zero payoff in default. This model explains one reason a credible borrower can get a larger loan than a less credible borrower through the rationing mechanism of collateral.[13] The collateral rate set for less credible

13. The result of traditional models that treat A as a direct control variable with a given r is obtained by solving equation (1) with respect to A as $r - i = (1 - \tau)p$, where the bank's profit margin is equal to its expected loss rate. If we disregard the collateral rate by

borrowers is higher than for more credible borrowers. In other words, a borrower who is charged a high collateral rate is regarded as having a high default probability.

We can easily find how τ reacts to changes in parameter values by checking the sign of the partial derivatives with respect to p, η, r, and i:

For $p > r - i$, thus $\eta > 1$,

$$\frac{\partial\tau}{\partial p} > 0, \quad \frac{\partial\tau}{\partial\eta} < 0, \quad \frac{\partial\tau}{\partial r} < 0, \quad \frac{\partial\tau}{\partial i} > 0. \tag{12}$$

For $p > r - i$, thus $\eta < 1$,

$$\frac{\partial\tau}{\partial p} < 0, \quad \frac{\partial\tau}{\partial\eta} > 0, \quad \frac{\partial\tau}{\partial r} > 0, \quad \frac{\partial\tau}{\partial i} < 0. \tag{13}$$

For a borrower whose default probability is higher than a bank's profit margin, the collateral rate will be increased if the default probability rises. If the default probability rises such that $p > \eta(r - i)$, then the collateral rate is set at more than 1 and a bank practically refuses to lend. On the other hand, the loan amount will be larger the lower the default probability, the higher the demand elasticity with respect to the collateral rate, the lower the loan rate, and the lower the cost of funds.

Conversely, the reaction of τ is completely opposite in the case of borrowers with low default probabilities, $p < r - i$. This asymmetry in a bank's reaction explains a lot of banks' lending behavior in the late 1980s.

Implications

If banks assess the default probability as lower for large firms and higher for small and medium-sized firms, this model explains the difference in the collateral rates for corporate borrowers of various sizes. Since banks recognized that the default probability of small and medium-sized firms is high, they charged these new borrowers a high collateral rate. If asset prices did not appreciate, the higher collateral rate imposed on small and medium-sized firms and the real estate industry would have severely limited new loans to these customers.

Unfortunately, in the late 1980s, soaring land and stock prices increased the perceived creditworthiness of these borrowers. In terms of the model, their demand curves with respect to the collateral rate shifted upward.

---

setting $\tau = 0$, then $r - i = p$, and the loan amount is determined at $\eta = 1$. This is the optimum solution for a normal monopoly with a zero cost of production.

Figure 4.22 Small and medium-sized firms: Increased demand

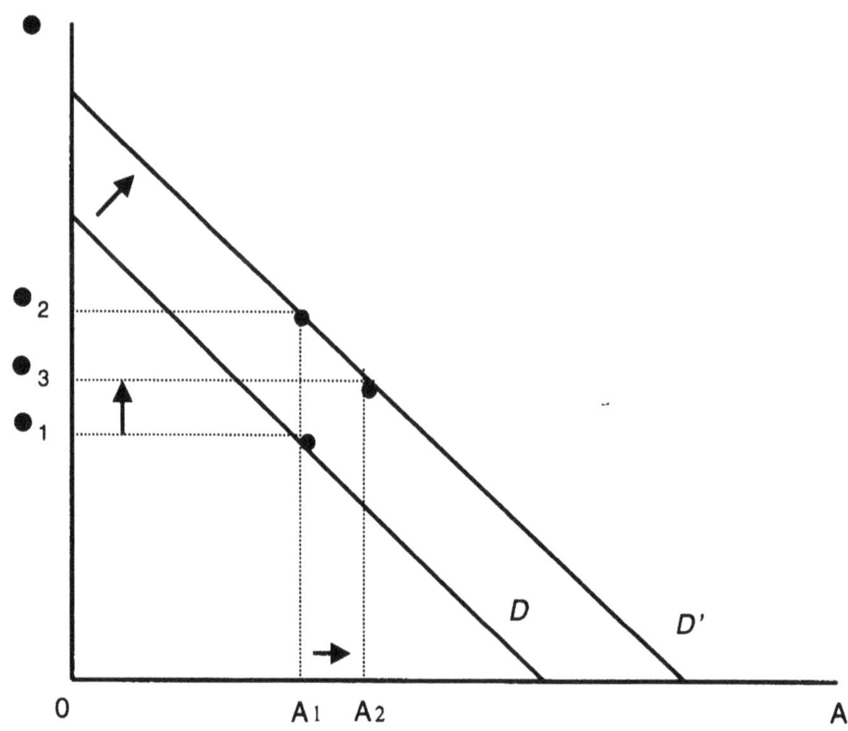

As shown in figure 4.22, this shift in the demand curve from D to D' implies a rise in η measured at the same loan amount A_1. For small and medium-sized firms with $p > r - i$, a rise in η reduces τ and thus increases the amount of the loan to A_2 at τ_3. This fall in τ remains somewhere between τ_1 and τ_2, because η is the same on D and D' measured at the original τ_1, and a rise in η does not occur.[14] Hence, a rise in land prices increases loans to small and medium-sized firms and raises the collateral rate from the original level to some extent.

Increased loans to riskier borrowers do not mean that banks were ignorant of the higher risks. On the contrary, because of their knowledge of the higher risks, banks increased τ from the original level and depended heavily on the value of collateral to secure the loan. As shown in equation (12), τ is higher for a borrower with a higher p.

On the other hand, the aggregate loan demand of large firms shifted downward from the middle 1970s and especially in the late 1980s. This downward shift was due to the decrease in the growth rate of the economy

14. If D and D' start from the same point on the vertical axis, η is identical at τ_1. Thus, the new collateral rate τ_3 cannot be less than the original τ_1. If D' shifts simply upward, as shown in figure 4.22, η is smaller on D' than on D at the same τ_1, and τ_3 must be higher than τ_1.

Figure 4.23 Large firms: Decreased demand

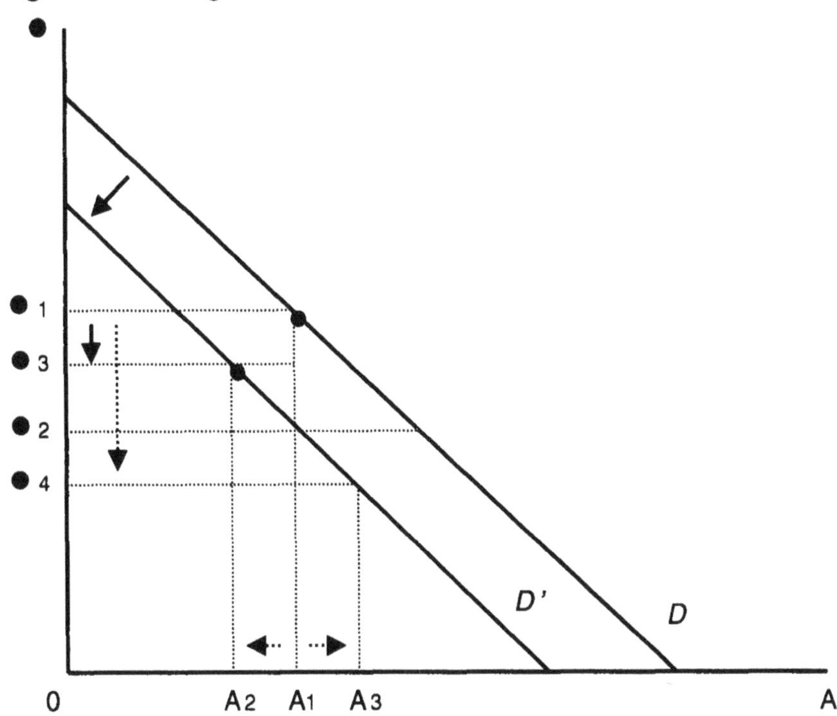

and therefore of investment demand by firms. Another factor was increased opportunities for large firms to raise funds directly from capital markets. The downward shift of D to D' in figure 4.23 implies a fall in η measured at A_1. For large firms with $p < r - i$, a fall in η unambiguously reduces the new τ to less than the original level τ_1. It is not clear whether τ_3 is higher or lower than τ_2, and thus whether the new loan amount is larger or smaller than A_1 depends on how the demand curve shifts.

For small and medium-sized firms, however, the same downward shift of the demand curve with respect to τ from D to D' affects them differently. A fall in η increases τ. So, as shown in figure 4.24, a fall in η at A_1 resulting from the shift from D to D' increases τ from τ_1 to τ_3.[15] So, for small and medium-sized firms, a downward shift of the demand curve, which happened after the asset price crashes, unambiguously increases τ and reduces the loan amount to A_2. This sharp downward shift for small firms' loan demand was caused by the collapse in their creditworthiness with the fall in land prices.

15. The level of τ_3 could be less than τ_1 in this particular case of the parallel shift of the demand curve. But τ_3 is never less than τ_2, and A_2 is always less than A_1. If the demand curve starts from the same point on the vertical axis, τ_3 is always higher than the original level τ_1.

Figure 4.24 Small and medium-sized firms: Decreased demand

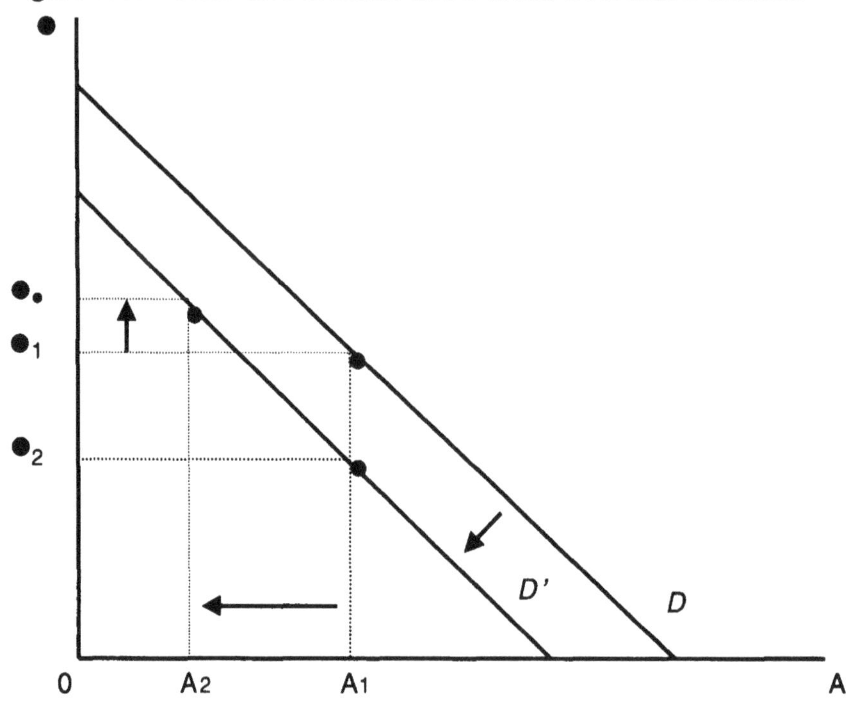

This implication of the model is confirmed by the evidence in figure 4.8 above, which shows the ratio of loans secured by real estate for each group of banks. Regional banks and second-tier regional banks lend mostly to small and medium-sized firms, and long-term-credit banks and trust banks lend mostly to large firms. In the late 1980s, this ratio slightly increased for regional banks and sharply decreased for long-term-credit banks and trust banks. The increasing ratio for city banks during the late 1980s is due to the increased loans to small and medium-sized firms, as well as mortgage loans to individuals.

This empirical observation implies that the banks' lending policy in the late 1980s was not inconsistent with profit-maximizing behavior. The problem was the failure to foresee the drastic fall in the land prices that occurred in the 1990s, which happened after prices had risen for four decades. The land price plunge in the 1990s was triggered by a sudden tightening of monetary policy and mandatory governmental restrictions on loans to the real estate industry, which were intended to reduce soaring land prices.

Bank Loans and Real Estate Prices

Real estate is the most important form of collateral for secured loans in Japan, being used in 73 percent of all loans (as shown in figure 4.8 above).

Although stocks and bonds increased their role as collateral for bank lenders in the late 1980s, these assets were owned mostly by large firms, and their share among total secured loans was only about 4 to 7 percent (as shown in figure 4.20 above). Generally, small and medium-sized firms do not have eligible collateral other than real estate. Since buildings depreciate quickly in Japan, land has been the most important asset used to secure bank loans.

Despite the importance in theory and in practice, the empirical relationship between collateral and bank loans has not been easy to identify econometrically, because of the difficulty in obtaining accurate loan data. The Japanese bank loan market in the late 1980s is a unique case for empirical study, since loan collateral was primarily represented by land prices and both collateral value and loan originations changed sharply over a short period of time.

It is already well established that there has been a strong causal link from land prices to total bank loans over the past four decades.[16] In the following analysis, we reexamine this relationship, disaggregating the data by borrower size category and by time period.

Data and Analysis Method

We examine monthly data over an observation period of March 1955 to March 1999.[17] Four different bank loan datasets are used in the study: (1) total loans by all domestically licensed banks, (2) loans to large firms, (3) loans to small and medium-sized firms, and (4) total credit guarantees by credit guarantee associations. Credit guarantees are made only for loans to small and medium-sized firms. We examine the relationship between land prices and credit guarantees, because a credit guarantee is theoretically equivalent to having sufficient collateral. Data on funding by companies listed on the Tokyo Stock Exchange are used as a proxy for the amount of funds raised in the capital market.

Two variables are used to measure land prices: (1) the land price index for Japan and (2) the land price index for the six largest cities. Monthly land price indices were obtained by interpolating semiannual data.

The period of analysis was (1) the entire observation period (March 1955 to March 1999), (2) the high-growth period (March 1955 to December 1974), (3) the low-growth and the bubble period (January 1975 to December 1990), and (4) the period of falling land prices (January 1991 to March 1999).

---

16. Shimizu (1997b, chapter 4, section 2). See appendix 4A of this chapter.

17. Data sources: *Economic Statistics Annual; Economic Statitics Monthly; Economic and Financial Data on CD-ROM;* Bank of Japan, *Price Indexes of Urban Areas;* Nippon Institute of Real Estate Research; and *Monthly Statistics of Tokyo Stock Exchange*. Software used for the analysis is RATS, Version 4.

We examined the relationship using the impulse response function of the VAR(2) model with 12 lags. The model can be expressed as:

$$Y_t = \sum_{i=1}^{12} a_i Y_{t-i} + \sum_{i=1}^{12} b_i X_{t-1} + u_{1t} \qquad \text{(I)}$$

$$X_t = \sum_{i=1}^{12} c_i X_{t-i} + \sum_{i=1}^{12} d_i Y_{t-1} + u_{2t} \qquad \text{(II)}$$

where X_t and Y_t are land price variables and bank loan variables, respectively, a_i, b_i, c_i, and d_i are parameter estimates, and u_{it} is an error term.

For the period after January 1975, the funds raised in the capital market by large firms are added as an additional explanatory variable, Z_t, and its relationship with X_t and Y_t is examined.

The Results

The *p*-values of the F-test of the impulse response functions are summarized in tables 4.1 and 4.2. Only the responses significant at the 5 percent level are shown in figures 4.25 and 4.26. In the following, we summarize the important findings with primary attention focused on the period after 1975.

Full period (March 1956 to March 1999). For all types of loans, there are highly significant univariate causal relationships from either land price index to bank loans. The impact of land prices is more significant for loans to small and medium-sized firms than for loans to large firms. No causality was found for any types of bank loans to land prices. In general, changes in land prices preceded changes in bank loans by about a year. The effect of changes in land prices on bank lending is transmitted more quickly for small and medium-sized firms than for large firms. The effect of land prices on bank lending is estimated to persist for more than 10 years. Our evidence suggests that monetary policy did not directly and specifically affect land prices. The BOJ did support the increase in credit creation in the 1980s, which was fueled by land prices increasing collateral.

High-growth period (March 1956 to December 1974). According to table 4.1, total loans were independently influenced by movements in both measures of land prices. Loans to large firms were not affected by land prices in this period. Only the all-Japan land price measure affected loans to small and medium-sized firms. This means that bank loans to small and medium-sized firms were especially sensitive to the enhanced creditworthiness induced by higher land prices during the high-growth period. On the other hand, large firms did not need to depend on the value of land for their creditworthiness and were much less affected by it.

Table 4.1 P values of the F-test of the impulse response functions, land prices, and bank loans

	Whole period		High-growth period		Low-growth and bubble period		Period of falling land prices	
	March 1956-March 1999		March 1956-December 1974		January 1975-December 1990		January 1991-March 1999	
Direction of the effect	All Japan	6 cities	All Japan	6 cities	All Japan	6 cities	All Japan	6 cities
Land P → loans								
Total loans	**0.00002**	**0.000007**	**0.009**	**0.007**	**0.0000003**	**0.00002**	0.351	0.253
Large firm loans	**0.015**	**0.028**	0.19	0.094	0.37	0.47	0.9	0.95
Small firm loans	**0.00004**	**0.0012**	**0.006**	0.075	**0.012**	**0.002**	0.6	0.15
Credit guarantee	**0.0000003**	**0.00000001**	**0.0005**	**0.0000004**	0.11	0.176	0.095	0.333
Loans → Land P								
Total loans	0.474	0.872	0.068	0.526	0.298	0.795	0.244	0.59
Large firm loans	0.46	0.77	0.62	0.74	**0.0004**	**0.0008**	0.27	0.32
Small firm loans	0.2	0.58	0.78	0.97	0.27	0.18	**0.046**	0.12
Credit guarantee	**0.002**	**0.0000007**	**0.02**	**0.000003**	0.124	0.149	0.042	0.21

Note: Bold numbers are those significant at less than 5 percent level.

Table 4.2 P values of the F-test of the impulse response function funds raised in the capital market (FRCM)

	Low-growth and bubble period	Period of falling land prices
	January 1975-December 1990	January 1991-March 1999
FRCM → loans		
Total loans	0.485	0.17
Large-firm loans	0.585	**0.002**
Small-firm loans	0.135	0.262
Loans → FRCM		
Total loans	0.256	0.285
Large-firm loans	0.62	**0.018**
Small-firm loans	0.331	0.485
Land prices of all Japan		
Land prices → FRCM	**0.014**	0.145
FRCM → land prices	**0.0001**	0.237
Land prices of 6 large cities		
Land prices → FRCM	**0.0029**	0.843
FRCM → land prices	**0.0006**	0.069

Note: Bold numbers are those significant at less than 5 percent level.

Low-growth and bubble period (January 1975 to December 1990). During this period, like the previous one, loans to large firms were not affected by land prices. Loans to small and medium-sized firms, and thus total loans, were significantly affected by both kinds of land prices (see table 4.1). Land prices in the six largest cities had larger effects on both total loans and loans to small and medium-sized firms (see figures 4.25j to 4.25m) As shown in figures 4.18 and 4.19 above, the contrast in the movements of land prices in the six largest cities and those in other cities is impressive. Land prices soared rapidly in the six largest cities, but not so much in other locations, remaining rather stable there. Therefore, the increased bank loans made to small and medium-sized firms were mainly a phenomenon for firms holding land in large cities.

Interestingly, in this period, bank loans to large firms significantly and negatively affected both measures of land prices, as shown in figures 4.25n and 4.25o. That is, the reduced growth in large-firm loans contributed to increased land prices both in all Japan and in the six largest cities. This is hard to interpret as a causal relationship. During this period, nonbank fund-raising directly from capital markets by large firms increased, and bank loans to large firms fell due to the reduced demand. At the same time, the increased funds raised in the capital market were invested in real estate and had significant effects on both kinds of land prices, as is explained below. The negative relationship between large-firm loans and land prices must be deemed a spurious relationship.

Figure 4.25 The impulse response functions: Land prices, bank loans, and credit guarantee

Figure 4.25a—Response of total loans to land prices (all Japan) (March 1956 to March 1999)

Figure 4.25b—Response of total loans to land prices in 6 large cities (March 1956 to March 1999)

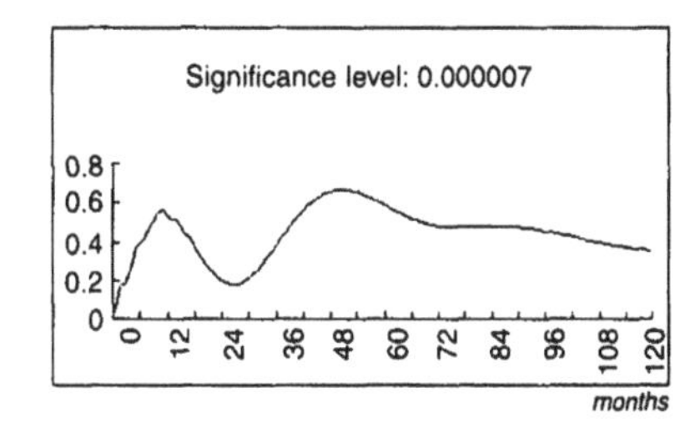

Figure 4.25c—Response of large-firm loans to land prices (all Japan) (March 1956 to March 1999)

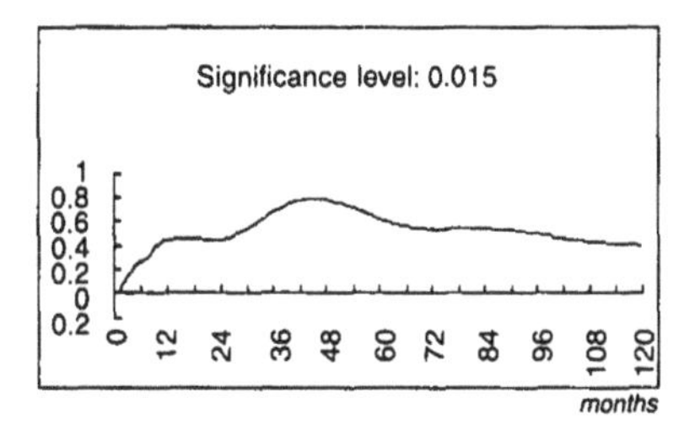

Figure 4.25d—Response of large-firm loans to land prices in 6 large cities (March 1956 to March 1999)

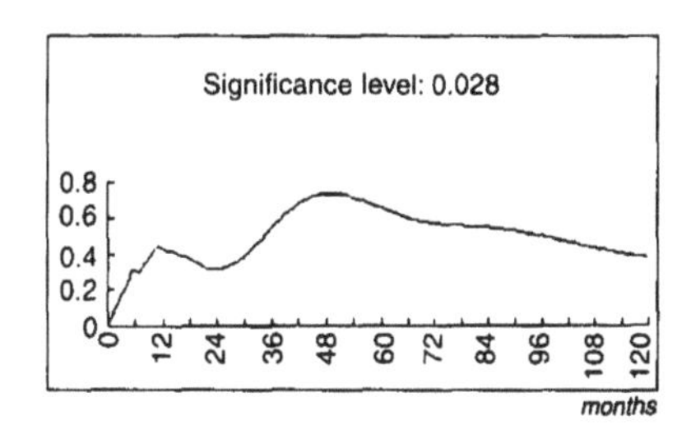

Figure 4.25e—Response of small and medium-sized firm loans to land prices (all Japan) (March 1956 to March 1999)

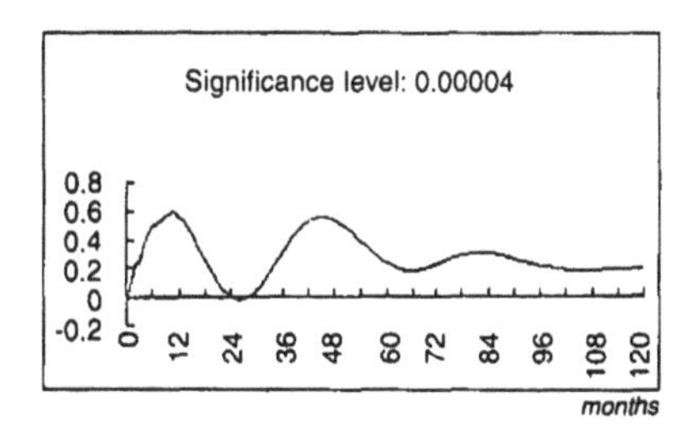

Figure 4.25f—Response of small and medium-sized firm loans to land prices in 6 large cities (March 1956 to March 1999)

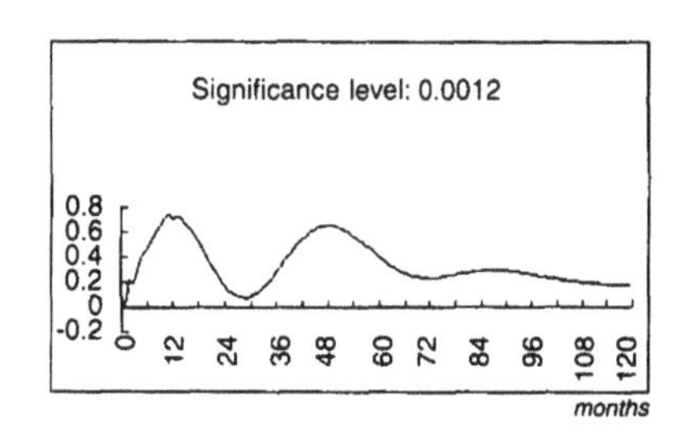

Figure 4.25g—Response of total loans to land prices (all Japan) (March 1956 to December 1974)

Figure 4.25h—Response of total loans to land prices in 6 large cities (March 1956 to December 1974)

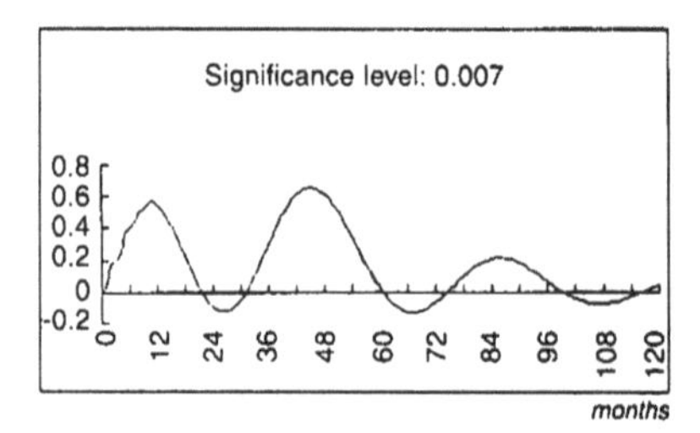

Figure 4.25i—Response of small and medium-sized firm loans to land prices (all Japan) (March 1956 to December 1974)

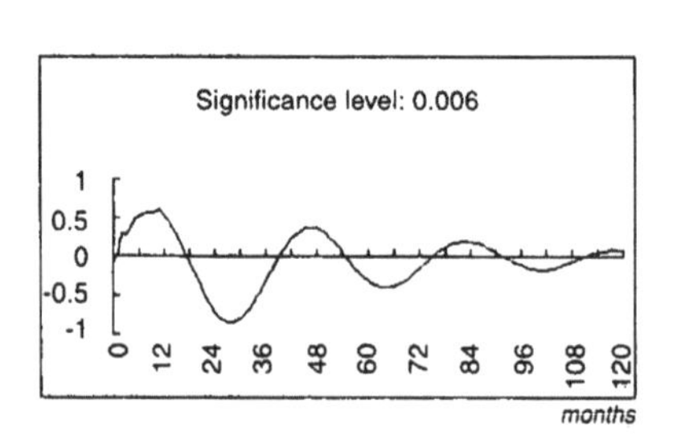

Figure 4.25j—Response of total loans to land prices (all Japan) (January 1975 to December 1990)

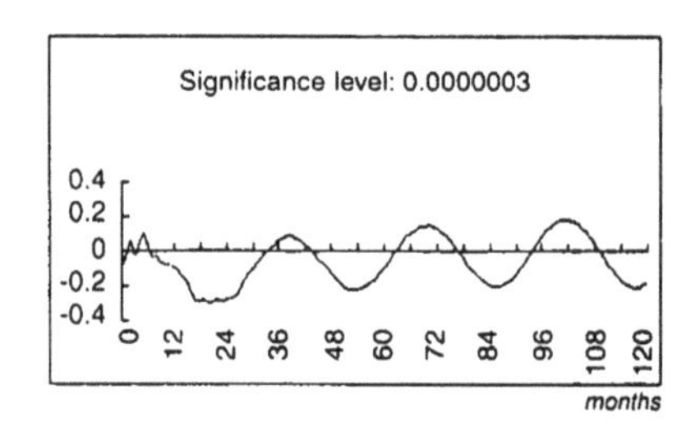

Figure 4.25k—Response of total loans to land prices in 6 large cities (January 1975 to December 1990)

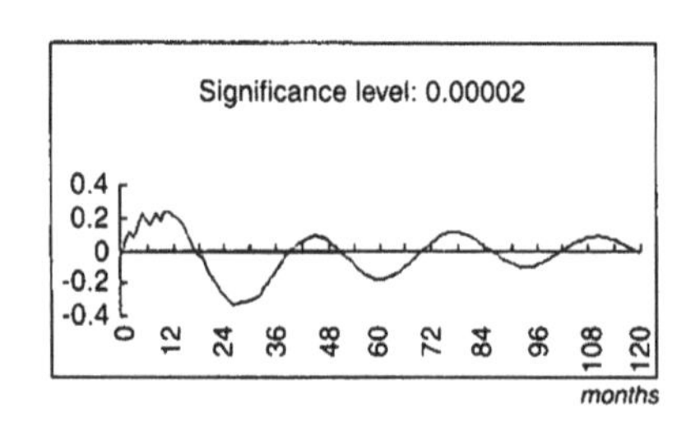

Figure 4.25l—Response of small and medium-sized firm loans to land prices (all Japan) (January 1975 to December 1990)

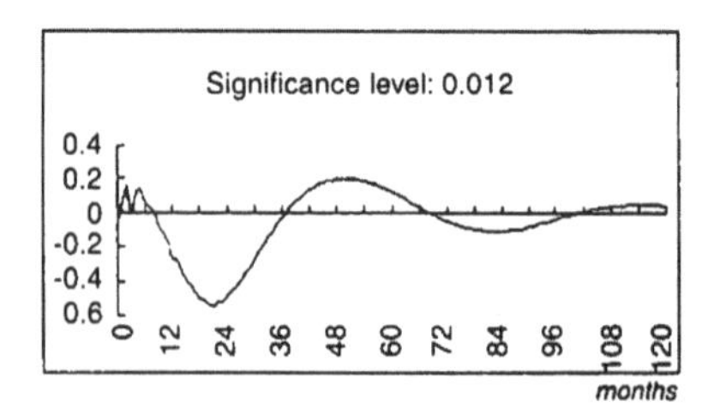

Figure 4.25m—Response of small and medium-sized firm loans to land prices in 6 large cities (January 1975 to December 1990)

Significance level: 0.002

0.8
0.6
0.4
0.2
0
-0.2
-0.4

0 12 24 36 48 60 72 84 96 108 120

months

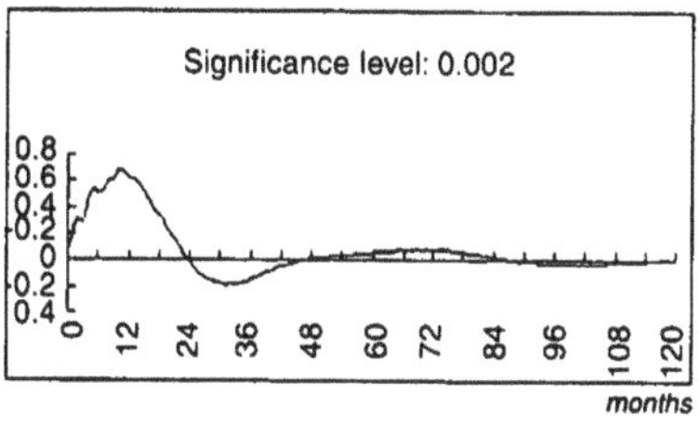

Figure 4.25n—Response of land prices in all Japan to large-firm loans (January 1975 to December 1990)

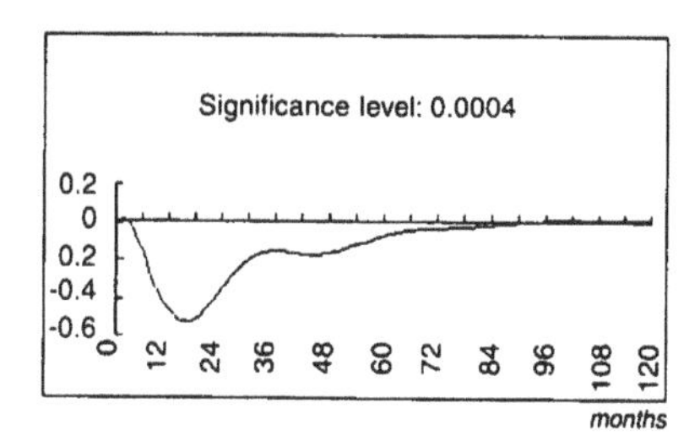

Figure 4.25o—Response of land prices in 6 large cities to large-firm loans (January 1975 to December 1990)

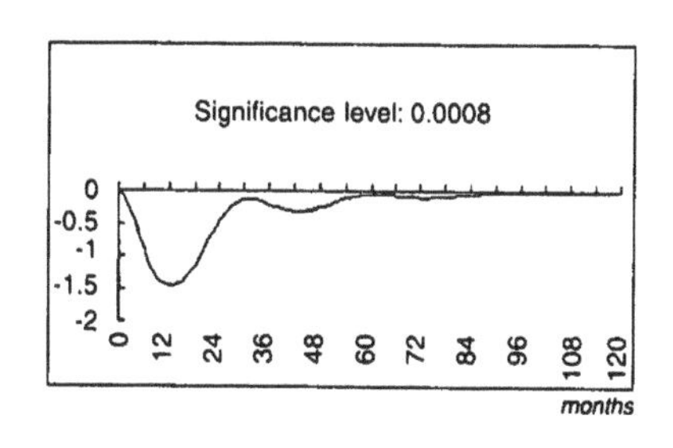

Figure 4.25p—Response of small and medium-sized firm loans to land prices in all Japan (January 1991 to March 1999)

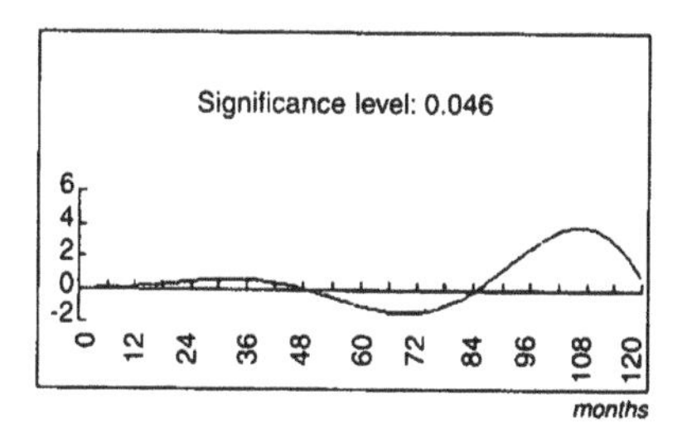

Figure 4.25q—Response of credit guarantee to land prices in all Japan (June 1960 to March 1999)

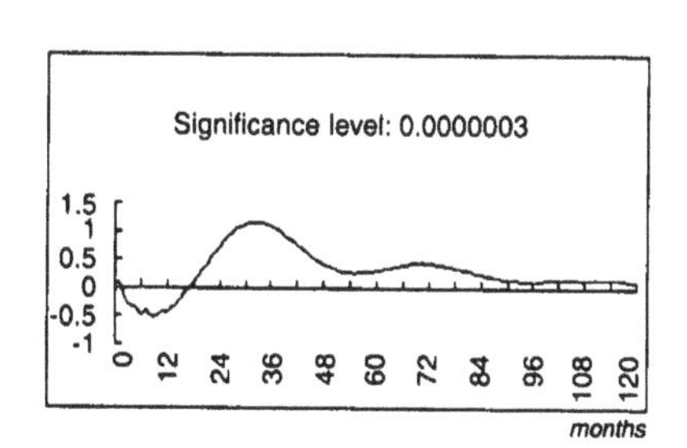

Figure 4.25r—Response of credit guarantee to land prices in 6 large cities (June 1960 to March 1999)

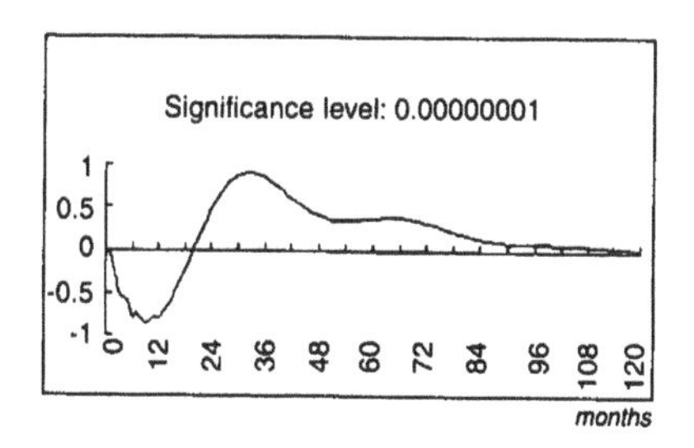

Figure 4.25s—Response of land prices of all Japan to credit guarantees
(June 1960 to March 1999)

Significance level: 0.002

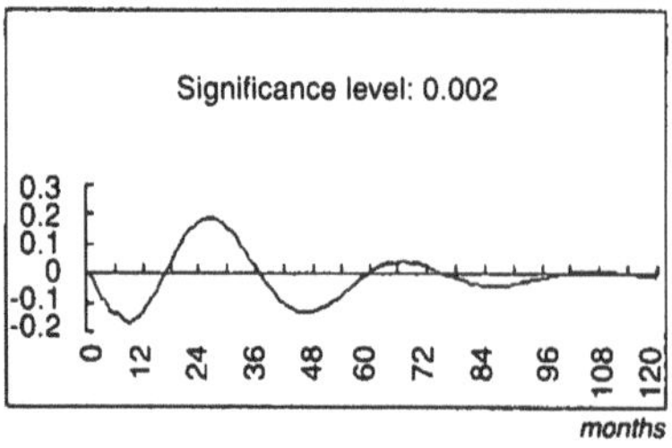

Figure 4.25t—Response of land prices of 6 large cities to credit guarantees
(June 1960 to March 1999)

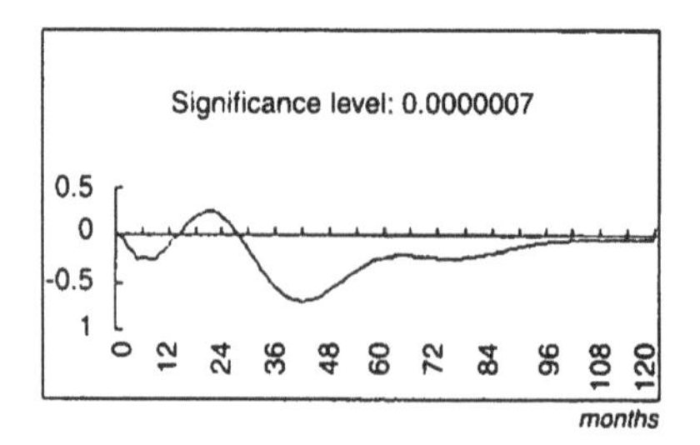

Figure 4.25u—Response of credit guarantees to land prices (all Japan) (June 1960 to December 1974)

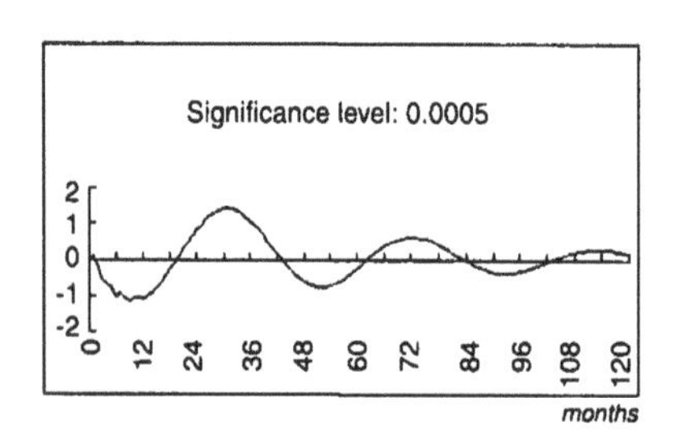

Figure 4.25v—Response of credit guarantees to land prices of 6 large cities (June 1960 to December 1974)

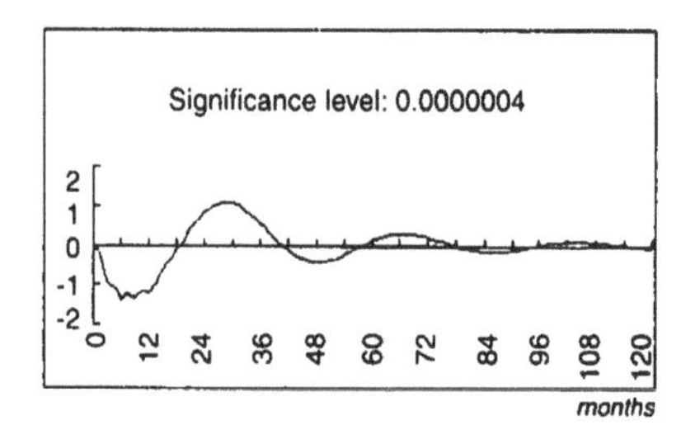

Figure 4.25w—Response of land prices of all Japan to credit guarantees
(June 1960 to December 1974)

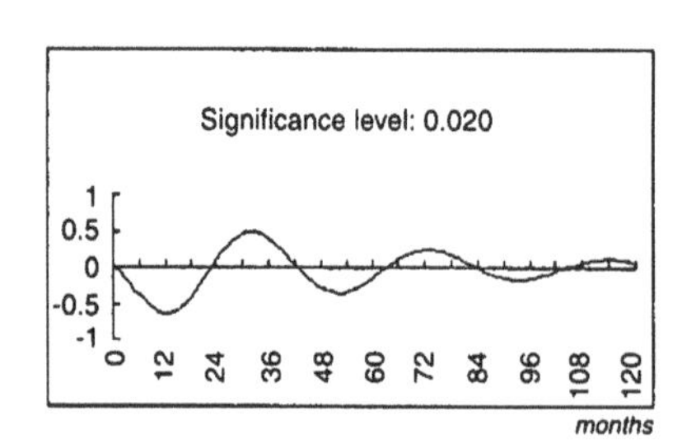

Figure 4.25x—Response of land prices of 6 large cities to credit guarantees
(June 1960 to December 1974)

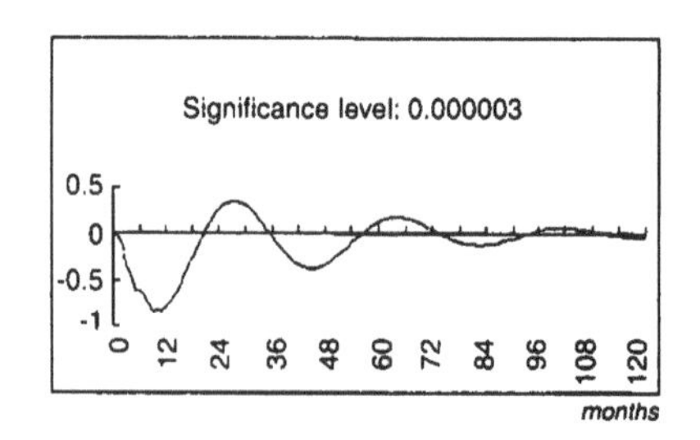

Figure 4.26 The impulse response functions: Funds raised in the capital market

Figure 4.26a—Response of funds raised in the capital market to land prices (all Japan) (January 1975 to December 1990)

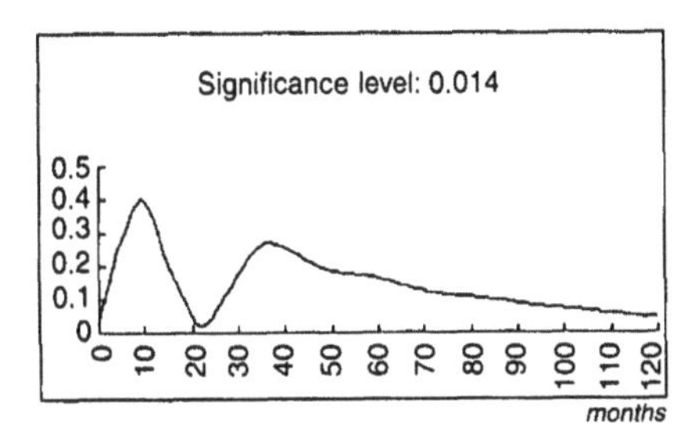

Figure 4.26b—Response of land prices in all Japan to funds raised in the capital market (January 1975 to December 1990)

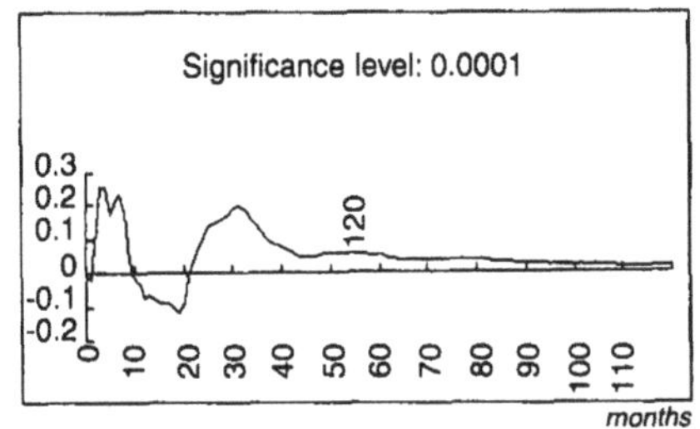

Figure 4.26c—Response of funds raised in the capital market to land prices in 6 large cities (January 1975 to December 1990)

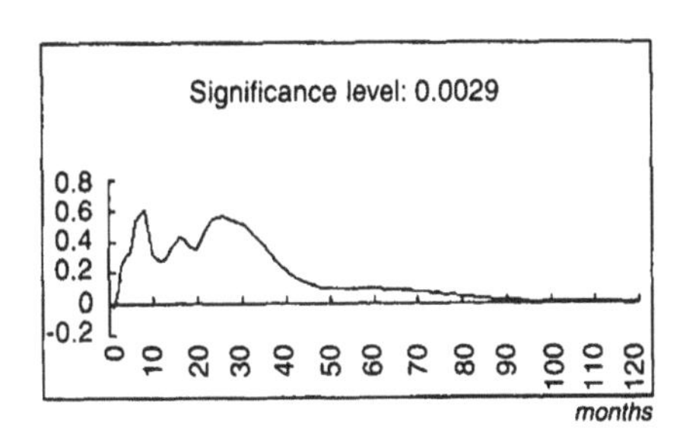

Figure 4.26d—Response of land prices in 6 large cities to funds raised in the capital market (January 1975 to December 1990)

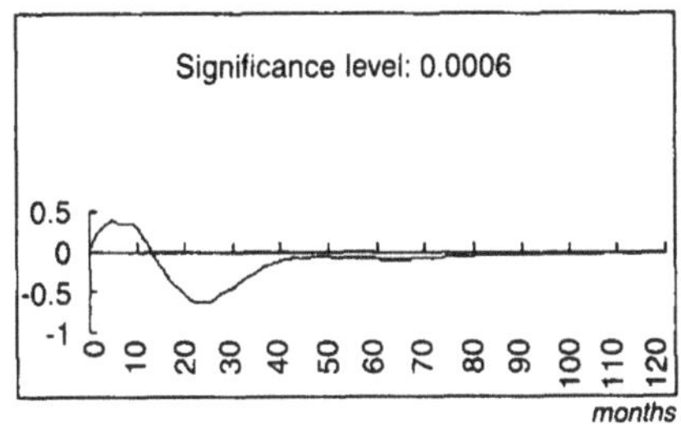

Figure 4.26e—Response of large-firm loans to funds raised in the capital market (January 1991 to March 1999)

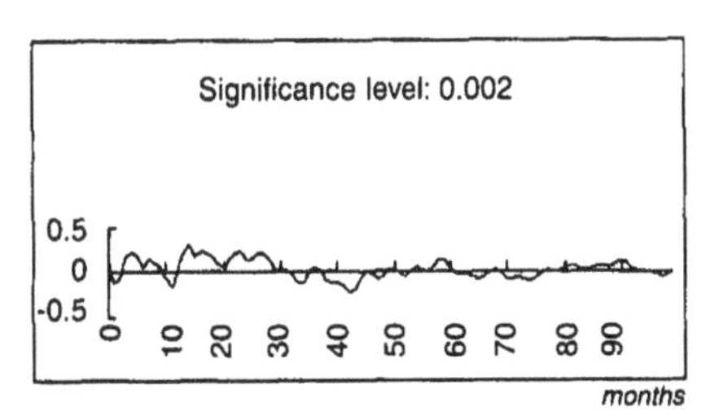

Figure 4.26f—Response of funds raised in the capital market to large-firm loans (January 1991 to March 1999)

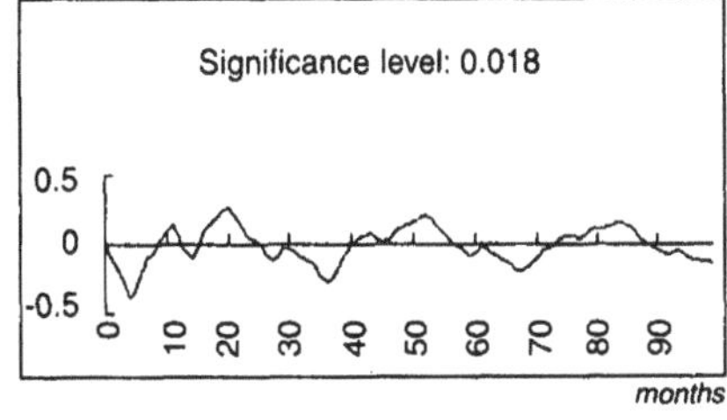

In table 4.2, the relationship between funds raised in the capital market and bank loans is not significant in either direction. On the other hand, the relationship between funds raised in the capital market and land prices is highly significant in both directions. As shown in figure 4.26c, the funds raised in the capital market are highly and positively affected by land prices in the six largest cities, and the effect remains positive for several years. The effect of land prices in all Japan on funds raised in the capital market shown in figure 4.26a is significant, but not as large as in figure 4.26c. This suggests that the increased land prices in the six largest cities mainly contributed to the increased fund-raising in the capital market.

The effects from funds raised in the capital market to land prices are also significant (figures 4.26b and 4.26d). The coefficients on land prices remain positive for more than a decade only for land prices in all Japan. These findings are consistent with the following observation. Land prices, especially in the six largest cities, encouraged large firms to raise funds from the capital market. Then these funds were themselves invested in land and equity holdings, and contributed to the further rise in asset prices. Thus, the collateral principle as it applies to corporate bond issuance could have been an important channel through which increased land prices encouraged increased fund-raising in the capital market.

Summarizing the above findings, we could characterize what happened in the Japanese financial market in the 1980s as follows: Deregulation of the capital market and low interest rates made it easy and profitable for large firms to raise money in the capital market. At the same time, a rise in land prices in the six largest cities increased the collateral value of land, and the soaring stock prices further encouraged fund-raising in the capital market. The funds raised by large firms were invested in land- and stock-holdings, further raising their prices, while reducing the demand for bank loans.

Then banks started to make loans secured by land to small and medium-sized firms, which was made possible due to the increased land prices in large cities. As a result, the small and medium-sized firms receiving larger loans were primarily located in large cities. The funds raised in the capital market by large firms played a major role in further raising land prices. Compared with the role of large firms, the role of increased bank loans to small and medium-sized firms in raising the land prices is less important.

Falling-land-price period (January 1991 to March 1999). All the causal relationships between land prices and bank loans disappear in this period, except that the effect of loans to small and medium-sized firms on land prices in all Japan is significant at the 4.6 percent level, as is seen in table 4.1. The direction of the causality and the patterns of the coefficients are very different from those in the earlier periods (figure 4.25p). This suggests that one cause of the land price decline could have been the credit crunch experienced by small and medium-sized firms in the 1990s.

The lack of significant causality indicates that the fall in bank loans in the 1990s was not proportional to the extremely large fall in land prices. This could imply that bank loans to small and medium-sized firms have not yet fallen enough to be consistent with the land's market value, based on the relationship that existed in the earlier periods. If bank loans had to be secured with collateral at the same rate through the 1980s, then the amount of bank loans outstanding is still too great. This strongly suggests the possibility of discovering further bad loans in the Japanese banking system.

The relationship between funds raised in the capital market and land prices is still significant for both directions, as shown in table 4.2 and in figures 4.26e and 4.26f. These results suggest that the reduced amount of fund-raising in the capital market might have contributed to the fall in land prices, and vice versa. But the coefficients representing this relationship are smaller than those in the earlier period. Therefore, in the 1990s, the role of land prices was far less significant than in earlier periods.

Credit guarantees. The guarantees of the Credit Guarantee Association cover only bank loans to small and medium-sized firms against default for a guarantee fee of 1 percent. The effects of the land prices both in the six largest cities and in all Japan on the credit guarantee are significant for the whole period and high-growth period (table 4.1). The effect is not significant for the period after 1991. Compared with the effect on bank loans, the pattern of the coefficients on credit guarantees suggests a positive effect that persists for about 2 years. The cyclical pattern of the coefficients on the credit guarantee is opposite to that for bank loans. That is, when land prices increase, bank loans to small and medium-sized firms increase, and credit guarantees fall. When the growth rate in land prices decreased, the credit guarantees increase. This suggests that small and medium-sized firms used increased land values to secure their borrowings when land prices were rising, and they depended on credit guarantees when the rate of the rise in land prices decreased.

Conclusion

Real estate plays an important role as a key form of collateral for obtaining credit not only in Japan but in nearly all Asian countries.[18] In the 1980s, financial deregulation encouraged large firms to raise long-term funds from the capital market. Regulated low interest rates facilitated a rise in stock prices and further encouraged the expansion of the capital market, reducing the demand for long-term bank loans by large firms. At the

18. The analysis for South Korea is shown in the appendix.

same time, deregulation helped banks increase the amount of funds they had available for lending. Banks tended to increase loans to small and medium-sized firms to substitute for the reduced demand for loans by large firms. The increased land prices helped to enhance the creditworthiness of these small and medium-sized firms, and the loans made to them increased markedly.

Under a regime of regulated deposit interest rates, bank profits were proportional to the size of their loan portfolios. Banks continued to follow their traditional lending behavior for maximizing profits in a newly liberalized market—with painful results. The common belief in Japan before 1992 that land prices never fall, the so-called myth of land, affected bank lending policy in the face of increased competition for originating loans. Our model of bank lending and collateral can explain the lending pattern as typical profit-maximizing behavior if we assume banks ignored the changing economic environment (which seems more than plausible). Banks increased the amount of real estate collateral needed to secure their loans because they clearly perceived higher credit risks involved in making the loans to these new borrowers. The problem was their persistent belief that land prices would never fall.

The empirical analysis based on the estimated impulse-response functions of the previous section indicates that causality between land prices and financial market activities existed in Japan. Loans to small and medium-sized firms and funds raised in the capital markets are significantly affected by land prices. The analysis implies that the asset inflation in 1980s planted seeds for a later financial crisis and the later government policy change to stop it abruptly triggered the financial crisis in Japan. In this sense, the monetary policy that brought about asset inflation in the 1980s was largely responsible for the current financial crisis.[19] Japan's experience shows how large the economic dislocation caused by the combination of regulating interest rates and allowing asset price fluctuations can be.

The dominant position of banks in Japan's financial market and the lack of an effective system of credit risk sharing through the capital market were the fundamental structures that brought about the ensuing financial crisis.[20]

In order to end the financial crisis, stabilization of land prices at an unregulated market equilibrium is needed. Deregulation of the real estate market is a promising policy measure for economic recovery; such measures as real estate tax reform and deregulation of real estate construction could increase both real estate demand and liquidity in this market.[21]

---

19. See Shimizu (1997c; 1998) for a discussion of Japanese monetary policy in the 1980s.

20. See Shimizu (1997b, chap. 8).

21. Thurow (1998) correctly makes this point.

The above analysis may offer a useful perspective on the causes of other Asian financial crises that have occurred in the years since Japan began to experience its financial difficulties. Certainly these economies share many common characteristics in their financial organization.

References

Asakura, Kokichi. 1978. *Ginko Eeiei no Keifu*. Nipponn Keizai Shinbunsha (in Japanese). Tokyo.

Demirguc-Kunt, Asli, and Encica Detragiache. 1998. Financial Liberalization and Financial Fragility. Working Paper. Washington: International Monetary Fund.

Friedman, Benjamin M. 2000. Japan Now and the United States Then: Lessons from the Parallels. Chap. 3 of this volume.

Lindgren, C. J., G. Garcia, and M. I. Saal. 1996. *Bank Soundness and Macroeconomic Policy*. Washington: International Monetary Fund.

Miller, Merton H. 1993. The Economics and Politics of Index Arbitrage in the US and Japan. *Pacific Basin Finance Journal* 1: 3-11.

Shimizu, Yoshinori. 1993. The Regulation of Financial Markets. *Hitotsubashi Journal of Commerce and Management* 28, no. 1: 1-14.

Shimizu, Yoshinori. 1997a. Speculative Bubbles, Depression and the Monetary Policy in Japan. *Hitotsubashi Journal of Commerce and Management* 32, no. 1: 23-58.

Shimizu, Yoshinori. 1997b. *Nippon no Kinyu to Shijo Mechanism* [*The Japanese Financial Market and the Market Mechanism*]. Tokyo: Thoyokeizai Shinposya.

Shimizu, Yoshinori. 1997c. *Macro Keizaigaku no Shinpo to Kinyuseisaku* [*The Progress of Macroeconomics and the Monetary Policy*]. Tokyo: Yuhikaku.

Shimizu, Yoshinori. 1998. International Policy Coordination and Central Bank Independence. *Hitotsubashi Journal of Commerce and Management* 33, no. 1: 20-41.

Stigler, George J. 1964. Public Regulation of the Securities Markets. *Journal of Business* 37: 117-42.

Stigler, George J. 1971. The Theory of Economic Regulation. *Bell Journal of Economics and Management Science* 2: 2-19.

Thurow, Lester C. 1998. *Japan's Economic Recovery* (Japanese edition). Tokyo: TBS Britannica.

Appendix 4.A
Land Prices and Total Bank Loans

The effect of land prices on bank loans can be demonstrated empirically. We analyzed the relationship using a generalized least squares regression with an autocorrelation adjustment at 3 degrees using monthly data from January 1956 to July 1994. The two regression equations are as follows:

$$\Delta ABL_t = \alpha + \beta\Delta LP_t + \gamma CR_t + u_t \quad \text{(i)}$$

$$\Delta ABL_t - \Delta IPI_t = \alpha + \beta\Delta LP_{t-12} + \gamma CR_t + u_t, \quad \text{(ii)}$$

where

ABL = Amount of bank loans by all banks
LP = Land price index of all territories
CR = Interest rate in the call money market
IPI = Industrial production index

The term Δ designates the rate of growth relative to the same month of the previous year; α, β, and γ are parameters; t shows the current period; $t-12$ shows the 12-month lag; and u is an error term.

The regression (2) intends to eliminate an effect from the economic activity by subtracting the growth rate of the industrial production index from the growth rate of bank loans. In this case, the best result is obtained by the 12-month lagged rate of change in land prices rather than the current one.

Table 4A.1 and figure 4A.1 show that the regression fits extremely well, and the coefficient of the land prices is highly significant at the 1 percent level.

We made the same empirical examination for Korea for the period from September 1974 to December 1996 with similar results, as shown in table 4A.2. The results clearly show that in Korea land prices also have a significant effect on the amount of bank loans.

Table 4A.1 Regression of bank loans on land prices: Japan

	ƒ	ƒ LP (t−12)	ƒ LP (t)	CR	D.W.	RSQ
ƒ ABL	10.32**		0.30**	−0.11*	1.96	0.99
	(7.88)		(5.68)	(−2.12)		
ƒ ABL − ƒ IPI	3.39	0.35**		−0.19	2.06	0.91
	(1.29)	(3.05)		(−1.06)		

D.W. = Durbin-Watson statistic
RSQ = r-squared
** = Significant at 1 percent level.
* = Significant at 5 percent level.

Figure 4A.1 Actual rate and estimated rate of bank lending [regression (1)]

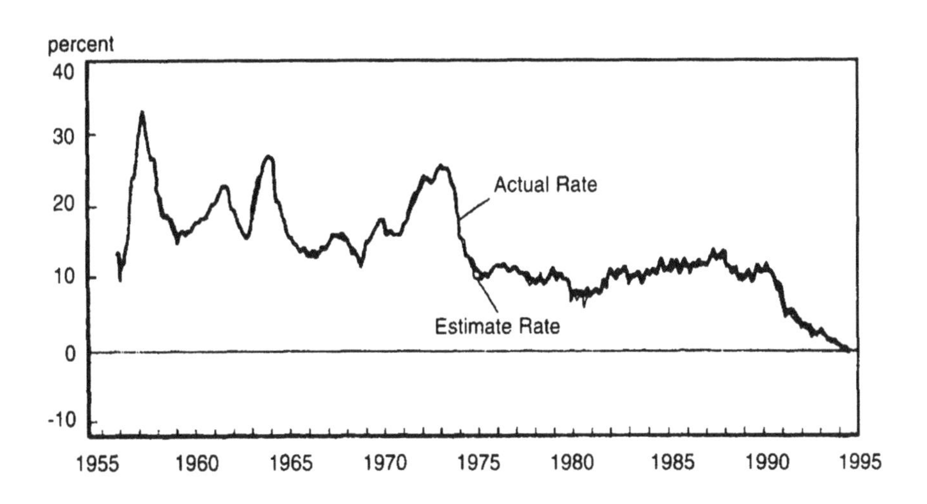

Table 4A.2 Regression of bank loans of land prices: South Korea

		f	*f* LP (t−12)	D.W.	RSQ
	(1)	6.553**	0.328**	0.195	0.4027
f ABL−*f* IPI		(9.952)	(13.617)		
	(2)	3.799	0.680**	1.039	0.926
		(1.656)	(20.913)		

** = Significant at 1 percent level.

(1) Ordinary least squares.

(2) Generalized least squares method with autocorrelation adjustment in error terms.

5

Discussions of the Financial Crisis: Robert Glauber and Anil Kashyap

ROBERT R. GLAUBER

My comments are directed to the parallels between the US banking and savings and loan (S&L) crises and Japan's ongoing banking crisis. I also want to suggest some lessons from US experience that may be relevant for Japan. To this purpose, let me start with some comments on the essays by Friedman and Shimizu.

Friedman puts forward a long, comprehensive, and entirely sensible list of similarities between US and Japanese banking experiences. Prominent among the similarities are the large role of real estate as collateral and the impact of falling real estate prices, regulatory relaxation, moral hazard arising from deposit insurance and deregulation, lax supervisory standards, substantial overcapacity in the banking system, regulatory forbearance, and governmental paralysis arising from the need to get public funds to rehabilitate the banking system. To this list of similarities I would add nontransparent accounting; the "too big to fail" doctrine, which engendered moral hazard behavior; and undercapitalization of the banking system arising from overcapacity.

Against this list of similarities, Friedman notes several differences between US and Japanese experiences. As he suggests, banks play a more important capital market role in Japan than in the United States, and the Japanese banking system is more concentrated. He also suggests that purchase and assumption (P&A) transactions, a process that "resolves" insolvent banks without reducing excess capacity in the banking system,

Robert R. Glauber is professor at the John F. Kennedy School of Government, Harvard University.

played a large role in Japan but not in the United States. In fact, in the 1980s, P&A transactions were the standard resolution procedure used by the Federal Deposit Insurance Corporation, and were as ill conceived in the United States as they were in Japan. Also, Friedman points to the corrosive effects of deposit insurance and the "too big to fail" (TBTF) doctrine, and he suggests that these were a far more serious problem in Japan than the United States. I would suggest that the same corrosive effects of deposit insurance and TBTF are evident in the sad history of the S&L debacle of the 1980s and the banking crisis of 1989-92.

In the same vein, Shimizu cites a number of differences between the two banking systems that have made it more difficult for the Japanese government to deal effectively with the banking crisis. Here I think he is letting the government off a bit too easily. The differences are not that great and hardly excuse the government's delay in dealing with the crisis. (In fairness, I should note that the US government's record in dealing with the S&L crisis is hardly one that engenders great pride.)

Shimizu's list begins with the large decline in the value of land and real estate collateral, which makes it hard to securitize loans and mortgages at current prices. But loans and mortgages on the balance sheets at US S&Ls were under water as well, and any sale through securitization or other means required recognizing losses. This is the essence of resolving these insolvent, or nearly insolvent, institutions. Bad assets must be written down to market value and sold to market buyers, and losses must be recognized and written off against equity. They simply cannot be disposed of at current prices.

The second distinctive characteristic of the Japanese crisis cited by Shimizu is the need for large amounts of public funds to close down insolvent institutions and pay off depositors. This need, he suggests, accounts for (and perhaps excuses) the delay in government action. But the same need for public funds existed in the United States; the S&L debacle cost US taxpayers about $175 billion, perhaps a "small" sum compared with the likely price tag in Japan, but large by US historical measures. In both countries, there is little doubt that the government's timidity in informing taxpayers of the full cost to resolve the crisis produced a large, unnecessary delay. The delay in both cases turned a relatively small cost into a staggeringly large one. Dealing with these crises takes political leadership, a quality often not in large supply.

The final point that Shimizu makes is that the real estate market recovered in the United States in the early 1990s, reducing banking and S&L problems and making it easier to resolve the crises. Here I think he has the cart before the horse. The US real estate market recovered *because* financial institutions were forced to sell their real estate assets into the market at whatever (low) prices the market dictated, and take the write-downs. Only when these assets passed from weak hands (S&Ls and banks) into strong hands (market participants that wanted to own real estate at marked-down prices) could the market recover. Markets do not recover when there is a large inventory overhanging them, waiting for sale. Waiting around for the market to recover before forcing distressed assets out of the banks is a hopeless endeavor.

These are all important lessons, many of which I fear the Japanese regulators have not fully comprehended. There are other lessons that can be learned from the US experience, and it is to them that I would like to turn. In doing so, I should emphasize that whatever wisdom can be found from analyzing the US experience comes in substantial measure from understanding the mistakes of US regulators. Japan has the opportunity to go to school on these mistakes.

Broadly speaking, the objective of any regulatory action in Japan should be to enhance the safety and soundness of the banking system, ensuring that there are strong banks capable of supporting creditworthy domestic companies and capable of competing successfully in the global financial markets. This objective will be best served by several broad regulatory initiatives: First, strict supervision that enforces capital requirements and takes prompt corrective action against banks that fail to meet these requirements; second, a commitment to close insolvent institutions to eliminate excess capacity; and third, increased reporting transparency to reassure the markets. The need to close insolvent banks cannot be overemphasized. Only by doing so will the Japanese banking system avoid cutthroat competition, avoid spreading the system's capital too thinly across too many institutions, and move to reallocate capital and borrowers from weak to healthy banks.

These broad initiatives will be supported by specific actions. First, regulators should close, either directly or through merger, all insolvent banks. In this process, shareholders suffer complete losses, and the senior bank management retires. This closing process is crucial both as a political necessity and to reduce excess capacity in the banking system. Second, the good assets and the franchise of a closed bank should be sold to other solvent institutions. As part of the process, corporate borrowers in good financial health would be transferred to the buying institution—but only healthy borrowers would be transferred. Foreign institutions would be candidates to become buyers. Third, the Financial Supervisory Agency (FSA), the new banking supervision authority, should require transparent reporting.

Fourth, the bad assets (loans and real estate) of closed banks would be transferred to the Resolution and Collection Bank (RCB). The RCB would sell these assets as quickly as feasible, which would require that they be marked down to market value and that the RCB show substantial losses. This is the same course the RTC followed in the US S&L resolution process. The longer the RCB holds assets off the market, the less these assets will be worth and the longer it will take for the real estate market to recover.

Measured against this roadmap, how do recent regulatory activities in Japan stack up? There is some good news. The FSA has been more effective than many expected. It has imposed rigorous supervision and mandated more transparent accounting and loan loss reporting. A substantial number of mergers has been announced, with the effect that, of the 19 largest banks 2 years ago, two have been (temporarily) nationalized and the remaining 17 merged into eight new banks. The largest of these mergers, Industrial Bank of Japan/Dai-Ichi Kangyo/Fuji and Sumitomo/Sakura, will produce very large institutions. Interestingly, the Sumitomo/Sakura merger unites banks formerly allied with two different keiretsus. These mergers can be a mechanism to close insolvent banks, downsize capacity, and sell off bad loans on the balance sheet. They can be the vehicles to do very real restructuring of the financial industry.

The bad news is that the same mergers can provide an excuse to avoid the hard decisions necessary to accomplish real restructuring, which is needed for Japanese banks to provide domestic credit and compete in the global financial market. Will the merger process provide the needed restructuring?

There are reasons for some skepticism. Bank mergers are difficult to accomplish effectively. Particularly in Japan, these mergers require combining large bureaucracies into even larger ones. The integration process must proceed across different corporate cultures, even across keiretsu lines in one case. The record of success in the United States is not altogether reassuring; there, fewer than 50 percent of merged banks have been more profitable after merging than before.[1] What has been difficult in the United States could be even more so in Japan.

I must admit to having several concerns about the prospects of these mergers. They may produce just more delay before the necessary restructuring is accomplished. The mergers are typically announced with 1 to 2 years lead time, during which the organizations can be paralyzed. Asset sales can be delayed, and efforts to enter new profitable businesses, needed to meet the imperatives of globalization, can be put on hold. There is in fact little evidence that asset sales have begun in earnest. Perhaps it would be better to sell assets first, then proceed with the merger, or at least to commit to doing both at the same time.

It also appears that the mergers are being used to keep insolvent industrial companies on financial life support. As a condition imposed by the government for the purchase of Long-Term Credit Bank by a group of US financial institutions, the buyers cannot reduce the size of the bank's loan portfolio for 3 years. So the bank must continue to lend to weak or bankrupt firms in the old economy—steel, shipbuilding, construction—

1. Pilloff, Steven J., and Anthony M. Santomero. 1996. *The Value Effects of Bank Mergers and Acquisitions.* Wharton Financial Institutions Center Working Papers 97-07. Philadelphia: Wharton Financial Institutions Center, University of Pennsylvania.

and has little capacity to lend to potentially healthy emerging growth companies.

In dealing with a serious crisis in its financial system, Japan's regulators appeared for many years to have learned little from mistakes made by US regulators facing similar challenges. Recently, the new Japanese financial regulator has taken some encouraging steps. But there is still much to do, and some cause for concern that the mistakes are not over.

ANIL K. KASHYAP

The essays in this volume nicely convey the range of opinions regarding both what happened in Japan in the 1990s and what policymakers might do to improve the current situation. Given the diversity of views, I will begin my remarks by reviewing the consensus position. Having set out the consensus, I will then identify the most novel observations made by the authors. I will close by pointing to the issues that I believe deserve the most attention at this time.

The Consensus Explanation for Japan's Economic and Financial Crises

Like most of the contributors to this volume, I believe that during the 1990s Japan faced both economic and financial crises, each of which was partially preventable. Because the causes of the financial collapse seem to be less controversial, let me begin my remarks by reviewing this evidence, before turning to the more contentious issue of the macroeconomic problems.

Background on the Banking and Financial Problems

According to most observers, the origins of the financial crisis can be traced to the financial liberalization that began in the late 1970s and is just now being completed (for an elaboration of what follows, see Hoshi and Kashyap 2000). Up until the middle of the 1970s, the financial system was heavily regulated, so corporations were virtually forced to rely on banks for funding (because other market options were restricted). Households also faced very restricted choices regarding where they could put their savings, so most of their wealth was held in deposit accounts. Although this system may not have been the most efficient way to fund corporate investment, it was at least internally consistent—as long as the banks did a good job of taking in deposits and making loans.

The system began to unravel with the onset of deregulation. The key problem came from three mutually inconsistent aspects of the changes. The first was the easing of restrictions on accessing capital markets, which undercut the banks' dominant position as suppliers of capital to the corporate sector (particularly for the largest firms). The second was slow and

---

Anil K. Kashyap is a professor at the Graduate School of Business, University of Chicago. He is a consultant with the Federal Reserve Bank of Chicago and research associate at the National Bureau of Economic Research. *The author thanks Takeo Hoshi for helpful discussions.* *The views in this essay do not reflect those of the Federal Reserve System or the Federal Reserve Bank of Chicago.*

incomplete easing of the restrictions on households' nonbank savings' options. The absence of full liberalization assured the banks of a large supply of deposits. The third was the even less complete expansion of bank powers and shareholders' rights, which not only prevented the banks from moving into new lines of business, but also made it difficult to force the banks to shrink as their traditional customers migrated to other sources of funding.

The inconsistencies among the changes played out during the 1980s as the deposit-bloated banks began looking for things to finance. Domestically, the banks shifted toward more small-business lending and really ramped up their real estate lending. There was also a large increase in overseas lending. By the end of the 1980s, the banks had transformed themselves so that they were more attached to these new customers, and they therefore faced a new set of risks.

The plummeting asset prices of the 1990s triggered the crisis by impairing the banks' capital. The banks were reluctant to recognize the losses, and regulators were slow to force them to do so (because this would have been an implicit acknowledgment of bungled supervision). This period of denial meant that the capital-impaired banks fell behind their international competitors in launching new products and offering new services that will be important once the financial services industry around the world is deregulated. Only when the losses became too large to hide did the government step in to force some reorganization.

Macroeconomic Events in the 1990s

The standard explanation for the macroeconomic stagnation in the 1990s also usually begins with the collapse of the stock market and subsequent decline in land prices. Most of the essays in this volume (except notably for that by Jinushi, Kuroki, and Miyao) do not say much about the cause of the break in asset prices, although it is common to point to monetary policy as having precipitated the decline. For our purposes, settling this issue is not essential, but I will offer some reasons to be skeptical about believing that the Bank of Japan (BOJ) caused a "bubble" to pop.

Regardless of the reason that asset prices did begin falling, it is clear that the price shifts adversely affected banks', consumers', and firms' balance sheets. This deterioration in net worth contributed to a spending decline, most clearly in investment. Initially, there was some easing by the BOJ, but in hindsight this was incomplete. Only by the end of the decade—when the BOJ had become independent and implemented its zero interest rate policy—did monetary policy become exceptionally loose.

Fiscal policy throughout most of the 1990s was also relatively tight. Although the government repeatedly announced stimulus packages, its actual spending was almost always far below the announced amounts. The major exception to this rule was the period 1995-96, during which growth was actually robust. The stance of fiscal policy shifted in April 1997, when the national consumption tax was increased from 3 to 5 percent. At the same time, the temporary income tax cut was discontinued and the copayment for national health insurance was increased. Growth during the rest of the year was much slower.

In the fall of 1997, the banking crisis came into full view as several large financial institutions failed. Bank credit and investment spending both dropped markedly, and nominal GDP growth for the next 2 years was actually negative. Banks were forced to accept some capital in the spring of 1998, but it took a year before a serious injection of public money was offered. By the beginning of 2000, a recovery had begun that appears to be taking hold.

Novel Observations Made by the Authors

Although this general picture is painted by almost all the authors of the essays in this volume, each chooses to emphasize slightly different things. To keep these comments brief, I will highlight only those observations that I find most intriguing. I will also add my reactions to these main points.

Perspectives on the Banking Crisis

Shimizu makes three noteworthy points. First, he argues persuasively that the long-term-credit banks were the most disenfranchised by the deregulation, so it is not surprising that they were the most hurt. Second, the banks' shift toward more real estate lending could be rationalized as an appropriate (and perhaps even optimal) response to having to switch to lending to more risky customers. Third, he notes that up until the 1990s there was clear evidence that land price shifts preceded loans, particularly for smaller firms.

I agree that the demise of the long-term-credit banks was in many respects inevitable: They were more dependent on large manufacturing firms than the other major banks, and they also had enjoyed the advantage of being the only serious long-term lenders. Once these niches disappeared, they became organizations with no clear reason to exist and no comparative advantage.

I am less convinced that the real estate lending boom was fully rational. As mentioned above, the lack of corporate control insulated the banks from a pressure to shrink and maintain profitability. More important, the terms of many of the loans were not always as conservative as one would expect if property lending were really being driven by concerns about risk. For instance, in the late 1980s it was common to hear of real estate loans for which the ratio of loan to value was above 100 percent at the time credit was extended, because "land prices never decline in Japan."

I also see this interpretation as being consistent with the potential shift in the correlation between lending flows and land price changes. In particular, perhaps one reason why the land price declines did not initially lead to a sharp drop in lending was the lack of strong corporate governance for the banks. Because there was no immediate pressure to maintain profitability, many loans with little chance of netting a profit were extended and then rolled over.

The political economy of the crisis figures heavily in Friedman's essay. He offers six strong pieces of advice about what should be done in Japan: (1) act "more" promptly; (2) avoid regulatory forbearance; (3) force consolidations; (4) sell the collateral; (5) penalize shareholders, not depositors; and (6) apply expansionary fiscal and monetary policies. I concur with all these suggestions.

However, I see the need to force consolidation as the most urgent priority. Throughout the 1990s, the major Japanese banks were simultaneously among the largest banks in the world, and the least profitable. This situation cannot continue much longer, and unfortunately it is hard to see how a recovery in profitability could occur. At this point, the banks have virtually no competitive advantage vis-à-vis the other global banks; put differently, it is hard to think of a single product or service line in which the Japanese banks could compete head-to-head with the world leaders and win much business. Thus, an attempt to take on the world's major financial services firms in offering new products and services is likely to fail.

Given these circumstances, the obvious alternative is for the banks to retreat from most global activities and focus on those core areas of banking within Japan for which full foreign competition is likely to be less acute. This would imply a major shakeout in the industry—one that is probably inevitable anyway, because during the next few years, savers will be able to access nondeposit financing more easily, and borrowers will continue to migrate to capital market financing.

The consolidation that I imagine involves significant downsizing, not just in the number of banks but, more important, in the *overall scale* of the banking sector. As a benchmark, table 5.1 reports data from Gilson (1998) showing that it was common for mergers between large banks in the United States in the late 1980s and early 1990s to involve targeted cost cuts of 30-40 percent. The contrast with the large Japanese mergers since the fall of 1999 is striking. For instance, in the merger of Dai-Ichi Kangyo Bank, Fuji Bank, and the Industrial Bank of Japan, only 3 extra branch closings and 38 additional employees were to be let go (relative to what the individual banks had announced when they received their

Table 5.1 Cost savings for selected large US bank mergers

Year	Acquiring bank / acquired bank	Cost savings as a percentage of smaller bank's expenses
1986	Wells Fargo / Crocker	31
1987	Hartford National / Shawmut	33
1987	Bank of New York / Irving	37
1989	MNC / Equitable	39
1989	Core States / First Pennsylvania	39
1991	Chemical / Manufacturers Hanover	33
1991	Commercial / Manufacturers National	37
1995	Fleet / Shawmut	43
1995	PNC / Midatlantic	33
	Average	36

Source: Gilson (1998, table TN.3).

capital infusion in the spring)! The tie-ups between Sakura and Sumitomo and between Asahi and Tokai were only slightly more ambitious. Unless these mergers result in significantly more downsizing, they will not help with the fundamental underlying problem.

Similarly, the capital injection that occurred in the spring of 1999 was also inefficient. Many of the banks that received support are destined to disappear or shrink massively, so it was probably unwise to spread public money so indiscriminately across the banks. I suggest that any policy proposal to address the continuing problems of the banks first be evaluated by checking whether it is consistent with the view that the Japanese banking sector needs to shrink.

Perspectives on Japanese Monetary Policy

The essays by Bernanke and by Jinushi, Kuroki, and Miyao each use very different approaches to arrive at the conclusion that Japanese monetary policy could have been used to foster growth during the 1990s. Because I also agree with this conclusion, I will not dwell on the details of these authors' arguments. Instead, I will pick up on three other observations that flow from their work.

First, I think it is important to recognize that the Jinushi, Kuroki, and Miyao essay stands out relative to the other contributions to this volume because it looks at what happened in the late 1980s as well as in the 1990s. Their assessment of the evidence from before the growth slowdown is very interesting: They conclude that during the period 1990-91 the BOJ's monetary policy was *too loose*! Their fitted rule for the call rate (shown in their table 4) clearly shows that one might have expected further monetary tightening during this period.

I find this observation intriguing in two respects. First, most textbook treatment of stock price determination would say that monetary policy would have a difficult time affecting any particular relative price in the economy (including the relative price of land or stocks). In a more recent context, Federal Reserve Chairman Alan Greenspan has been expressing his concerns over US stock prices for years, but stock prices have soared since his now famous quote about "irrational exuberance."

No doubt, if the United States does have a crash, there will be some who blame Greenspan, but to do so would ignore the impotence of his remarks for years. More important, in the Japanese context, why did the overall inflation rate in the late 1980s not explode, if monetary policy was so loose? Thus, there are good theoretical reasons to be cautious in asserting that the BOJ started or stopped an asset price bubble.

Furthermore, others who have looked for fundamentals-based explanations for the stock price movements have had some success in explaining this period. For instance, Ueda, in an essay published in *1990*, found that the land price increase in the 1980s can be fully explained by the growth in rental prices (Ueda 1990). In spite of the high rate of land price increases, the ratio of land price to rent hardly changed.

Because many Japanese firms hold substantial amounts of land, Ueda (1990) also found that the increase in corporate assets implied by the increase in land prices goes a long way toward explaining the stock price increase. If investors believed that the low interest rates and healthy growth in corporate earnings of the 1980s would continue forever, fundamental factors (including the land price increase) can fully explain the increase in stock prices. (See also Frankel 1993 for a similar account.) Thus, I believe we should add the Jinushi, Kuroki, and Miyao essay to the stack of evidence challenging the claim that the BOJ really triggered the collapse of the stock and land markets.

If the BOJ did not cause the collapse in asset prices that triggered this whole debacle, what did? As Jinushi, Kuroki, and Miyao note, there were also some direct credit controls on land and stock purchases that were put in place during this time, and these factors may well have been important. But I think this topic is still ripe for further study.

Bernanke's essay focuses more on recent events and argues strongly for two points. He first argues that part of the poor growth of the 1990s was due to insufficient aggregate demand. He then argues that a looser monetary policy focusing on depreciating the exchange rate would be a good first step toward stimulating spending; if that is tried and fails, he proposes a variety of other monetary actions.

I am a bit skeptical of the overall importance of the deflationist story of insufficient aggregate demand. To play devil's advocate, my concern comes from evidence on forward interest rates (e.g., published each month in BOJ's *Monthly Bulletin*). These rates suggest (at least since the fall of 1999) that the expected 1-year rate, 3 to 4 years ahead, has been about 2 percent; it is even higher going out a few years further. Taking Bernanke's estimate of a 1 percent real rate, this seems consistent with the view that the strong growth of narrow money is expected to slowly lead to a modest amount of inflation—not too far from the preferred level for many countries that are pursuing inflation targets.

Although this evidence gives me pause, I am equally puzzled by the movement in the exchange rate since the fall of 1998. It is hard to understand why the yen has appreciated so much—unless one gives some credence to the concerns over deflation. Moreover, I agree with Bernanke that a depreciation of the yen would improve growth in Japan in the near term. Given the low rate of inflation, it is hard to argue against this on the grounds of harming price stability; at the same time, a depreciation is almost certain to at least spur exports. So, despite my minor doubts about Bernanke's diagnosis, I am in full agreement with his policy prescription.

Unfortunately, this view is not shared by the BOJ. As Bernanke notes, the BOJ has argued that it cannot intervene on its own in the foreign exchange market. Like Bernanke, I am troubled by this argument. For one thing, it is quite possible that, even by stating its preference for a weaker yen, the depreciation would occur with little or no intervention. Moreover, even if the "open mouth" operations did not work, the BOJ could legitimately fight for the right to intervene to offset deflationary pressures. I think it is unfortunate that the turf battles between the Ministry of Finance and the BOJ over how to manage this issue have ruled out the depreciation strategy thus far.

What Next?

Having discussed most of the relevant economic issues already, I close by pointing to two concerns regarding the political economy of the banking and macroeconomic crises. Both these issues are related to the observation that, despite the size of these problems, the Japanese public does not seem to have decided who really is responsible for the mess. Furthermore, within the government there is likely to be further jockeying to attempt to get credit for resolving the crises.

Blame Shifting

By the end of the US savings and loan crisis, there was lots of blame to go around. Most important, many people went to jail, and in textbook descriptions of the crises certain figures such as Charles Keating became the poster boys of the crisis. In Japan, this has yet to happen. I believe it will need to occur before the public will be completely satisfied and prepared to support measures to fully resolve the crisis.

Against this backdrop, I found the essay by Sakakibara extremely incredible. In particular, he writes that "US ambivalence about the infusion of public money had been a big factor in making Japanese public opinion largely antagonistic toward such an infusion." This is a stunning attempt at historical revisionism! For instance, Thomas F. Cargill (2000), in his summary of why the public support was missing, makes no mention of the US position. Instead, he attributes the tepid support to the scandals inside the Ministry of Finance and the BOJ, the bungled handling of the *jusen* resolution, and the perception that in the first round of capital injections the banks seemed to receive very few sanctions. To assert now that the Japanese public's opposition to the bailout was driven by the United States is absurd. However, I believe this example proves my basic point that there is likely to be considerable posturing over who is responsible.

The other troubling thing about blaming foreigners is that it does not inspire confidence that foreign firms seeking to enter Japan will be treated fairly. I believe that the best chance for Japanese financial-services firms to become efficient and competitive is for them to learn from competing against foreign firms. This process may be hindered if the Japanese authorities are dickering with their international counterparts over these matters.

To move forward in determining who should be held accountable for the need to use public money, I believe it would be helpful to focus on the question posed by Friedman: What happened to the money? It is remarkable that the winners who managed to sell land at such high prices have not surfaced. I hope that there will be more work on this question, by both academics and journalists.

Who Will Get the Credit?

Although a macroeconomic recovery does seem to be under way, there is still quite a bit of controversy over whether further steps could be taken to make sure it will persist. Of the many potential debates, I will focus on the discussions of the mix between monetary and fiscal policy and the question of whether tax reform or bank recapitalization ought to come next.

Until the recovery is fully apparent, the BOJ likely will be under continued pressure to maintain a loose monetary policy. Part of this pressure will come from the Ministry of Finance, which is concerned with the impending social security obligations associated with the aging of the population and therefore is hesitant to keep running up budget deficits. I am sympathetic to these longer-term budget concerns. Accordingly, if stimulative policy is needed, I would prefer to see it come from the monetary side.

Ironically, Ueda (Kazuo Ueda, "Why the BOJ Won't Target Inflation," *Asian Wall Street Journal*, 6 March 2000) and others at the BOJ have argued that the BOJ's capital could be wiped out if it continues to expand its balance sheet when interest rates rise. Not surprisingly, BOJ officials are nervous about having to beg for capital from the Ministry of Finance. The Ministry ought to eliminate this concern by setting a framework to recapitalize the BOJ immediately.

If the BOJ is going to continue to aggressively expand its balance sheet, the question then is what securities should be purchased. Here, I would like to see the BOJ buying the bonds that will be issued to finish recapitalizing the banks and other financial institutions. It is clear that losses by the commercial banks are still not fully covered. Moreover, other financial institutions also may need assistance. I favor Friedman's prescription of shutting the insolvent institutions promptly; but doing so will require funding. Monetization is my preferred option.[1]

Furthermore, there is likely to be a debate over how aggressively to proceed on this front. As we saw during the time when Michio Ochi was the minister for financial reconstruction, there is considerable sentiment within the government for going slow and hoping that a recovery can occur without any tough steps. Even with Ochi's departure there is only so far that the Financial Supervisory Agency (FSA) can go without strong support throughout the government. A further advantage of agreeing that the BOJ is going to begin the refinancing operations is that it would provide cover for the FSA to take a tough line with the weaker institutions that need to be closed. As I said above, the sooner that happens, the better!

References

Cargill, Thomas F. 2000. What Caused Japan's Banking Crisis? In *Crisis and Change in the Japanese Financial System*, eds. Takeo Hoshi and Hugh Patrick. Boston, MA: Kluwer Academic Publishers.

Gilson, Stuart C. 1998. Chase Manhattan Corporation: The Making of America's Largest Bank (Teaching Note), May 12. Watertown, MA: Harvard Business School Publishing.

Hoshi, Takeo, and Anil Kashyap. 2000. The Japanese Banking Crisis: Where Did It Come From and How Will It End? In *NBER Macroeconomics Annual* 14, eds. B. Bernanke and J. Rotemberg. Cambridge, MA: National Bureau of Economic Research.

Frankel, Jeffrey A. 1993. The Japanese Financial System and the Cost of Capital. In *Japanese Capital Markets*, ed. Shinji Takagi. Cambridge, MA: Basil Blackwell.

Ueda, Kazuo. 1990. Are Japanese Stock Prices Too High? *Journal of the Japanese and International Economies* 3: 351-70.

1. In some respects, this may be inevitable, because the Deposit Insurance Funds that are being used for much of the restructuring activity come from a credit line from the BOJ. If the BOJ forgives (or cannot collect) on these loans, this would amount to monetizing the losses.

6

Monetary Policy in Japan Since the Late 1980s: Delayed Policy Actions and Some Explanations

TOSHIKI JINUSHI, YOSHIHIRO KUROKI, and RYUZO MIYAO

Introduction

Japan's monetary policy is now at a crossroads. The overnight call rate, the primary instrument of monetary policy in Japan, had been virtually zero for almost a year at the time of this writing (February 2000). There are increasing requests for further monetary easing, from both inside and outside the country, to prompt economic recovery. The requests often come with the proposal that the central bank should purchase some specific assets, such as government bonds, stocks, foreign currencies (implying unsterilized intervention), or even real estate. These proposals are in some cases accompanied by the policy strategy of "managed inflation," in which the central bank makes an exclusive commitment to achieve some targeted inflation, or, more broadly, "inflation targeting."

In contemplating further policy actions, it may be worthwhile to look back at the history of Japan's monetary policy and seek to draw some lessons from the past. This essay reviews how monetary policy has func-

---

Toshiki Jinushi is professor in the department of economics, Kobe University. Yoshihiro Kuroki is a professor in the Department of Economics, Osaka Prefecture University. Ryuzo Miyao is an associate professor in the Research Institute for Economics and Business Administration, Kobe University. *The authors wish to thank Ryoichi Mikitani, Benjamin Friedman, Adam Posen, Olivier Blanchard, Ben Bernanke, Patricia Kuwayama, Yoshinori Shimizu, Kosuke Aoki, Kengo Inoue, Takayoshi Kitaoka, Yuzo Honda, Kazuo Ogawa, Naoyuki Yoshino, and seminar and workshop participants at Chuo University, Doshisha University, Kobe University, and Tohoku University for helpful comments and discussions. They are also grateful to Takami Kanayama for editorial assistance.*

tioned in Japan, especially since the late 1980s, and attempts to draw some implications for the current discussions about Japan's monetary policy.[1]

In the subsequent section, we first apply a Taylor-rule-type policy reaction function to Japan and document possible delays of monetary policy actions in the late 1980s and early 1990s. In the middle of the 1980s, Japan's monetary control since the late 1970s was viewed by some observers as a success in holding down and stabilizing money growth (e.g., Friedman 1985; Hamada and Hayashi 1985). We therefore treat the reaction function estimated for 1975-85 as the benchmark for a "good" policy rule and compute the call rate after 1985 using the policy rule before 1985. From this exercise, we detect some policy delays (i.e., the deviations of the computed call rate from the actual rate), especially the delay of monetary tightening in 1987-88 and the delay of loosening since 1992.

We then seek explanations for these delays from the following two perspectives. The first explanation is based on a narrative analysis. We attempt to identify the sources of these delays by inspecting various issues of the Bank of Japan's (BOJ) *Monthly Bulletin*. The inspection suggests that the delays in policy action may be attributed to the political pressures based on international policy coordination in 1986-87 and delays in judgment by the BOJ in the early 1990s.

The second explanation is based on a time-series analysis. Using Svensson's (1997) framework of inflation forecast targeting, we show that there may be a shift in the implied policy rule relationship in 1987. We then interpret the estimated shifts in the inflation and output coefficients as suggesting that there may be a shift in the underlying economic structure (a flatter aggregate supply/Phillips curve relationship) and a shift in the monetary policy weight toward a more strict (or rule-like) inflation targeting. The observed policy delays since the late 1980s can be attributed to shifts in the policy reaction function.

On the basis of these results, we finally make some remarks on the current policy discussions of Japanese monetary policy. The suggested shift toward stricter inflation targeting may have led to destabilization of Japan's real economy in the late 1980s and early 1990s. Too strict an inflation target is not a desirable strategy to take, as emphasized in the existing literature. The current proposal for "managed inflation" in Japan implies nothing but such inflation targeting as an absolute rule. More moderate inflation targeting as a "framework" may also lead to inflation targeting as a strict rule under the particular circumstances in Japan. This signals the need to take extra caution in the current policy discussion on this issue. It is still premature to conclude that Japan should adopt an explicit inflation target at present in such a very-low-inflation (if not deflationary) environment.

---

1. See, e.g., Miyao (1999a; 1999b) for other recent discussions.

Delayed Policy Actions Since the Late 1980s

In this section, we apply the Taylor-rule-type policy reaction function to Japanese monetary policy in order to examine its appropriateness in the period since the late 1980s. We find that the monetary-policy actions were delayed, primarily during the periods 1987-88, 1992-95, and 1997-98.[2]

A "Good" Policy Rule

We first estimate the BOJ's reaction function in the "pre-bubble" period of 1975-85. This is the period during which the Japanese economy enjoyed rather better performance than the other industrial countries. The monetary-policy rule in this period can be considered one contributing factor to the country's relative prosperity with lower inflation. If this is true, the estimated-policy rule in this period is a "good" policy rule for Japan, as long as the economic structure remains unchanged.

We basically adapt the empirical specification of Clarida, Gali, and Gertler (1998) but add an exchange rate term:[3]

$$r_t = b_0 + b_1(\pi_t - \pi_t^*) + b_2(y_t - y_t^*) + b_3(x_t - x_t^*) + \gamma r_{t-1} + e_t, \quad (1)$$

where r_t stands for the real "call rate"[4] and e_t is a disturbance term. The call rate is the interbank overnight lending rate in Japan and is considered to be the main policy instrument of the BOJ. Following the original Taylor-rule specification, all the explanatory variables are in gap form, defined as follows. The inflation rate term is the gap between π_t, the actual inflation rate, and π_t^*, the 10-year average inflation rate around the period t. The gross domestic product (GDP) term is the gap between y_t, the log of actual real GDP, and y_t^*, the quadratic trend value of y_t. The exchange rate term is the gap between x_t, the actual exchange rate, and the 10-year average

2. A similar illustration of policy delays can be found in Bernanke and Gertler (1999). In the exercise of Bernanke and Gertler, the deviations between the actual and targeted call rate basically reflect the presence of the assumed partial adjustment mechanism. In the present essay, we not only document the deviations but also explore possible explanations at some length from several perspectives in the sections below.

3. We added this term because strong attention is paid to it in the arguments about monetary policy in Japan. However, it often turns out to be not significant, as in the preceding analysis. In addition, the basic results do not change if this term is deleted. Actually, most of the results, the deviations and the changes, are robust against other specification changes, such as deleting the lagged dependent variable or discriminating the positive and negative inflation gaps.

4. The real rate is calculated using the actual inflation rate.

Figure 6.1 Inflation rate and its 10-year average (percent)

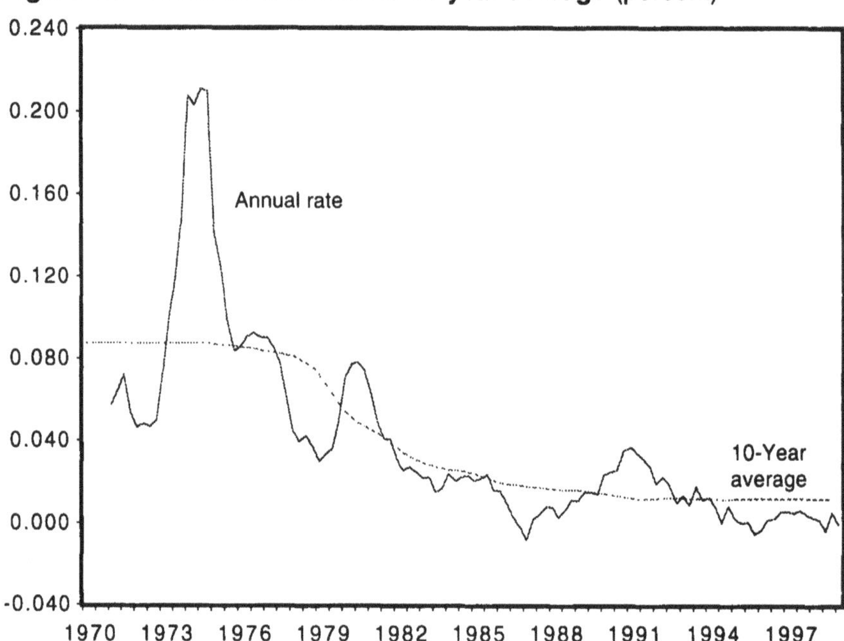

exchange rate around the period t. These three gap variables are depicted in figures 6.1 through 6.3.[5]

We also followed Clarida, Gali, and Gertler's empirical method of Generalized Method of Moments (GMM) estimation in order to take care of the endogeneity bias. The correlation between the error term and the explanatory variables comes partly from the contemporaneous causal relationship between the policy instrument and policy goals. It is also caused by the measurement error in the policy goal variables; for example, the revision of GDP is significant, and the level of potential GDP is the focus of the discussions.[6] The instruments are the own lags (up to 4 lags) of the explanatory variables.[7]

---

5. In calculating the inflation rate, we used the consumer price index (CPI) series adjusted for the changes in the sales tax rate and the copayment rate for public health insurance. We used the seasonally adjusted real GDP series. Its quadratic trend is estimated with a rolling-regression method using the data up to the period t. We used the yen-dollar exchange rate as the exchange rate series; it is known that the nominal effective exchange rate for the Japanese yen moves closely with the yen-dollar rate.

6. Aoki (1999) shows the important implications of measurement errors for monetary policy in the theoretical model.

7. For the GMM estimation to be valid, we rely on the assumption that all the gap variables as well as the real call rate can be characterized as I(0) for the sample period 1975-85. Using the standard Dickey-Fuller tests, the null of a unit root is rejected for the real call rate and the exchange rate term. The null is not rejected for the output gap and inflation gap, yet we view this acceptance as due to the low power of the test for our short sample period.

Figure 6.2 Real GDP and its quadratic trend (percent)

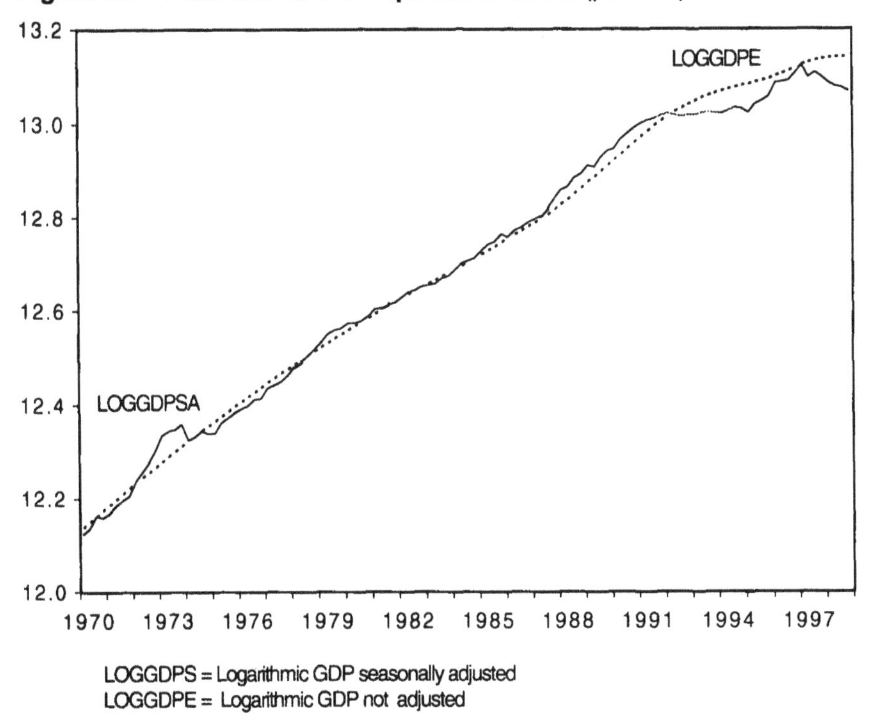

The results are given in table 6.1, which reports the estimation results from several different specifications. In addition to the basic specification, which utilizes the contemporary explanatory variables, we tried two other specifications; they respectively use the 1-period lag and the autoregressive (AR) forecast of each explanatory variable.[8] The main purpose is to check the robustness of the results. In all three specifications, all the coefficients have the right signs. Both the inflation term and the GDP-gap term are always significant. However, the exchange rate term is mostly not significant; its t-statistic is barely in the basic specification. There are some differences in the coefficient estimates, but most of them seem to be caused by the different coefficient estimates (γ) on the lagged dependent variable. The long-run reaction coefficients, calculated as $b_i/(1 - \gamma)$, are much closer over the specifications. The basic specification has a smaller estimate of γ, which reflects the stronger explanatory power

A similar treatment can be found in Clarida, Gali, and Gertler (1998). The optimal weight matrix and robust standard errors are computed using Newey and West's (1987) covariance matrix with the truncation of four lags. We also employ two and three lags, but the results are unaffected.

8. Ordinary least squares (OLS) is used for these estimations.

Figure 6.3 Exchange rate and its 10-year average

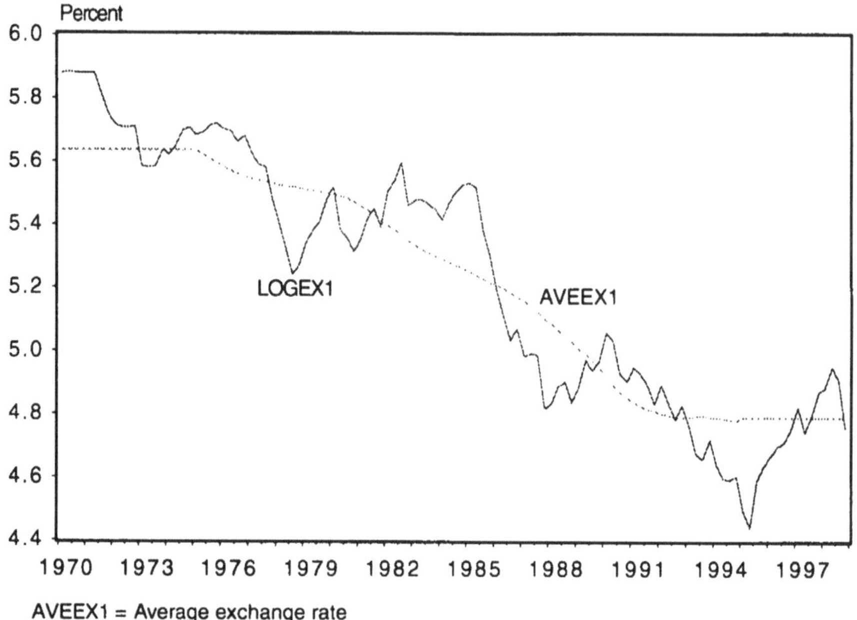

AVEEX1 = Average exchange rate
LOGEX1 = Log exchange rate

Table 6.1 The "good" policy rule in 1975-85

Specification		Estimation						R^2
π	y and x	method	b_0	b_1	b_2	b_3	γ	SEE[a]
Current value	Current value	GMM	1.39 (0.34)	0.27 (0.14)	1.14 (0.37)	0.03 (0.02)	0.39 (0.14)	0.87 (1.21)
1-quarter lagged value	1-quarter lagged value	OLS	1.01 (0.21)	0.17 (0.06)	0.70 (0.20)	0.01 (0.01)	0.65 (0.08)	0.92 (0.97)
Forecast[b] current value	Forecast[b] current value	OLS	1.02 (0.21)	0.25 (0.09)	0.68 (0.22)	0.01 (0.01)	0.66 (0.08)	0.91 (0.97)
1-year lead value	Current value	GMM	1.13 (0.34)	0.17 (0.16)	0.62 (0.26)	0.03 (0.01)	0.57 (0.11)	0.88 (1.15)

GMM = Generalized Method of Moments.
OLS = Ordinary least squares regression.

a. SEE = standard error of estimation.

b. Forecast values are based on autoregressive equations.

Note: Empirical specification: $r_t = b_0 + b_1(\pi_t - \pi_t^*) + b_2(y_t - y_t^*) + b_3(x_t - x_t^*) + \gamma r_{t-1} + e_t$ (see text for explanation). Numbers in parentheses are standard errors.

Figure 6.4 Call rate and the rate implied by the "good" policy rule

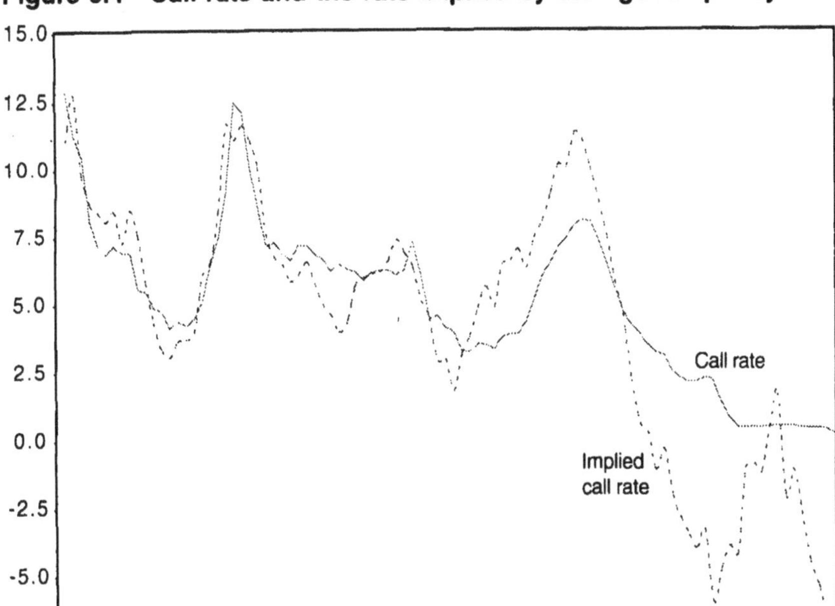

of the contemporary variables compared with those of the 1-period lags or the AR forecasts. Thus, hereafter we adapt the basic specification.

Further, we tried one more specification, which uses the actual 1-year lead value for inflation. Several researchers have adapted this, because the variable may represent the inflation forecasts. The result is reported in the last row of table 6.1. It shows that the 1-year lead value for inflation is not significant. This may suggest that 1-year lead value is not close to the inflation forecast the BOJ used at the time.

Delayed Policy Actions: Identifying Deviations from the "Good" Policy Rule

Next, we apply the estimated "pre-bubble" policy rule to the "bubble" and the "post-bubble" periods. We followed Taylor's (1998) "historical" approach. We try to find the major deviations of the actual monetary policy from the estimated "good" policy rule. The result is depicted in figure 6.4, which shows the call rate implied by the good policy rule.

There seem to be four major deviations:

1. The delay in policy restraint, 1987-88.

2. Insufficient policy restraint, 1990-91.

3. The delay in easing policy restraint, 1992 to early 1995.

4. The delay in easing policy restraint, 1997 to early 1998.

The first deviation is the well-known policy mistake. Three factors are often mentioned as the main reasons for this prolonged delay. The typical argument goes as follows. First, in the implementation of "international policy coordination" after the Plaza Accord of 1985, the BOJ was pushed to keep a low interest rate. Second, market instability caused by the US stock market crash in October 1987 kept the BOJ from tightening policy in late 1987. Third, in 1988, the domestic political requirements pushed the BOJ to delay restraint until the sales tax was successfully introduced in April 1989.[9]

The second deviation seems to be against the popular opinion that monetary policy overkilled the bubble in 1990-91. However, in the final stage of restraint, a couple of major nonmarket restrictions were mobilized by the Ministry of Finance, such as the total volume limit on the lending to the real estate business. Thus, this result might be interpreted as suggesting that, in 1990-91, monetary policy was not too restrictive but that direct credit control was.

The third delay has not been much argued. The BOJ eased rapidly after the bubble burst but stopped further easing in 1994. However, figure 6.4 suggests that the BOJ should have continued to ease more. Further easing in 1994 might have blocked the abnormal appreciation of the yen in March 1995. The BOJ lowered rates quickly to below the 1 percent level after the appreciation.

The fourth deviation was the focus of debate at the time. The BOJ finally adopted the so-called zero interest rate policy in February 1998. However, the result suggests that it should have done so in early 1997, when the short-lived recovery, which was caused mainly by the unusual fiscal policy, ended.

It should be noted that the focus of this essay is monetary policy and that therefore we will not dig deeper into fiscal policy. Of course, few would doubt that fiscal policy played as big a role in the current depression as monetary policy.[10] However, its examination requires another essay.

We further discuss the reasons for these deviations in the next section, using a "narrative" approach based on BOJ publications. We found sub-

9. Some discussions that emphasize the first and third factors can be found in Shimizu (1997).

10. For example, see Posen (1998).

stantial material for the first and third deviations. The first deviation is confirmed again below through the structural test in the cointegration analysis.

Explanation from a Narrative Analysis

In this section, we utilize a "narrative" approach.[11] We examined the publications of the BOJ in order to search for the reasons behind the policy-action delays, which we identified as the deviations of the actual policy from the "good" rule. We first deal with the period of 1986-87 when "international policy coordination" was much emphasized. Second, we look at the period from 1988 to early 1989. The delay in monetary restraint is attributed to the shift in the relative weights of the policy goals. The third period is the first half of the 1990s, when the policymakers could have been misled by the delay in their judgment of the economic situation.

International Policy Coordination, 1986-87

Monetary Policy Stance in 1985 and the Plaza Accord

Loose money policy—which was followed beginning in August 1980 to ride out the recession caused by the second oil crisis in 1979—brought about relatively low but stable growth. Real GDP grew 3 percent on average in the first half of the 1980s, and even faster in 1984.

The BOJ's statements show that the Japanese economy was enjoying relatively good performance in 1985: "Production and shipment are still increasing" (*Monthly Bulletin,* January 1985, 23). "Domestic demand such as capital investment and consumer expenditure steadily increase" (*Monthly Bulletin,* March 1985, 28). "The business firms' judgment on the economic situation is still cautiously optimistic" (*Monthly Bulletin,* June 1985, 32). Monetary growth, measured in M2+CD, was also effectively managed and well controlled in a reasonable range (around 7-8 percent) for most of the early 1980s.

The BOJ ascertained these situations and did not plan to change its policy stance. Then-Governor of the BOJ Sumita told the 39th National Bankers Conference that they must check the cost against the benefit of stimulating domestic demand by monetary and fiscal policies, and of further monetary expansion to redress the trade imbalance (8 July 1985). It seems clear that he was reluctant to conduct further monetary expansion.

This policy stance, however, was obliged to change by the pressure of the Plaza Accord on 22 September. The leading countries thereby agreed

11. The narrative analysis in this section draws heavily on Kuroki (1999, chap. 6).

on a "commitment" to cooperative interventions in the foreign exchange market to force down the appreciated dollar and stimulate domestic demand through expansionary policy to rectify the international balance of payments situation (see table 6.2). The relatively good economic performance of Japan in those days surely depended on the weak yen, which did not correctly reflect the fundamentals of the Japanese economy, in particular large trade surpluses. The international coordination was reasonable in the sense that the attainment of economic prosperity should not involve sacrifices by other countries. However, we have to keep in mind that the policy coordination brought a change in the domestic policy stance.

Discount Rate Policy, 1986-87

The coordinated intervention in the foreign exchange market by the leading countries based on the Plaza Accord produced an upsurge in the yen. The yen's rate shifted from $1 = ¥240 in August 1985 to ¥150 in mid-1986. This rapid appreciation of the yen brought about recessionary effects, and domestic production and capital investment declined (this is the so-called yen-appreciation recession). The decline in industrial production was accelerating, and real GDP growth shifted down from 5 to 3 percent in 1986. The business circumstances of the manufacturing sector worsened, and investment in that sector rapidly cooled down.

Fortunately, the yen hike also brightened the outlook for the Japanese economy. The strong yen and the low price of imported oil encouraged consumer expenditures, such as individual consumption and housing investment, as well as capital investment by the nonmanufacturing sector. The decline in the prices of imported goods and services as well as oil also resulted in lower domestic price levels, and both consumer and retail prices were moving in a stable direction. These benefits, driven by the appreciation of the yen, helped make the 1986 recession relatively mild.

Under these economic conditions, the BOJ reduced the official discount rate five times between January 1986 and February 1987. The discount rate was pushed down from 5 percent to 2.5 percent, which was the lowest level up to that time. These successive reductions aimed to (1) stabilize exchange rates and (2) redress the trade imbalance by stimulating domestic demand. Monetary policy goals, then, emphasized the importance of external affairs. It is not legitimate to assert that Japan's economic structure is solely export oriented, that is, imports are hard to increase and exports are hard to decrease. A monetary policy stance that stimulates the domestic economy might be useful in recovering from a mild recession. However, the issue here is whether revisions in the policy stance and the timings of these revisions were based upon the BOJ's own judgment. We will solve this problem by investigating the circumstances that led to the policy change.

Table 6.2 Aims of changes in the discount rate level

Date of change in discount rate	Tight or loose discount rate level (percent)	Targets	Statements by chairman of policy board (extracts)
29 January 1986	Loose, 5.0-4.5	Redress trade imbalance	"Redress the trade imbalance by stimulating domestic demand."
		Stabilize exchange rates	"Closely watch the movement of exchange rates."
7 March 1986	Loose, 4.5-4.0	Redress trade imbalance	"Redress of the trade imbalance by stimulating domestic demand."
		Stabilize exchange rates	"Avoid drastic exchange fluctuations."
19 April 1986	Loose, 4.0-3.5	Redress trade imbalance	"Take more steps to correct the trade imbalance by stimulating domestic demand in coordination with the government's package of economic policies."
		Stabilize exchange rates	"Contribute to stabilizing the yen exchange rate."
31 October 1986	Loose, 3.5-3.0	Redress trade imbalance Stabilize exchange rates	"Since the government has prepared a supplementary budget for this fiscal year for the package of economic policies, the BOJ . . . eagerly expects stable exchange rates to lead to continuous economic growth."
20 February 1987	Loose, 3.0-2.5	Redress trade imbalance	"Lately, Japan and the United States reconfirmed their cooperation in solving problems of the foreign exchange market, and we expect that the leading countries will closely coordinate efforts to stabilize exchange rates."
		Stabilize exchange rates	"Contribute to stabilizing exchange rates and encourage steady expansion of domestic demand."
30 May 1989	Tight, 2.5-3.25	Redress trade imbalance	"Redress our trade imbalance and promote sound development of the world economy."
		Stabilize domestic prices	"Contribute to attaining continuous economic growth based on the expansion of domestic demand, and keeping prices stable as well."

Tables 6.3 and 6.4 show the discount rate policy in 1986-87 and both international and domestic political trends at the time. These tables imply that the third to the fifth reductions of the discount rate were brought about by the political pressure of international policy coordination.

First, let us look at the reduction of 19 April 1986. In March, the US Federal Reserve demanded the third reduction from the BOJ right after the second reduction of the discount rate (*Nikkei* newspaper, 2 April 1986). On 8 April, the Japanese government prepared the package of economic policies, and an additional expansionary move in monetary policy was listed in the first place to stimulate domestic demand. Moreover, the Takeshita-Baker meeting reached an agreement on 9 April that both countries were in a favorable environment for coordinated reduction of the discount rate.

During the course of these political movements, however, the BOJ started moral suasion to reduce bank lending, and BOJ Governor Sumita stated that he was closely watching the speculative transactions of land and the hike of stock prices based on loose money (*Nikkei* newspaper, 3 April 1986).

We can see the same kind of political pressure on domestic monetary policy in the cases of the fourth and fifth reductions in the rate. The conference of G-7 finance ministers agreed that the country bearing the trade surplus should attain the faster economic growth (27 September). At the IMF-World Bank annual meetings, Japanese Finance Minister Miyazawa pledged publicly to stimulate domestic demand and US Secretary of the Treasury Baker requested that Japan and Germany further reduce their discount rates (1 October).

Again, the BOJ had a different policy stance. Governor Sumita stated that we would not need further monetary loosening (*Nikkei* newspaper, 5 October 1986). The BOJ's *Monthly Bulletin* said, "We will continue to watch carefully the movements of economic situations, including the money supply. We hope that financial institutions will keep a deliberate lending attitude" ("Kouteibuai hikisageni tsuite" [On the reduction of the discount rate], *Monthly Bulletin*, November 1986).

Table 6.4 shows the BOJ's judgment of the economic situations and political trends in 1987. We can see from this table that the BOJ sounded the alarm about the dangers of the financial and economic conditions. For example, "The money supply is considerably high compared with real economic activities. . . . The discount rate is at the lowest level up to today" (*Monthly Bulletin*, January 1987). "Excessive monetary expansion, however, does not contribute to real economic growth, but will quite possibly support speculative transactions of existing assets" (*Monthly Bulletin*, April 1987). "The deflationary shock can be widespread once asset prices start falling, since the hike in those prices has been aided by

Table 6.3 Policy stance of the Bank of Japan and political trends as reported in the *Monthly Bulletin*, 1986

Month	Judgments of the economic situations by the Bank of Japan	Monetary policy (discount rate)	Political trends (international and domestic)
January	"The quantity of exports clearly hit a peak because of the yen appreciation." "Production of the mining and manufacturing sectors is now gradually decreasing." "Domestic demand has been basically steady." "Wholesale prices declined again in December, and consumer prices were stable."	Reduction (29 January 1986)	
March	"Mining and manufacturing production are tending to mildly decline." "Increase in capital investment in manufacturing has been slowing down." "Wholesale prices declined drastically." "The yen has further appreciated." "The current account has been running a large surplus."	Reduction (7 March 1986)	(6 March) Bundesbank: cooperative reduction of the discount rate. (7 March) US Federal Reserve Board: Cooperative reduction of discount rate.
April	"Mining and manufacturing production are tending to mildly decline." "Domestic demand has been still steady as a whole." "Wholesale prices declined further in March." "Stock prices continue to soar." "The current account surplus was still high in February."	Reduction (19 April 1986)	(8 April) The Japanese government prepared the package of economic policies. (9 April) Takeshita-Baker meeting reached an agreement—"Both countries are in a favorable environment for cooperative reduction of the discount rates."
September	"Consumer prices have fallen for 3 consecutive months." "Money supply grows even faster than it did last month." "Flow of money into the stock market goes on."		(19 September) The Japanese government prepared a package of economic policies. (27 September) G-7 finance ministers conference.
October	Almost the same as above.	Reduction (31 October 1986)	

Table 6.4 Policy stance of the Bank of Japan and political trends as reported in the *Monthly Bulletin*, 1987

Month	Judgments of the economic situations by Bank of Japan	Political trends (international and domestic)
January	"Money supply is considerably high compared with real economic activities." "The discount rate is at the lowest level up to today." "Business finance has been getting easier." "Monetary policy stance supporting speculative transactions of assets can damage long-run price stability."	(21 January) Miyazawa-Baker meeting—"The Japanese government would urge BOJ to make a fifth reduction of the discount rate." (22 January) Bundesbank decided to reduce discount rate.
February	Reduction of the discount rate (22 Feb.).	(20 February) Louvre Agreement at G-6 conference asserted that the BOJ would reduce the discount rate by 0.5 percent.
April	"The velocity of money has been declining." "It is appropriate to keep today's stance of easy money for a while to attain continuous expansion of domestic demand and stable exchange rates." "Excessive monetary expansion, however, does not contribute to real economic growth, but will quite possibly support speculative transactions of existing assets."	(8 April) G-7 conference reconfirmed the Louvre Agreement. (24 April) Package of economic policies is decided on to conduct appropriate and mobile monetary policy such as reducing deposit rate to the Fund Management Bureau (Shikin Unyoubu) at the Ministry of Finance.
May	"The deflationary shock can be widespread once asset prices start falling, since the hike in those prices has been aided by speculative transactions." "Excessive monetary expansion will have an adverse effect on sound and stable economic growth in the long run, although it is appropriate to maintain today's easy-money policy for a while."	(1 May) Nakasone-Reagan meeting—Nakasone referred to open-market operations to reduce short-term interest rates. (29 May) Package of urgent economic policies is decided on to conduct appropriate and mobile monetary policy and reduce policy interest rates.
July	"Decline of the velocity of money is now larger than that in 1971-72." "Money stock becoming inactivated in comparison with the activity level of the real economy."	

(continued next page)

Table 6.4 *(continued)*

Month	Judgments of the economic situations by Bank of Japan	Political trends (international and domestic)
July *(cont.)*	"Lending by financial institutions has come to be active." "Prevent harmful effects of excessive expansion while keeping policy stance of today."	
September	"Monetary growth has fairly accelerated."	(4 September) US Federal Reserve Board raised the discount rate.
October	"We do not have to worry about the effects of Black Monday in October." "Money supply has been accelerating faster than the real economy." "The velocity of money has declined drastically." "Activity of financial institutions is firmly expanding."	(26 September) G-7 communiqué—Some of the countries bearing current account surplus need to attain further increase in domestic demand. Each country needs to stabilize exchange rates around current levels. (October) Black Monday
December	"Monetary growth has fairly accelerated."	

speculative transactions. . . . Excessive monetary expansion will have an adverse effect on sound and stable economic growth in the long run, although it is appropriate to maintain today's easy-money policy for a while" (*Monthly Bulletin,* May 1987, 5-7).

Contrary to these alarms, though, the BOJ reduced the discount rate again on 20 February and also started lowering short-term interest rates. The Miyazawa-Baker meeting agreed that the Japanese government would urge the BOJ to make a fifth reduction of the discount rate (21 January 1987). The Louvre Agreement at the G-6 conference asserted that the BOJ would reduce the discount rate by 0.5 percent (20 February). The G-7 conference in April reconfirmed the Louvre Agreement. The package of economic policies decided on by the government included the appropriate and flexible monetary policy, as well as the reduction of the deposit rate to the Fund Management Bureau (*Shikin Unyoubu*) at the Ministry of Finance (8, 24 April). At the Nakasone-Reagan meeting on 1 May, Prime Minister Nakasone referred to open-market operations to reduce short-term interest rates.

As we now have seen, it is clear both that the BOJ had a policy stance against further monetary expansion and that there is a common pattern in these episodes. Requests from foreign governments and public commitments between foreign and domestic governments preceded the monetary decision of the BOJ, and the BOJ then changed its policy stance and undertook excessive monetary expansion. The third to the fifth reductions of the discount rate were brought about by political pressure. Both domestic and international political pressure, based on international policy coordination, distorted monetary policy from mid-1986 to 1987.

Change in Policy Judgment, 1987-88

Bank of Japan's Judgment of the Financial Situation, 1986-87

As we saw above, the BOJ comprehended that monetary growth was in a reasonable range and did not plan to change its policy stance in 1985. After the spring of 1986, the BOJ came to sound the alarm about the monetary growth. "The cumulative decline of the velocity (nominal aggregate demand / M2 + CD) is larger than that of the last easy-money period. . . . We cannot deny the speculative aspects of land transactions based on the quantitative ease of money" (*Monthly Bulletin,* April 1986, 17). "Backed up by the increasing funds' inflow to the stock market, those prices are going higher, regardless of business prospects" (*Monthly Bulletin,* July 1986, 17). "Money supply is considerably high compared with real economic activities" (*Monthly Bulletin,* September 1986, 25).

The BOJ's caution regarding excessive monetary loosening had become fairly clear by 1987. "A large proportion of the increased money supply is used in speculative transactions, with the result that the velocity has been drastically declining. . . . These are] supported by the aggressive lending attitude of financial institutions" (*Monthly Bulletin,* May 1987, 5). "We are afraid that there will be widespread deflationary shocks, which will include financial institutions." (*Monthly Bulletin,* May 1987, 45).

It is in fact remarkable that the BOJ was aware that monetary policy, distorted by political pressure, caused the bubble and already pointed out the danger of widespread "debt-deflation," including that of the overall financial system in the early stage of 1987.

Change in Bank of Japan's Judgment, 1988

Despite the alarms by the BOJ, the excessive loosening stance continued in the first half of 1987, due to the political pressures. Then came the US stock market crash in October 1987—known as Black Monday—and this led to a further delay of a preemptive tightening in Japan. Nevertheless, it is fortunate that Black Monday did not have crucial negative effects on the Japanese economy. In fact, domestic demand grew faster than before, and real GDP growth was 6-7 percent in 1988, which was the highest level since the middle of the 1970s. Business profits, in both manufacturing and nonmanufacturing sectors, rapidly recovered, and fixed investments were also active. Exchange rates were largely stable, and the world economies were steadily expanding on the basis of the reasonable monetary conditions.

Under the circumstances, the Bundesbank decided to raise its discount rate on 30 June and 25 August 1988. Some of the other European countries followed this decision, and the Federal Reserve also raised its discount rate in August 1988. The reasons the Bundesbank decided to raise the rate were (1) powerful expansion of the economy, (2) rapid increase of the money supply, and (3) depreciation of the deutsche mark. This was a precautionary tightening to avoid the inflationary pressures brought on by easy money theretofore.

Why, then, did the BOJ not move on to monetary tightening in early 1988? The Japanese economy faced almost the same situation in which the Bundesbank decided to raise the rate, and the yen-dollar exchange rate was stable. The political pressures to maintain loose money policy were still observed, for example, in Prime Minster Takeshita's announcement at the US-Japan leaders' meeting in January 1988 and in the G-7 communiqué in September 1988. The second and more important factor, however, is that the BOJ changed its policy stance and that the relative weight of its policy concerns shifted from asset prices and possible debt deflation to the prices of goods and services.

In the very beginning of 1988, the BOJ was still worried about the financial situation. "We cannot ignore the fact that excessive monetary expansion can disturb the financial and capital markets" (*Monthly Bulletin*, January 1988, 3). However, the alarm about the hazardous by-products of the redundant monetary expansion almost disappeared in the spring of 1988. Instead, the basic stance of the BOJ became: "Monetary policy that attaches weight to price stability will contribute to the long-lasting expansion of domestic demand.... The BOJ will take appropriate and mobile actions with closely monitoring movements in prices and exchange rates" (*Monthly Bulletin*, April 1988, 2). At the time, the money supply was large enough compared with the real economy, and this inactivated part of money, which did not reflect the real activities, had still pushed up the bubble of existing assets.[12]

The mistake of the BOJ in 1988 is that it slighted the movements of asset prices (prices of "stock" variables) and their possible disastrous effects and stressed the prices of "flow" variables. In the next section, we will see, using time-series analyses, that the relative policy weight on GDP relative to inflation goals decreased in the second quarter of 1987. Here, the narrative approach can give fairly robust explanations for the statistical result.

---

12. Monetary growth was still high, and the velocity of money continued to decline in 1988. Meanwhile, the liquidity of businesses (as scaled by monthly sales) was drastically increasing.

Optimistic Policy Operations and Delays in Judgment in the Early 1990s

Bursting of the Bubble and Optimistic Policy Operations

In May 1989, the BOJ abandoned the easy-money policy that had lasted for a decade and started monetary contraction. Its goal was to maintain price stability and contribute to continuous growth based on domestic demand. The BOJ raised the discount rate five times, and its level reached 6 percent in August 1990, which was higher than the level at the time of the Plaza Accord. The policy stance of the BOJ at the time was to prevent a rise in inflationary expectation in the early stage to attain price stability (*Monthly Bulletin*, May 1990, 35). Again, the BOJ's policy stance emphasized stabilizing prices of goods and services.

The Ministry of Finance also introduced restrictive laws and regulations to land transactions. These devices possibly triggered the bursting of the bubble. The increasing rate of stock prices hit a peak in 1989 and turned negative in the second half of 1990. Land prices also started reducing their increase rates in the middle of 1990, and recorded negative rates in the fourth quarter of 1991.

In the face of this situation, the BOJ began loosening monetary conditions in July 1991. However, the BOJ's judgment of the situation was quite optimistic, and hence it did not recognize that the bubble had already burst and that the economy was at the entrance gate of the debt-deflation cycle. For instance, "Since economic activities are still high, we shouldn't fail to watch price movements" ("On the Reduction of the Discount Rate," *Monthly Bulletin*, July 1991). "The policy action of this time hopefully contributes to continuous growth based on price stability. . . . We will conduct deliberate policy operations pursuing price stability" ("On the Reduction of the Discount Rate," *Monthly Bulletin*, December 1991). "This will contribute to our country's smooth and steady movement toward a balanced economy based on price stability" ("On the Reduction of the Discount Rate," *Monthly Bulletin*, January 1992).

It is clear that the BOJ did not recognize the prospect of debt deflation at that time and pursued an "optimistic anti-inflation policy." In the early summer of 1992, we can see that the BOJ recognized that the situation was more serious than it had expected and also used the expression "the bursting of the bubble" in the *Monthly Bulletin* (see, for example, *Monthly Bulletin*, June 1992, 37-39).

Delays in Judgment in the Early 1990s

After April 1992, the BOJ reduced the discount rate five times in addition to the previous reductions. Finally, the discount rate was reduced to 0.5 percent, the lowest level in the BOJ's history, in September 1995. Its goal, of course, was to recover from the prolonged stagnation. However, the large amount of debt that had accumulated during the period of the bubble put a heavier burden on consumers, business firms, and financial institutions than the BOJ had expected. Many economic indicators and indices showed pessimistic figures. We do not need to show each figure here, since Japan's economic conditions in the 1990s are well known. Consumption and business investments have declined. The unemployment rate has been rising. The long-range prospects for households and businesses have been doubtful and gloomy.

While the Japanese economy has suffered from prolonged stagnation for almost a decade, the situation was not monotonic. There was a faint but favorable sign that the economy would improve in 1994 and 1995. The confidence indices on consumption and the index of business prospects hit bottom in the last quarter of 1993 and started to improve. The ratio of current profits to sales of firms also turned upward in the same year, although the growth rate was still stagnating.

In these situations, the BOJ maintained a loose money policy. The problem was that the BOJ might have misjudged how serious the economic situation was, so that the pace of monetary loosening lagged events. Of course, the BOJ knew that the large amount of debt prevented the economy from recovering and that the economy was still in a severe condition. We can read this fact in the *Monthly Bulletins* for those days, in which the BOJ referred to a "demand-supply gap." However, as far as we can tell, the BOJ did not use the expression "deflationary gap" or "debt deflation" in the early 1990s. This fact would seem to suggest that the BOJ did not recognize the potential seriousness of debt deflation, and it therefore can be interpreted as a delay in judgment by the BOJ during that time. A further loosening in 1994 might have prevented the abnormal yen appreciation in March 1995 and might have accomplished stronger recovery afterward. This is the possible explanation for the delay in loosening in 1992-95 that we observed above (figure 6.4).

Explanation from Time-Series Analyses

In this section, we seek another explanation for the delayed policy actions documented above by reexamining the time-series characteristics of the policy rule relationship. The motivation for this exercise is as follows. The coefficients of a monetary policy reaction function are in general determined by the structural parameters of the underlying economy and the relative weight placed on the policy objectives (say, inflation and output) in the loss function of the central bank. If there is a shift in the underlying economic structure, or if there is a shift in the relative weight on the central bank's goals, then the optimal policy response should change accordingly, and we should observe some shift in the coefficients in the policy rule relationship. This would cause the observed deviations of the actual call rate from the rate computed by the Taylor rule with fixed coefficients. We document time-series evidence of a possible shift in the policy reaction function of Japan and examine these possible sources for that shift.

Reaction Function Implied by Svensson

For our purpose, we employ a policy reaction function implied by the theoretical framework of Svensson (1997). In Svensson's (1997) framework, the economy is characterized by a simple Phillips curve and aggregate demand relationships together with the central bank's intertemporal loss function. As we illustrate in the appendix, the framework is quite useful for explaining the link between structural parameters and the implied reaction function. The optimal policy reaction function in this setting can be written as:

$$i_t = b_0 + b_1\pi_t + b_2 y_t + e_t, \qquad (2)$$

where i_t is the monetary policy instrument (here the nominal call rate), π_t is the inflation rate, y_t is real output, and b_1 and b_2 are policy rule coefficients (b_0 denotes a constant, and e_t is a disturbance term). The coefficients b_1 and b_2 are in particular linked with the slope coefficient of the Phillips curve and the relative policy weight set by the central bank between inflation and output stabilization. These two parameters are denoted as a and λ, respectively, in the appendix and will be used as primary factors in the interpretation of our empirical results below.

This reaction function appears similar to the Tayloresque reaction function we used above in equation (1). In the specification above, the real call rate was used, and all the explanatory variables were expressed in "gap" terms. Here, the call rate is in nominal terms, and the explanatory variables are not specified in gap terms. The important advantage in using the present Svenssonesque specification is that, as we will argue below, we are able to apply the idea of cointegration to the present policy reaction function and therefore to make more reliable statistical inferences about a possible shift in the reaction function.[13]

---

13. Above, the GMM analysis of a Clarida-Gali-Gertler type reaction function hinges on the validity of the assumption that all the variables, including gap variables on the lefthand side, are $I(0)$. As we discuss in footnote 7, the issue of whether this assumption is really supported by the actual evidence is not completely resolved, especially due to the short sample period of 1975-85. Here, we examine the reaction function and its possible shift using the full sample of 1975-95, and in fact the unit root test results below lend consistent support to employing the idea of cointegration in equation (2). And when cointegration really exists here, the estimates of the cointegrating vector (i.e., the coefficients in the reaction function [2]) have a favorable property that is known as "superconsistency," so that we can make fairly reliable statistical inferences for the estimation results.

Time-Series Evidence

We now examine time-series evidence on the policy rule relationship (equation [2]) that is implied by Svensson's (1997) inflation targeting framework.

The econometric procedure consists of the following four steps. In the first step, we run unit root tests for each of the variables in the reaction function, i_t, π_t, and y_t. Here two unit root tests are performed—the augmented Dickey-Fuller (1979) tests of a unit root against no unit root (ADF); and a modified Dickey-Fuller test based on GLS detrending series (DF-GLS), which is a powerful univariate test proposed by Elliot, Rothenberg, and Stock (1996). The sample period is the first quarter of 1975 through the fourth quarter of 1995 (these and other similar periods are hereafter abbreviated "1975:1-1995:4").[14] For each of the variables in levels, these two tests do not reject the null of a unit root, and for the variables in first differences, both tests find strong rejections. Thus each of the variables can be characterized as a unit root $I(1)$ process.[15]

In the second step, we examine whether there is a "long-run" or cointegrating relationship among these variables. A standard trivariate model of cointegration can be applied to the policy reaction function of equation (2) above to examine whether the inflation forecast targeting framework implied by Svensson (1997) is consistent with the Japanese data.

Here, two conventional cointegration tests are performed: the augmented Dickey-Fuller (1979) test of no cointegration against cointegration (denoted as ADF) and Johansen's (1988) and Johansen and Juselius's (1990) maximal eigenvalue test of no cointegration against one cointegrating vector (denoted as JOH).[16] The second and third columns of table 6.5 show the cointegration test results. Each of the ADF and JOH tests does not reject the null of no cointegration, suggesting that there is no cointegrating policy rule relationship in Japan.

The third step of our analysis concerns the cointegration analysis that allows for a possible structural shift. Although the evidence from conventional ADF and Johansen procedures does not support the presence of cointegration, there is some possibility that cointegration is detected when a struc-

---

14. The sample ends in 1995:4 because the call rate was lowered to a decimal level in late 1995 and there has been virtually no movement in this policy instrument since 1996.

15. Detailed results can be obtained upon request.

16. Note that all the tests are detrended. The lag length for ADF is chosen based on the step-down procedure of Campbell and Perron (1991) with the maximum lag length equal to six. For the Johansen test, the lag length is set to four. Since Johansen's procedure has a well-known problem of large size distortions in finite samples (see, e.g., Stock and Watson 1993), we correct critical values to avoid a possible over-rejection of the test as proposed by Cheung and Lai (1993).

Table 6.5 Cointegration test statistics

Sample	ADF	JOH	ADF*	Break date
1975:1-1995:4	−2.71(1)	16.96	−4.30(5)	
1978:1-1995:4	−3.30(5)	11.74	−5.65(0)*	87:2 (0.53)
1980:1-1995:4	−3.88(5)	13.79	−6.36(0)**	87:2 (0.47)

Note: ADF is the augmented Dickey-Fuller test of no cointegration against cointegration (detrended case). JOH is Johansen's maximal eigenvalue test of no cointegration against one cointegrating vector (detrended case). ADF* is the augmented Dickey-Fuller test of the null of no cointegration against the alternative of cointegration with a structural break, proposed by Gregory and Hansen (1996). The lag lengths for ADF and ADF* are chosen based on the step-down procedure, with the maximum lag length equal to six and shown in parentheses, and the lag length for JOH set to four. The estimated break date is indicated in the last column (and the corresponding fraction of the total sample is shown in parentheses). Critical values for each of the three tests are tabulated by MacKinnon (1991) for ADF, by Osterwald-Lenum (1992, table 1) for JOH with Cheung and Lai's (1993) correction method, and by Gregory and Hansen (1996, table 1) for ADF*. Superscripts to statistics †, *, and ** indicate rejections at the 10 percent, 5 percent, and 1 percent significance levels, respectively.

		10 percent (†)	5 percent (*)	1 percent (**)
ADF	1975:1-1995:4	−3.95	−4.26	−4.89
	1978:1-1995:4	−3.96	−4.29	−4.94
	1980:1-1995:4	−3.98	−4.31	−4.97
JOH	1975:1-1995:4	21.60	24.42	29.72
	1978:1-1995:4	22.27	25.18	30.64
	1980:1-1995:4	22.90	25.90	31.52
ADF*		−5.23	−5.50	−5.97

tural break is appropriately incorporated into the analysis. This in fact corresponds to a shift in the policy rule relationship we are interested in here.

To examine this possibility, we apply Gregory and Hansen's (1996) residual-based test for cointegration with a regime shift, where the null of no cointegration is tested against the alternative of cointegration, with a break in the cointegrating vector in an unknown timing. In Gregory and Hansen's procedure, the following dummy variable is defined to introduce a regime shift:

$$D_{\tau t} = \begin{cases} 1.0 \ (t > [\tau T]) \\ 0.0 \ (otherwise), \end{cases} \tag{3}$$

where τ is the unknown timing of the structural break in a relative term defined over the (0, 1) interval and $[T]$ is its integer part. Therefore, $[\tau T]$ denotes the break date. Using this dummy variable, we consider the cointegration model where a possible break occurs in both constant and slope coefficients (C/S model):

$$i_t = b_0 + b_1\pi_t + b_2 y_t + c_0 D_{\tau t} + c_1 \pi_t D_{\tau t} + c_2 y_t D_{\tau t} + e_{\tau t}, \tag{4}$$

where c_0, c_1, and c_2 denote the shifts in the intercept and the policy rule coefficients.

Under this model, Gregory and Hansen's procedure can be implemented as follows. We first estimate the above regression model with a break by ordinary least squares regression (OLS) for each possible breakpoint τ, and obtain the estimated residual $\hat{e}_{\tau t}$. For the actual computation, we consider τ as a step function over (0.15, 0.85) that jumps every $1/T$ period. Thus, the possible breakpoints here consist of all integers over ([0.15*T*], [0.85*T*]), and corresponding to each of these points we compute the residual $\hat{e}_{\tau t}$. Then an augmented Dickey-Fuller (ADF) test is applied to each of those residual series, and the ADF statistic is calculated (in each round, we select an optimal lag length using Campbell and Perron's step-down procedure, with the maximum lag equal to six). In the end, we obtain a time series of the ADF statistics corresponding to all possible break dates. We report the minimum value in the ADF series as the test statistic of the Gregory-Hansen procedure.

The third and fourth columns of table 6.5 display the Gregory-Hansen test results. (See the notes to the table for critical values tabulated by Gregory and Hansen 1996, table 1, 109.) Using the sample of 1975:1-1995:4, we cannot reject the null hypothesis of no cointegration. On the other hand, when the sample period starts at 1978:1 or at 1980:1, we detect strong rejection results. The estimated break dates are consistently 1987:2 for both rejection cases. The evidence here is in fact indicative of the presence of a cointegrating policy rule relationship in Japan that includes a shift in the coefficients in the middle of 1987.

Finally, in the fourth step, we estimate the policy rule coefficients before and after the structural break. To estimate the shift, we use a dynamic OLS (DOLS) procedure proposed by Stock and Watson (1993). Under the maintained hypothesis that the short-run dynamics stay constant, the regression model can be written as:

$$\begin{aligned} i_t = {} & b_0 + b_1\pi_t + b_2 y_t + c_0 D_{\hat{\tau} t} + c_1 \pi_t D_{\hat{\tau} t} + c_2 y_t D_{\hat{\tau} t} \\ & + d_1(L)\Delta\pi_t + d_2(L)\Delta y_t + e_t, \end{aligned} \tag{5}$$

where $D_{\hat{\tau} t}$ is a dummy variable equal to 1.0 after the estimated break point $\hat{\tau}$, and $d_j(L)$ ($j = 1, 2$) is a polynomial of the lag operator, which contains both leads and lags ($d_j(L) = \Sigma_{j=-K}^{K} d_{rj} L^j$), and K is the number of leads and lags. Therefore (b_1, b_2) is the optimal policy rule coefficient before the break, and (c_1, c_2) represents the structural shifts in these coefficients. We compute DOLS estimates for the sample period of 1978:1-1995:4 with the break date equal to 1987:2 (or $\hat{\tau}$ equal to 0.53) using two leads and lags ($K = 2$). Standard errors are computed using Newey and West's (1987) covariance matrix with the truncation of two lags.

Table 6.6 Estimates for policy rule coefficients with a break

b_1	b_2	c_1	c_2	Wald statistic
1.134	0.132	0.940	−0.251	104.73
(0.176)	(0.038)	(0.214)	(0.044)	(0.000)

Note: All the estimates are computed using the dynamic OLS procedure of Stock and Watson (1993) with two leads and lags. The sample period is 1978:1-1995:4, and the break date is 1987:2. Standard errors, shown in parentheses, are calculated using the Newey and West (1987) covariance matrix with truncation of two lags. The Wald statistic in the last column tests the hypothesis that all the shift parameters (c's) are jointly equal to zero and have χ^2 (3) distribution. Below the coefficients, the p-value is shown in parentheses.

Table 6.6 summarizes the estimation results. Before the break of 1987:2, the point estimates for b_1 and b_2 are positive and significant. In particular, b_1 is estimated to be larger than 1, which corresponds to the prediction of the theoretical framework. After 1987:3, the inflation coefficient rises and the output coefficient falls, both significantly (positive c_1 and negative c_2). The Wald statistic of the last column of table 6.6 tests the null hypothesis that the shift parameters (c's) are jointly equal to zero and have $\chi^2(3)$ distribution. We clearly reject the null hypothesis (see p-value shown in parentheses).

Interpretations

Interpreting these empirical results, we first note that the evidence above suggests the possibility that Japanese monetary policy was largely consistent with Svensson's (1997) framework of "inflation forecast targeting." The call rate was (at least until recently) regarded as the best monetary policy instrument in Japan (see, e.g., Okina 1993; Ueda 1993). And we obtain the time-series evidence in support of a long-run cointegrating relationship among the policy instruments, inflation, and output in Japan (with a break), which suggests that the BOJ may have adopted *implicit* inflation targeting (again with a break) after the late 1970s. This in fact sounds plausible. Japan's monetary policy in the early 1970s is often viewed as a "mistake" that led to double-digit inflation in 1973-74.[17] It is conceivable that the BOJ learned some lessons from the experience of the early 1970s and has adopted a strategy of implicit inflation targeting since then.[18]

17. See, e.g., Ito (1992) for details of the mistake of Japanese monetary policy in the early 1970s. Ito (1992, 127) states that "In retrospect, it was a mistake to put forward a particular exchange rate as an absolute target with priority over considerations of inflation and growth."

18. The success of the Bank of Japan's monetary management for the late 1970s-early 1980s was also acknowledged by Friedman (1985) and Hamada and Hayashi (1985) in terms of holding down money supply growth for that decade.

Having said that, let us now discuss the implications of the estimated shift in the policy reaction function in 1987, namely, the rise in the inflation coefficient and the fall in the output coefficient. Using Svensson's (1997) framework, we may be able to interpret these changes from two perspectives—a shift in some parameters in the underlying structural model, such as α and β's; and a shift in the policy weight placed by the central bank λ. Among other things, we provide the following two interpretations that would seem most plausible.

The first interpretation is that there may be a significant decline in α, which implies that the aggregate supply/Phillips curve relationship becomes flatter. As seen in equation (A7) in the appendix, if there is a decline in α, this leads to a rise in θ and thus a decline in a_2 unambiguously. This is also followed by a direct negative impact on the denominator of a_1. If this direct effect through the denominator is larger than the indirect effect on the numerator, then a_1 will increase. It appears that these shifts in a_1 and a_2 explain the result of table 6.6. A recent study by Nishizaki and Watanabe (1999) also finds evidence that the short-run Phillips curve in Japan became flatter in the 1990s than before, which seems to support this interpretation.

The second interpretation incorporates a shift in the weights on monetary policy goals into the first interpretation. In addition to the shift in the Phillips curve (the decline in α), we consider the case of a possible decline in λ. This implies that the central bank places a lower weight on output fluctuations and a higher weight on inflation (i.e., "stricter," or more "rule-like," inflation targeting). The decline in λ is followed by a decline in θ and therefore a rise in a_1 and a_2. Accordingly, this strengthens the rise in a_1 and weakens the decline in a_2, which is suggested in the first interpretation. Note that the narrative section above actually lends support to the change in the BOJ's policy judgment in 1988, which corresponds to the shift in the BOJ's policy weight in this interpretation. Adding the shift in the policy weight λ would seem to account for such a large significant increase in the inflation coefficient and a relatively small decline in the output coefficient shown in table 6.6.

These two interpretations should not be viewed as definitive. Nevertheless, we argue that the second interpretation, which builds on the first one, seems to explain the situation in the late 1980s reasonably well and therefore is quite suggestive. By a downward shift in the slope of the aggregate supply/Phillips curve relationship, fluctuations in aggregate demand lead to the relatively small movements in prices and inflation and large fluctuations in real output that were actually observed in the late 1980s and early 1990s. At the very time when the shift in the economic structure took place, the BOJ shifted its relative weight on the policy objectives toward stricter, more rule-type inflation targeting. Imposing a larger weight on inflation under a low and stable inflation environment implies that the central bank is simply content with the fact of low and stable inflation and does little to stabilize the real economy. Consequently, with both factors combined, the business fluctuations could actually become unprecedentedly large, as we observed they did in the late 1980s and early 1990s.

Conclusion and Current Policy Discussions

This essay has documented arguable delays in BOJ monetary policy responses to macroeconomic events in the late 1980s and early 1990s using a Taylor-rule-type reaction function, and has sought explanations. In the narrative analysis based on the Bank of Japan's *Monthly Bulletins*, we have argued that the political pressure resulting from international policy coordination is a major factor in explaining the policy delays to tighten policy of the late 1980s. In the time-series analysis, where we have employed Svensson's (1997) model of inflation forecast targeting, we have indicated that there may have been a shift in the cointegrating policy rule relationship in mid-1987, which may have led to the post-1987 deviations detected in figure 6.4. Then we have interpreted the time-series evidence as suggesting that in the late 1980s there may have occurred both a shift in the underlying economic structure (flatter Phillips curve) and a shift in the monetary policy weight toward stricter inflation targeting. We have argued that the BOJ's shift in policy weight destabilized Japan's real economy and unnecessarily amplified the business fluctuations from the late 1980s to the early 1990s.

The literature on inflation targeting actually lends support to this conclusion. Adopting inflation targeting as a strict rule (or "inflation-only targeting") would destabilize the real economy and therefore would lead to a suboptimal outcome (see, e.g., Rogoff 1985). Friedman and Kuttner (1996) raised a serious concern regarding the "Economic Growth and Stability Act" that was then proposed to impose the constraint of exclusive price level (or inflation) targeting on US Federal Reserve policy. Because of this concern, the literature emphasizes again and again that inflation targeting should be implemented not as a strict, absolute rule, but as a flexible "framework" in which output stabilization should also be appropriately targeted in the policy decision (see, e.g., Bernanke and Mishkin 1997; Bernanke et al. 1999). As we have shown, Japanese monetary policy in the late 1980s provides an actual example in which the problem of strict, rule-type inflation targeting is indeed a serious one.

The conclusion of this essay has an important implication for current discussions of Japan's monetary policy.[19] The requests for further monetary easing are in many cases accompanied by a proposal for inflation

19. See, e.g., Krugman (1999), Posen (1998), and Okina (1999).

targeting. The most extreme proposal would be known as "managed inflation," through which the central bank should make an exclusive commitment to raise inflation to a targeted level for some period of time (according to Krugman 1999, 4 percent inflation for 15 years). Whatever the targeted level of inflation is (4 percent or, say, 2-3 percent), the absolute commitment to hit the target would in fact imply "inflation-only" targeting, which is severely criticized in the literature. The problem of strict inflation targeting should also be obvious from our main conclusion. Thus, managed inflation is not a realistic option to take.

Then how about a more moderate proposal of inflation targeting as a "framework"? As long as inflation targeting is carried out as a flexible framework and output stabilization is also appropriately taken into consideration, this would presumably raise the accountability and discipline of monetary policy and therefore may be recommended in normal times (see, e.g., Kuttner and Posen 1999 for a recent empirical study).

Under present circumstances in Japan, however, there is a calculated risk that explicit inflation targeting as a framework would be confused with inflation targeting as an absolute rule. There are increasing requests for further monetary loosening by the BOJ from inside and outside the country. As expansionary fiscal policy measures almost reach a limit, these requests from the political sector will come in a more extreme fashion, such as demanding that the central bank purchase newly issued government bonds, stocks, and even real estate (or sometimes real estate abroad).

The requests for further monetary loosening would be legitimate if in fact the Japanese economy faced further (and serious) downside risks, or actually was in a deflationary spiral situation. We tend to agree that Japan's current recovery will not be strong because it will take more time to resolve the balance sheet problem in Japan. But it is safe to say that the crisis-like situation of 1997-98 is over and that the economy is not currently in a deflationary spiral situation, and probably will not be for some time to come. Given these observations, requests for further expansionary measures at any cost may not be relevant. Put differently, the expected advantage of avoiding a serious deflationary spiral may not be greater than the expected disadvantage that would occur should monetary policy turn out to be too expansionary and destabilize the economy.

With the call rate and other short-term interest rates staying at virtually 0 percent, what is left for the central bank is an unfamiliar, less reliable policy instrument, such as excess reserves or the monetary base. More important, the transmission mechanism of monetary policy in Japan is quite uncertain at present. The conventional transmission through the banking sector does not and will not function with nonperforming loans and the associated balance sheet problem for some time to come. Accordingly, further monetary easing would affect aggregate demand and prices with an uncertain, much longer lag than usual. Then the political pressures requesting that the BOJ meet the inflation target would possibly become intense, even under the flexible framework.

Let us elaborate on the issue of the credit channel. It was shown that the credit channel in Japan was significant before 1990 (e.g., Kuroki 1997). Bank credit was the imperfect substitute for other assets or liabilities for both banks and business firms. However, the following observations suggest the possibility that the credit channel has been severed and the massive liquidity supply by the BOJ does not flow into real investment activity. First, banks' lending attitude, as judged by business firms, has been severe since the last half of 1997. The recent lending attitude toward small business is the most strict in the past 25 years. Financial conditions have also been tight for them since 1990, and have gotten even worse since 1997. Second, business firms have increased the issuance of commercial paper and borrowing from public financial institutions since 1997. These facts imply that firms face the reduction in bank lending and try to offset it by raising funds from other sources; but it seems to be unsuccessful. It is clear that bank credit is still an imperfect substitute for other sources of finance for business firms. On the other hand, commercial banks have been reducing their credits since 1998 despite the massive injection of liquidity by the BOJ. The growth rate of commercial bank lending (total of city banks, local banks, second-tier local banks, trust banks, and long-term-credit banks) has been negative for the past 2 years, and the negative rate in absolute terms has been increasing. At the end of 1999, it reached approximately −6 percent, and there is no sign of reversal of this negative growth trend.[20]

The Japanese banks are now shrinking their business loans and total assets to meet the Bank for International Settlements standard and to reduce nonperforming loans. The massive liquidity injected by the BOJ has been used to purchase marketable assets, such as government bonds, and to reinforce their capital account, but has not led to the increase of credit supply. It has also piled up in the deposit account of call market dealers. All these observations are indicative of the fact that the credit channel in Japan has broken down in the supply side of credits in recent years.[21]

---

20. This number is taken from a figure of commercial bank lending in the BOJ's *Monthly Bulletin* (January 2000), which is also available at the download section of the BOJ Web site http://www.boj.or.jp.

21. The Japanese banks have refused making loans because of the shortage of collaterals of firms. However, city banks now plan to increase loans to small and medium-sized firms in the IT sector from the end of 2000, based on their growth prospects (*Nikkei* newspaper, 31 July 2000).

Given that the conventional credit channel is not working and that the effects of other channels through foreign exchange rates or asset prices are also unknown quantitatively, it would be reasonable to assume that, despite the massive quantitative easing, actual inflation will stay below the given target, if it is, say, in the 2-3 percent range. This would then make the pressure to request further monetary easing more intense. The BOJ would not easily overcome such pressures, because it is all the more difficult to provide a convincing estimate for the path of future inflation—which is needed to defend its own policy stance—under the present circumstances, where structural changes are widely under way. After all, a moderate inflation targeting framework within the 2-3 percent target range may end up being treated as an absolute rule, and this would destabilize the economy once again.

Let us elaborate our argument by making two observations. First, Krugman's managed inflation proposal has had a big impact on the policy discussion in Japan, and an influential national newspaper (as well as some other media outlets) has made a big campaign to support the proposal. Yet, Krugman's policy is in essence "strict rule" type inflation targeting, especially as it has been described in Japan. So, although it has not been implemented, strict inflation targeting actually has become very familiar to the public as a policy alternative, especially in certain media circles. Second, it is quite arguable that a 2-3 percent inflation target would be difficult to achieve due to the ongoing balance sheet problem, and the associated breakdown in the credit channel, as well as the likelihood of generally weak demand for another year or so. Given these two conditions, it is highly likely that a failure by the BOJ to meet an announced target would lead to a media campaign calling for still further monetary loosening to achieve the target at any cost. This likely scenario is why we argue that a moderate inflation targeting framework may be treated (or mistaken) as a strict rule in Japan today. This is a situation in which the setting of policy instruments would be determined as much by public or media pressures as by the BOJ's own judgment. In this sense, then, instrument independence would be seriously undermined.

This scenario would also jeopardize the instrument independence that was finally assured in the new Bank of Japan Law of April 1998. Article 3 of the new law states that "the BOJ's autonomy regarding currency and monetary control shall be respected," which implies the instrument independence of the BOJ. In retrospect, there was no clear assurance of central bank independence in the late 1980s. Consequently, the BOJ's policymaking was quite vulnerable to domestic and international political pressures at that time, which actually led to the unnecessary easing of early 1987. As we argued above, the current proposal for explicit inflation targeting, if it is mistaken as an absolute rule, would lead to further requests for loosening with extreme policy measures, and this would seriously undermine the instrument independence of the BOJ.

The new BOJ law clearly states its policy goal in Article 2: "Currency and monetary control shall be aimed at, through the pursuit of price stability, contributing to the sound development of the national economy." In our view, the policy goal for which the BOJ must be accountable is indeed given by this passage in the law. Yes, there is no numerical inflation target, but we do not view this as fundamentally deficient. Rather, it would be more hazardous to set a hard-to-achieve numerical goal because it might cause dangerously large fluctuations in macroeconomic conditions. This danger would be especially likely in the current zero-inflation environment with a flat Phillips curve. Obviously, such destabilization would be undesirable in the achievement of the ultimate policy goal: "the sound development of the national economy."

Before we conclude, let us stress again the main findings that are related to the current discussions of inflation targeting. An inflation targeting strategy was implicitly implemented in Japan after the late 1970s and worked well until the mid-1980s. Then the central bank appeared to change its behavior and set a wrong policy weight in the late 1980s that implied too strict inflation targeting. We view this suggested shift in the policy weight as a mistake that since then has actually led to destabilizing the real economy. This mistake has nothing to do with the fact that inflation targeting was implicit at that time. Even if explicit inflation targeting had been adopted in the late 1980s, the mistake would have been likely because inflation was actually reduced to a very low level at that time (CPI inflation was below 1 percent in 1987-88), resulting from favorable supply shocks associated with the decline in the oil price. What is important for the central bank is an appropriate balance between inflation and output stabilization objectives in its policymaking. Japan's experience in the late 1980s was an actual example of such an inappropriate balance that implies the strategy of "too strict" inflation targeting.

From all these issues raised above, it is still premature to conclude that Japan should adopt an explicit inflation targeting framework in the present environment with very low (virtually zero) inflation. Further discussions are definitely needed. Especially, how the central bank should maintain an appropriate balance between inflation and output stabilization objectives in a low-inflation environment seems to be a more important issue than the introduction of explicit inflation targeting itself.

References

Aoki, Kosuke. 1999. On the Optimal Monetary Policy Response to Noisy Indicators. Photocopy. Princeton, NJ: Princeton University.

Bernanke, Ben S., and Mark Gertler. 1999. Monetary Policy and Asset Price Volatility. In *1999 Symposium: New Challenges for Monetary Policy*, 77-128. Kansas City: Federal Reserve Bank of Kansas City.

Bernanke, Ben S., Thomas Laubach, Frederic S. Mishkin, and Adam S. Posen. 1999. *Inflation Targeting*. Princeton, NJ: Princeton University Press.

Bernanke, Ben S., and Frederic S. Mishkin. 1997. Inflation Targeting: A New Framework for Monetary Policy? *Journal of Economic Perspectives* 11: 97-116.

Campbell, John Y., and Pierre Perron. 1991. Pitfalls and Opportunities: What Macroeconomists Should Know about Unit Roots. *NBER Macroeconomics Annual* 6: 141-201. Cambridge, MA: National Bureau of Economic Research.

Cheung, Yin-Wong, and Kon S. Lai. 1993. Finite-Sample Sizes of Johansen's Likelihood Ratio Tests for Cointegration. *Oxford Bulletin of Economics and Statistics* 55: 313-28.

Chinn, Menzie D., and Michael P. Dooley. 1997. *Monetary Policy in Japan, Germany, and the United States: Does One Size Fit All?* NBER Working Papers 6092. Cambridge, MA: National Bureau of Economic Research.

Clarida, Richard, Jordi Gali, and Mark Gertler. 1998. Monetary Policy Rules in Practice: Some International Evidence. *European Economic Review* 42: 1033-67.

Dickey, D. A., and W. A. Fuller. 1979. Distribution of the Estimators for Autoregressive Time Series with a Unit Root. *Journal of the American Statistical Association* 74: 427-31.

Elliot, Graham, Thomas J. Rothenberg, and James H. Stock. 1996. Efficient Tests for an Autoregressive Unit Root. *Econometrica* 64: 813-36.

Friedman, Benjamin M., and Kenneth N. Kuttner. 1996. *A Price Target for U.S. Monetary Policy? Lessons from the Experience with Money Growth Targets*. Brookings Papers on Economic Activity 1: 77-146. Washington: Brookings Institution.

Friedman, Milton. 1985. Monetarism in Rhetoric and in Practice. In *Monetary Policy in Our Times*, eds. A. Ando, H. Eguchi, R. Farmer, and Y. Suzuki. Cambridge, MA: MIT Press.

Fuller, W. A. 1976. *Introduction to Statistical Time Series*. New York: John Wiley and Sons.

Gregory, Allan W., and Bruce E. Hansen. 1996. Residual-Based Tests for Cointegration in Models with Regime Shifts. *Journal of Econometrics* 70: 99-126.

Hamada, Koichi, and Fumio Hayashi. 1985. Monetary Policy in Postwar Japan. In *Monetary Policy in Our Times*, eds. A. Ando, H. Eguchi, R. Farmer, and Y. Suzuki. Cambridge, MA: MIT Press.

Ito, Takatoshi. 1992. *The Japanese Economy*. Cambridge, MA: MIT Press.

Johansen, Soren. 1988. Statistical Analysis of Cointegrating Vectors. *Journal of Economic Dynamics and Control* 12: 213-54.

Johansen, Soren, and Katarina Juselius. 1990. Maximum Likelihood Estimation and Inference on Cointegration—With Application to the Demand for Money. *Oxford Bulletin of Economics and Statistics* 52: 169-210.

Krugman, Paul R. 1999. It's Baaack: Japan's Slump and the Return of the Liquidity Trap. *Brookings Papers on Economic Activity* 2: 137-205.

Kuroki, Yoshihiro. 1997. The Significance of Credit Rationing on Real Investment Activity: A Test for the Significance of Capital-Market Imperfection in Japan. *Japanese Economic Review* 48: 424-44.

Kuroki, Yoshihiro. 1999. *Kinyu Seisaku no Yukousei* [The Effectiveness of Monetary Policy]. Tokyo: Toyo Keizai Shinposha (in Japanese).

Kuttner, Kenneth N., and Adam S. Posen. 1999. Does Talk Matter After All? Inflation Targeting and Central Bank Behavior. Photocopy. Institute for International Economics Working Paper 99-10, September. Washington: Institute for International Economics.

MacKinnon, James G. 1991. Critical Values for Cointegration Tests. In *Long-Run Economic Relationships*, eds., R. F. Engle and C. W. J. Granger. Oxford: Oxford University Press.

Miyao, Ryuzo. 1999a. The Effects of Monetary Policy in Japan. RIEB Discussion Paper 107. Kobe: Kobe University.

Miyao, Ryuzo. 1999b. The Role of Monetary Policy in Japan: A Break in the 1990s? Photocopy. Kobe: Kobe University.

Newey, Whitney K., and Kenneth D. West. 1987. A Simple, Positive Semi-Definite, Heteroscedasticity and Autocorrelation Consistent Covariance Matrix. *Econometrica* 55: 703-08.

Nishizaki, Kenji, and Tsutomu Watanabe. 1999. Output-Inflation Tradeoff at Near-Zero Inflation Rates. Paper presented at NBER-CEPR-TCER conference on monetary policy in a low-inflation environment, Tokyo (16-17 December).

Okina, Kunio. 1993. Market Operations in Japan: Theory and Evidence. In *Japanese Monetary Policy*, ed. K. J. Singleton. Chicago: University of Chicago Press.

Okina, Kunio. 1999. *Monetary Policy under Zero Inflation: A Response to Criticisms and Questions Regarding Monetary Policy*. Discussion Paper 99-E-20. Tokyo: Institute for Monetary and Economic Studies, Bank of Japan.

Osterwald-Lenum, M. 1992. A Note with Quantiles of the Asymptotic Distribution of the Maximum Likelihood Cointegration Rank Test Statistics. *Oxford Bulletin of Economics and Statistics* 54: 461-72.

Phillips, P. C. B., and S. Ouliaris. 1990. Asymptotic Properties of Residual Based Tests for Cointegration. *Econometrica* 58: 165-93.

Posen, Adam S. 1998. *Restoring Japan's Economic Growth*. Washington: Institute for International Economics.

Rogoff, Kenneth. 1985. The Optimal Degree of Commitment to an Intermediate Monetary Target. *Quarterly Journal of Economics* 100: 1169-89.

Shimizu, Yoshinori. 1997. *Makuro Keizaigaku no Shinpo to Kinyu Seisaku* [The Progress of Macroeconomic and Monetary Policy]. Tokyo: Yuhikaku (in Japanese).

Stock, James H., and Mark W. Watson. 1993. A Simple Estimator of Cointegrating Vectors in Higher Order Integrated Systems. *Econometrica* 61: 783-820.

Svensson, Lars E. O. 1997. Inflation Forecast Targeting: Implementing and Monitoring Inflation Targets. *European Economic Review* 41: 1111-46.

Taylor, John. 1993a. Discretion Versus Policy Rules in Practice. *Carnegie-Rochester Conference Series on Public Policy* 39: 195-214.

Taylor, John. 1993b. *Macroeconomic Policy in a World Economy: From Econometric Policy Design to Practical Application*. New York: W. W. Norton.

Taylor, John. 1998. An Historical Analysis of Monetary Policy Rules. In *Monetary Policy Rules*, ed. J. Taylor. Chicago: University of Chicago Press.

Ueda, Kazuo. 1993. A Comparative Perspective on Japanese Monetary Policy: Short-Run Monetary Control and the Transmission Mechanism. In *Japanese Monetary Policy*, ed. K. J. Singleton. Chicago: University of Chicago Press.

Appendix 6A
Svensson's Framework of Inflation Forecast Targeting

In this appendix, we illustrate the theoretical framework of inflation forecast targeting developed by Svensson (1997). Svensson's model is used to derive the reaction function above.

The economy is characterized by the following Phillips curve and aggregate demand relationships:

$$\pi_{t+1} = \pi_t + \alpha y_t + \epsilon_{t+1} \tag{A1}$$

$$y_{t+1} = \beta_1 y_t - \beta_2(i_t - \pi) + \eta_{t+1}, \tag{A2}$$

where π_t is the inflation rate, y_t is real output, i_t is the monetary policy instrument (here the call rate), and ϵ_t and η_t are structural disturbances of the economy. α, β_1, and β_2 are structural parameters of the underlying economy.

Suppose further that the central bank conducts monetary policy with an inflation target π^* as well as an output stabilization target. Then one period loss function of the central bank can be written as

$$L(\pi_t, y_t) = \frac{1}{2}[(\pi_t - \pi^*)^2 + \lambda y_t^2], \tag{A3}$$

where λ denotes the relative weight on output stabilization (the natural rate of output is normalized as zero here). The intertemporal loss function is expressed as

$$E_t \Sigma_{j=t}^{\infty} \delta^{j-t} L(\pi_j, y_j). \tag{A4}$$

Now the central bank is considered to determine the policy instrument $\{i_j\}_{j=t}^{\infty}$ by minimizing (A4) subject to (A1), (A2), and (A3). Then the derived first-order condition implies that

$$\pi_{t+2|t} = \pi^* + \theta(\pi_{t+1|t} - \pi^*), \tag{A5}$$

where $\pi_{t+i|t}$ is the i-year inflation forecast ($= E_t \pi_{t+i}$, $i = 1, 2$) and the coefficient θ can be shown as a function of λ, α, and δ and, in particular, increasing in λ and decreasing in α. Then the optimal policy reaction function in this setting can be written as

$$i_t = \pi_t + a_1(\pi_t - \pi^*) + a_2 y_t, \tag{A6}$$

where

$$a_1 = \frac{1 - \theta}{\beta_2 \alpha}, \quad a_2 = \frac{1 - \theta + \beta_1}{\beta_2}. \tag{A7}$$

The optimal monetary policy rule derived by Svensson can be used to discuss the possible effects of a change in structural parameters such as α and a change in the central bank weight λ. This reaction function can be further rewritten as

$$i_t = b_0 + b_1 \pi_t + b_2 y_t + e_t, \tag{6.2}$$

where b_0 denotes a constant, b_1 and b_2 are policy rule coefficients corresponding to a_1 and a_2, and e_t is an $I(0)$ disturbance term. This is an empirical specification we used above.

7

Japanese Monetary Policy: A Case of Self-Induced Paralysis?

BEN S. BERNANKE

The Japanese economy continues in a deep slump. The short-range International Monetary Fund (IMF) forecast was that, as of the last quarter of 1999, Japanese real gross domestic product (GDP) would be 4.6 percent below its potential. This number is itself a mild improvement over a year earlier, when the IMF estimated Japanese GDP at 5.6 percent below potential. A case can be made, however, that these figures significantly underestimate the output losses created by the protracted slowdown. From the beginning of the 1980s through the fourth quarter of 1991 (hereafter abbreviated 1991Q4, etc.), a period during which Japanese real economic growth had already declined markedly from the heady days of the 1960s and 1970s, real GDP in Japan grew by nearly 3.8 percent a year. In contrast, from 1991Q4 through 1999Q4, the rate of growth of real GDP was less than 0.9 percent a year. If growth during the 1991-99 period had been an even 2.5 percent a year, Japanese real GDP in 1999 would have been 13.6 percent higher than the value actually attained.[1]

Ben S. Bernanke is professor of economics at Princeton University. *He wishes to thank Refet Gurkaynak for expert research assistance and Olivier Blanchard, Alan Blinder, Adam Posen, and Lars Svensson for comments.*

1. I thank Paula DeMasi of the IMF for providing their data. A major source of the difference in my calculation and the IMF calculation is that the IMF bases its potential output estimate on the actual current value of the capital stock. Relatively low investment rates throughout the 1990s resulted in a lower Japanese capital stock than would have been the case if growth and investment had followed more normal patterns.

Some perspective is in order. Although, as we will see, there are some analogies between the policy mistakes made by Japanese officials in recent years and the mistakes made by policymakers around the world during the 1930s, Japan's current economic situation is not remotely comparable to that of the United States, Germany, and numerous other countries during the Great Depression. The Japanese standard of living remains among the highest in the world, and poverty and open unemployment remain low. These facts, and Japan's basic economic strengths—including a high savings rate, a skilled labor force, and an advanced manufacturing sector—should not be overlooked. Still, Japan also faces important long-term economic problems, such as the aging of its workforce, and the failure of the economy to achieve its full potential during the 1990s, which may in some sense be more costly to the country in the future than it is today. Japan's weakness has also imposed economic costs on its less affluent neighbors, which look to Japan both as a market for their goods and as a source of investment.

The debate about the ultimate causes of the prolonged Japanese slump has been heated. There are questions, for example, about whether the Japanese economic model, constrained as it is by the inherent conservatism of a society that places so much value on consensus, is well equipped to deal with the increasing pace of technological, social, and economic change we see in the world today. The problems of the Japanese banking system, for example, can be interpreted as arising in part from the collision of a traditional, relationship-based financial system with the forces of globalization, deregulation, and technological innovation (Hoshi and Kashyap 2000). Indeed, it seems fairly safe to say that, in the long run, Japan's economic success will depend largely on whether the country can achieve a structural transformation that increases its economic flexibility and openness to change without sacrificing its traditional strengths.

In the short to medium run, however, macroeconomic policy has played, and will continue to play, a major role in Japan's macroeconomic (mis)fortunes. My focus in this essay will be on monetary policy in particular.[2] Although it is not essential to the arguments I want to make—which concern what monetary policy should do now, not what it has done in the past—I agree with the conventional wisdom that attributes much of Japan's current dilemma to exceptionally poor monetary policymaking over the past 15 years (see Bernanke and Gertler 1999 for a formal econometric analysis).

Among the more important monetary-policy mistakes were (1) the failure to tighten policy during 1987-89, despite evidence of growing inflationary pressures, a failure that contributed to the development of the "bubble

---

2. Posen's (1998) survey of the issues discusses the somewhat spotty record of Japanese fiscal policy; see especially his chapter 2.

economy"; (2) the apparent attempt to "prick" the stock market bubble in 1989-91, which helped to induce an asset-price crash; and (3) the failure to ease policies adequately during the 1991-94 period, as asset prices, the banking system, and the economy declined precipitously. Bernanke and Gertler (1999) argue that if Japanese monetary policy after 1985 had focused on stabilizing aggregate demand and inflation, rather than being distracted by the exchange rate or asset prices, the results would have been much better.

Bank of Japan (BOJ) officials would not necessarily deny that monetary policy has some culpability for the current situation. But they would also argue that now, at least, the BOJ is doing all it can to promote economic recovery. For example, in his vigorous defense of current BOJ policies, Okina (1999, 1) applauds the "BOJ's historically unprecedented accommodative monetary policy." He refers, of course, to the fact that the BOJ has for some time now pursued a policy of setting the call rate, its instrument rate, virtually at zero, its practical floor. Having pushed monetary ease to its seeming limit, what more could the BOJ do? Isn't Japan stuck in what Keynes called a "liquidity trap"?

I will argue here that, to the contrary, there is much that the Bank of Japan, in cooperation with other government agencies, could do to help promote economic recovery in Japan. Most of my arguments will not be new to the policy board and staff of the BOJ, who of course have discussed these questions extensively. However, their responses, when not confused or inconsistent, have generally relied on various technical or legal objections—objections that, in my opinion, could be overcome if the will to do so existed. Far from being powerless, the BOJ could achieve a great deal if it were willing to abandon its excessive caution and its defensive response to criticism.

Diagnosis: An Aggregate Demand Deficiency

Before discussing ways in which Japanese monetary policy could become more expansionary, I will briefly discuss the evidence for the view that a more expansionary monetary policy is needed. As already suggested, it cannot be denied that important structural problems, in the financial system and elsewhere, are constraining Japanese growth. But there is compelling evidence that the Japanese economy is suffering as well from an aggregate demand deficiency. If monetary policy could deliver increased nominal spending, some of the difficult structural problems that Japan faces would no longer seem so difficult.

Tables 7.1 through 7.3 contain some basic macroeconomic data for the 1991-99 period that bear on the questions of the adequacy of aggregate

Table 7.1 Measures of inflation in Japan, 1991-99 (percent change)

Year	(1) GDP deflator	(2) PCE deflator	(3) CPI deflator	(4) WPI deflator	(5) Nominal GDP	(6) Monthly earnings
1991	2.89	2.13	2.30	−1.29	5.30	2.84
1992	0.94	1.44	2.08	−1.69	1.09	1.78
1993	0.44	0.96	0.91	−4.07	0.91	1.82
1994	−0.62	0.60	0.50	−1.25	0.04	2.70
1995	−0.38	−0.90	0.07	−0.06	0.79	1.87
1996	−2.23	0.34	0.30	−0.33	2.43	1.87
1997	1.00	1.91	2.23	1.42	0.39	0.81
1998	0.17	−0.02	−0.32	−3.64	−2.78	−0.10
1999	−0.79	−0.14	0.00	−4.12	0.12	0.84

PCE = personal consumption expenditure.
CPI = consumer price index.
WPI = wholesale price index.

Note: Growth rates are measured fourth quarter to fourth quarter, except for 1999, which is third quarter over third quarter. The CPI measure excludes fresh foods.

Sources: Data are from the Bank of Japan and the Management and Coordination Agency of Japan.

demand and the stance of monetary policy. The data in table 7.1 provide the strongest support for the view that aggregate demand is too low, and that the net impact of Japanese monetary and fiscal policies has been and continues to be deflationary. Columns (1)-(4) of the table show standard measures of price inflation, based on the GDP deflator, the personal consumption expenditure (PCE) deflator, the consumer price index (CPI) (excluding fresh food), and the wholesale price index (WPI), respectively. Considering the most comprehensive measure, the GDP deflator, we see that inflation has been 1 percent or less in every year since 1991 and has been negative in four of those years. Cumulative inflation, as measured by the GDP deflator, has been effectively zero since 1991: In the fourth quarter of 1991, the GDP deflator stood at 106, compared with a value of 101 in the third quarter of 1999, the latest number I have available.

Inflation has been slightly higher in the consumer sector, as measured by the rate of change of the PCE deflator and the CPI, but even there since 1991 inflation has exceeded 1 percent only twice, in 1992 and in 1997. Wholesale prices have dropped dramatically, having fallen about 10 percent since 1991. Moreover, increased deflationary pressure since 1997 is evident in all four of the inflation indicators. Taken together with the anemic performance of real GDP, shown in table 7.2, column (5), the slow or even negative rate of price increase points strongly to a diagnosis of aggregate demand deficiency. Note that if Japan's slow growth were due entirely to structural problems on the supply side, inflation rather than deflation would presumably be in evidence.

Table 7.2 Additional economic indicators for Japan, 1991-99

	(1) Yen-dollar rate	(2) Real yen-dollar rate	(3) Land prices (percent change)	(4) Stock prices (percent change)	(5) Real GDP (percent change)
1991	129.5	72.2	0.55	2.38	2.41
1992	123.0	69.4	−5.11	−32.03	0.14
1993	108.1	62.4	−5.13	16.91	0.47
1994	98.8	58.5	−3.82	0.47	0.66
1995	101.5	61.5	−4.30	−4.90	2.49
1996	112.8	71.2	−4.43	5.47	4.66
1997	125.2	79.4	−3.62	−20.85	−0.61
1998	119.8	76.8	−4.38	−15.37	−2.94
1999	113.6	76.9	−5.67	23.00	0.91

Notes: Columns (1)-(2): Exchange rates are fourth-quarter averages, except for 1999 figures, which are third-quarter averages. Real exchange rate is relative to 1978: 1 = 100. Columns (3)-(5): Land price is nationwide index, stock prices are TOPIX index. Percentage changes are fourth quarter over fourth quarter, except for 1999, which is third quarter over third quarter.

Sources: Data are from Datastream, except for real GDP, which is from the Bank of Japan.

As always, it is important to maintain a historical perspective and resist hyperbole. In particular, the recent Japanese experience is in no way comparable to the brutal deflation of 10 percent per year that ravaged the United States and other economies in the early stages of the Great Depression. Perhaps more salient, it must be admitted that there have been many periods (e.g., under the classical gold standard or the price-level-targeting regime of interwar Sweden) in which zero inflation or slight deflation coexisted with reasonable prosperity. I will say more below about why, in the context of contemporary Japan, the behavior of the price level has probably had an important adverse effect on real activity. For now I only note that countries that currently target inflation, either explicitly (e.g., United Kingdom or Sweden) or implicitly (United States), have tended to set their goals for inflation in the 2-3 percent range, with the floor of the range as important a constraint as the ceiling (see Bernanke et al. 1999 for a discussion.)

Alternative indicators of the growth of nominal aggregate demand are given by the growth rates of nominal GDP (table 7.1, column 5) and of nominal monthly earnings (table 7.1, column 6). Again, the picture is consistent with an economy in which nominal aggregate demand is growing too slowly for the patient's health. It is remarkable, for example, that, except for 1996, nominal GDP has grown by less than 1 percent per annum in every year since 1992, when it grew by 1.09 percent. As with the inflation measures in columns (1)-(4), there is evidence of even greater deflationary pressure since 1997. Indeed, nominal GDP declined by nearly 3 percentage points in 1998.

Table 7.3 Monetary indicators for Japan, 1991-99

Year	(1) Call rate	(2) Prime rate, short term	(3) Prime rate, long term	(4) Monetary base (percent change)	(5) M2 + CDs (percent change)
1991	6.45	6.88	6.95	2.89	2.14
1992	3.91	4.71	5.59	1.39	-0.54
1993	2.48	3.29	4.05	3.94	1.56
1994	2.27	3.00	4.90	4.12	2.64
1995	0.46	1.63	2.80	6.20	2.93
1996	0.48	1.63	2.74	6.78	3.17
1997	0.46	1.63	2.35	8.18	3.22
1998	0.23	1.50	2.29	6.34	4.43
1999	0.03	1.38	2.20	5.61	3.50

Note: Columns (1)-(3): Interest rates are fourth-quarter averages, third-quarter average for 1999. Columns (4)-(5): Percentage changes are fourth quarter over fourth quarter, except for 1999, which is third quarter over third quarter.

Sources: Data on call rate and monetary aggregates are from the Bank of Japan; data on prime rates are from Dow Jones Telerate.

Table 7.2 provides some additional macroeconomic indicators for Japan for the 1991-99 period. Columns (1) and (2) of the table show the nominal yen-dollar rate and the real yen-dollar rate, respectively. The yen generally strengthened over the period, which is consistent with the deflationist thesis. As I will discuss further below, even more striking is the surge of the yen since 1998, a period that has coincided with weak aggregate demand growth and a slumping real economy in Japan. As column (2) shows, however, the fact that inflation in Japan has been lower than in the United States has left the real terms of trade relatively stable. My interpretation is that the trajectory of the yen during the 1990s indicates strong deflationary pressures in Japan, but that a too-strong yen has not itself been a major contributor to deflation, except perhaps very recently.

Columns (3) and (4) of table 7.2 show rates of change in the prices of two important assets, land and stocks. As is well known, the stock market (column 4) has fallen sharply from its peak and has been quite volatile. The behavior of land prices (column 3), which is less often cited, is particularly striking: Since 1992 land prices have fallen by something between 3 and 6 percent *every year*. To be clear, it is most emphatically *not* good practice for monetary policymakers to try to target asset prices directly (Bernanke and Gertler 1999). Nevertheless, the declining nominal values of these assets, like the behavior of the yen, are also indicative of the deflationary forces acting on the Japanese economy.

So far, we have looked at broad macroeconomic indicators. Table 7.3 provides some measures more directly related to the stance of monetary policy itself. The first three columns of table 7.3 show fourth-quarter values (1991-99) for three key nominal interest rates: the call rate (the BOJ's instrument rate), the short-term prime rate, and the long-term prime rate. Prime rates are affected by conditions in the banking market as well as monetary policy, of course, and they may not always fully reflect actual lending rates and terms; but they are probably more indicative of private-sector borrowing costs than are government bill and bond rates. Columns (4) and (5) show, respectively, the fourth-quarter-to-fourth-quarter growth rates of the monetary base and of M2 + CDs, the broader monetary aggregate most often used as an indicator by the Japanese monetary authorities.

A glance at table 7.3 suggests that the stance of monetary policy has been somewhat different since 1995 than in the 1991-94 period. As mentioned above, there seems to be little debate even in Japan that monetary policy during 1991-94 was too tight, reacting too slowly to the deflationary forces unleashed by the asset-price crash. Interest rates came down during this period, but rather slowly, and growth of both narrow and broad money was weak. However, one can see that there has been an apparent change in policy since 1995: In that year, the call rate fell to under 0.5 percent, on its way down to effectively a zero rate in 1999, and lending rates fell as well. The fall in the nominal interest rate was accompanied by noticeable increases in the rates of money growth, particularly in the monetary base, in the period 1995 to present.

Monetary authorities in Japan have cited data like the 1995-99 figures in table 7.3 in defense of their current policies. Two distinct arguments have been made. The first is that policy indicators show that monetary policy in Japan is today quite expansionary in its thrust—"historically unprecedented accommodative monetary policy," in the words of Okina quoted above. Second, even if monetary policy is not truly as expansionary as would be desirable, there is no feasible way of loosening it further—the putative liquidity trap problem. I will address each of these two arguments in turn (the second in more detail in the next section).

The argument that current monetary policy in Japan is in fact quite accommodative rests largely on the observation that interest rates are at a very low level. I do hope that readers who have gotten this far will be sufficiently familiar with monetary history not to take seriously any such claim based on the level of the *nominal* interest rate. One need only recall that nominal interest rates remained close to zero in many countries throughout the Great Depression, a period of massive monetary contraction and deflationary pressure. In short, low nominal interest rates may just as well be a sign of expected deflation and monetary tightness as of monetary ease.

A more respectable version of the argument focuses on the *real* interest rate. With the rate of deflation under 1 percent in 1999, and the call rate effectively at zero, the realized real call rate for 1999 was under 1 percent, significantly less than, say, the real federal funds rate in the United States for the same period. Is this not evidence that monetary policy in Japan is in fact quite accommodative?

There are at least two responses to the real-interest-rate argument. First, I agree that the low real interest rate is evidence for the view that monetary policy is not the primary *source* of deflationary pressure in Japan today, in the way that, for example, the policies of Federal Reserve Chairman Paul Volcker were the primary source of disinflationary pressures in the United States in the early 1980s (a period of high real interest rates). But neither is the low real interest rate evidence that Japanese monetary policy is doing all that it can to offset deflationary pressures arising from other causes (in particular, the effects of the collapse in asset prices and of banking problems on consumer spending and investment spending). In textbook *IS-LM* terms, sharp reductions in consumption and investment spending have shifted the *IS* curve in Japan to the left, lowering the real interest rate for any given *LM* curve. Although monetary policy may not be directly responsible for the current depressed state of aggregate demand in Japan (leaving aside for now its role in initiating the slump), it does not follow that it should not be doing more to assist the recovery.

A second response to the real-interest-rate argument is to note that today's real interest rate may not be the best indicator of the cumulative effects of tight monetary policy on the economy. I will illustrate by discussing a mechanism that is highly relevant in Japan today, the so-called "balance-sheet channel of monetary policy" (Bernanke and Gertler 1995). Consider a hypothetical small borrower who took out a loan in 1991 with some land as collateral. The long-term prime rate at the end of 1991 was 6.95 percent (table 7.1, column 3).[3] Such a borrower would have been justified, we may speculate, in expecting inflation between 2 and 3 percent over the life of the loan (even in this case, he would have been paying an expected real rate of 4-5 percent), as well as increases in nominal land prices approximating the safe rate of interest at the time, say 5 percent per year. Of course, as tables 7.1 and 7.2 show, the borrower's expectations would have been radically disappointed.

To take an admittedly extreme case, suppose that the borrower's loan was still outstanding in 1999, and that at loan initiation he had expected a 2.5 percent annual rate of increase in the GDP deflator and a 5 percent annual rate of increase in land prices. Then by 1999 the real value of his principal obligation would have been 27 percent higher, and the real value of his collateral some 42 percent lower, than he anticipated when he took out the loan. These adverse balance sheet effects would certainly impede the borrower's access to new credit and hence his ability to consume or make new investments. The lender, faced with a nonperforming

3. Note that this rate was still 4.90 percent at the end of 1994.

loan and the associated loss in financial capital, might also find her ability to make new loans to be adversely affected.

This example illustrates why one might want to consider indicators other than the current real interest rate—for example, the cumulative gap between the actual and the expected price level—in assessing the effects of monetary policy. It also illustrates why zero inflation or mild deflation is potentially more dangerous in the modern environment than it was, say, in the classical gold-standard era. The modern economy makes much heavier use of credit, especially longer-term credit, than the economies of the nineteenth century. Further, unlike the earlier period, rising prices are the norm and are reflected in nominal-interest-rate setting to a much greater degree. Although deflation was often associated with weak business conditions in the nineteenth century, the evidence favors the view that deflation or even zero inflation is far more dangerous today than it was 100 years ago. Of course there are other reasons to aim for positive inflation as well, such as the measurement bias in price indices.

The second argument that defenders of Japanese monetary policy make, drawing on data such as those in table 7.3, is as follows: "Perhaps past monetary policy is to some extent responsible for the current state of affairs. Perhaps additional stimulus to aggregate demand would be desirable at this time. Unfortunately, further monetary stimulus is no longer *feasible*. Monetary policy is doing all that it can do." To support this view, its proponents could point to two aspects of table 7.3. The first is the fact that in 1999 the BOJ's nominal instrument rate (column 1) fell effectively to zero, its lowest possible value, where it remains today. Second, accelerated growth in base money after 1995 (column 4) did not lead to equivalent increases in the growth of broad money (column 5)—a result, it might be argued, of the willingness of commercial banks to hold indefinite quantities of excess reserves rather than engage in new lending or investment activity. Both of these facts seem to support the claim that Japanese monetary policy is in an old-fashioned Keynesian liquidity trap (Krugman 1999).

It is true that current monetary conditions in Japan limit the effectiveness of standard open-market operations in short-term Treasury debt. However, as I will argue in the remainder of the essay, monetary policy in Japan nevertheless retains considerable power to expand nominal aggregate demand and, consequently, to promote real economic recovery.

How to Get Out of a Liquidity Trap

Contrary to the claims of at least some Japanese central bankers, monetary policy is far from impotent today in Japan. In this section, I discuss some options that the monetary authorities have to stimulate the economy.[4] Overall, my claim has two parts. First—despite the apparent liquidity trap—monetary policymakers retain the power to increase nominal aggregate demand and the price level. Second, increased nominal spending and rising prices will lead to increases in real economic activity. The second of these propositions is empirical but seems to me overwhelmingly plausible; I have already provided some support for it in the discussion of the previous section. The first part of my claim will be, I believe, the more contentious one, and it is on that part that the rest of the essay will focus. However, in my view one can make what amounts to an arbitrage argument—the most convincing type of argument in an economic context—that it must be true.

The general argument that the monetary authorities can increase aggregate demand and prices, even if the nominal interest rate is zero, is as follows: Money, unlike other forms of government debt, pays zero interest and has infinite maturity. The monetary authorities can issue as much money as they like. Hence, if the price level were truly independent of money issuance, then the monetary authorities could use the money they create to acquire indefinite quantities of goods and assets. This is manifestly impossible in equilibrium. Therefore money issuance must ultimately raise the price level, even if nominal interest rates are bounded at zero. This is an elementary argument, but, as we will see, it is quite corrosive of claims of monetary impotence.

Rather than discuss the issues further in the abstract, I now consider some specific policy options of which the Japanese monetary authorities might now avail themselves. Before beginning, I add two more caveats. First, although I discuss a number of possible options below, I do not believe by any means that all of them must be put into practice to have a positive effect. Indeed, as I will discuss, a policy of aggressive foreign exchange intervention to put downward pressure on the yen would by itself probably suffice to get the Japanese economy moving again. Second, I am aware that several of the proposals to be discussed are either not purely monetary in nature, or require some cooperation by agencies other than the BOJ, including perhaps the Diet itself.

Regarding the concern that not all these proposals are "pure" monetary policy, I will say only that I am not here concerned with fine semantic distinctions but rather with the fundamental issue of whether there exist feasible policies to stimulate nominal aggregate demand in Japan. As to the need for interagency cooperation or even possible legislative changes: In my view, in recent years BOJ officials have—to a far greater degree than is justified—hidden behind minor institutional or technical difficulties in

4. For further discussion of monetary policy options when the nominal interest rate is close to zero, see Svensson (1999) and Clouse et al. (1999). Blinder (1999) discusses the Japanese case explicitly.

order to avoid taking action. I will discuss some of these purported barriers to effective action as they arise, arguing that in many if not most cases they could be overcome, given the will to do so.

Commitment to Zero Rates—with an Inflation Target

In February 1999, the BOJ adopted what has amounted to a zero-interest-rate policy. Further, to the BOJ's credit, it has since also announced that the zero rate will be maintained for some time to come, at least "until deflationary concerns subside," in the official formulation. Ueda explains, "By the commitment to maintain the zero rate for some time to come, we have tried to minimize the uncertainties about future short-term rates, thereby decreasing the option value of long-term bonds, hence putting negative pressure on long-term interest rates" (1999, 1). The announcement that the zero rate would be maintained did in fact have the desired effect on the term structure: Interest rates on government debt up to 1-year maturity or more fell nearly to zero when the policy was made public. Government rates up to 6-year maturity also fell, with most issues yielding less than 1 percent.

The BOJ's announcement that it would maintain the zero-rate policy for the indefinite future is a positive move that may well prove helpful. For example, in a simulation study for the United States, using the US Federal Reserve's macroeconometric model, Reifschneider and Williams (1999) found that tactics of this type—that is, compensating for periods in which the zero bound on interest rates is binding by keeping the interest rate lower than normal in periods when the constraint is not binding—may significantly reduce the costs created by the zero-bound constraint on the instrument interest rate.

A problem with the current BOJ policy, however, is its vagueness. What precisely is meant by the phrase "until deflationary concerns subside"? Posen (1998), Krugman (1999), and others have suggested that the BOJ quantify its objectives by announcing an inflation target, and further that it be a fairly high target. I agree that this approach would be helpful, in that it would give private decision makers more information about the objectives of monetary policy. In particular, a target in the 3-4 percent range for inflation, to be maintained for a number of years, would confirm not only that the BOJ is intent on moving safely away from a deflationary regime but also that it intends to make up some of the "price-level gap" created by 8 years of zero or negative inflation. Further, setting a quantitative inflation target now would ease the ultimate transition of Japanese monetary policy into a formal inflation-targeting framework—a framework that would have avoided many of the current troubles, I believe, if it had been in place earlier.

BOJ officials have strongly resisted the suggestion to publicly commit to an explicit inflation target. Their often-stated concern is that announcing a target that they are not sure they know how to achieve will endanger the Bank's credibility; and they have expressed skepticism that simple announcements can have any effects on expectations. On the issue of announcement effects, theory and practice suggest that "cheap talk" can in fact sometimes affect expectations, particularly when there is no conflict between what a "player" announces and that player's incentives. In technical language, announcements can serve as equilibrium selection devices. The effect of the announcement of a sustained zero-interest-rate policy on the term structure in Japan is itself a perfect example of the potential power of announcement effects.

With respect to the issue of inflation targets and BOJ credibility, I do not see how credibility can be harmed by straightforward, honest dialogue between policymakers and the public. In stating an inflation target of, say, 3-4 percent, the BOJ would be giving the public information about its objectives and hence the direction in which it will attempt to move the economy. (And, as I will argue, the Bank does have tools to move the economy.) But if BOJ officials feel that, for technical reasons, when and whether they will attain the announced target is uncertain, they could explain those points to the public as well. It is better for the public to know that the BOJ is doing all it can to reflate the economy, and that it understand why the Bank is taking the actions it does. The alternative is for the private sector to be left to its doubts about the willingness or competence of the BOJ to help the macroeconomic situation.

Depreciation of the Yen

We saw in table 7.2 that the yen has undergone a nominal appreciation since 1991, a strange outcome for a country in deep recession. Even more disturbing is the very strong appreciation that has occurred since 1998Q3, from about ¥145 per dollar in August 1998 to ¥100-105 per dollar range since December 1999, as the Japanese economy fell back into recession. Because interest rates on yen assets are very low, this appreciation suggests that speculators are anticipating even greater rates of deflation and yen appreciation in the future (the data from the futures markets confirm this view).

I agree with the recommendations of Meltzer (1999) and McCallum (1999) that the BOJ should attempt to achieve substantial currency depreciation through large open-market sales of yen. Through its effects on import-price inflation (which has been sharply negative in recent years), on the demand for Japanese goods, and on expectations, a significant yen depreciation would go a long way toward jump-starting the reflationary process in Japan.

BOJ stonewalling has been particularly pronounced on this issue, for reasons that are difficult to understand. The BOJ has argued that it does not have the legal authority to set yen policy; that it would be unable to reduce the value of the yen in any case; and that even if it could reduce the value of the yen, political constraints prevent any significant depreciation. Let us briefly address the first and third points, then turn to the more fundamental question of whether the BOJ could in fact depreciate the yen if it attempted to do so.

On legal authority, it is true that technically the Ministry of Finance retains responsibility for exchange rate policy. (The same is true for the United States, by the way, with the Treasury playing the role of Ministry. I am not aware that this has been an important constraint on Fed policy.) The obvious solution is for the BOJ and the Ministry to agree that yen depreciation is needed, abstaining from their ongoing turf wars long enough to take an action in Japan's vital economic interest. Alternatively, the BOJ could probably undertake yen depreciation unilaterally; because the BOJ has a legal mandate to pursue price stability, it certainly could make a good argument that, with interest rates at zero, depreciation of the yen is the best available tool for achieving its mandated objective.

The "political constraints" argument is that, even if depreciation is possible, any expansion thus achieved will be at the expense of trading partners—a so-called beggar-thy-neighbor policy. Defenders of inaction on the yen claim that a large yen depreciation would therefore create serious international tensions. Whatever validity this political argument may have had at various times, it is of no relevance at the moment, for Japan has recently been urged by its most powerful allies and trading partners to weaken the yen—and refused! Moreover, the economic validity of the beggar-thy-neighbor thesis is doubtful, as depreciation creates trade—by raising home-country income—as well as diverting it. Perhaps not all those who cite the beggar-thy-neighbor thesis are aware that it had its origins in the Great Depression, when it was used as an argument against the very devaluations that ultimately proved crucial to world economic recovery. A yen trading at 100 to the dollar or less is in no one's interest.

The important question, of course, is whether a determined Bank of Japan would be able to depreciate the yen. I am not aware of any previous historical episode, including the period of very low interest rates in the 1930s, in which a central bank has been unable to devalue its currency. Be that as it may, there are those who claim that the BOJ is impotent to affect the exchange rate, arguing along the following lines: Because (it is claimed) monetary policy has been made ineffective by the liquidity trap, BOJ intervention in foreign exchange markets would amount, for all practical purposes, to a sterilized intervention. Empirical studies have often found that sterilized interventions cannot create sustained appreciations or depreciations. Therefore the BOJ cannot affect the value of the yen, except perhaps modestly and temporarily.

To rebut this view, one can apply a reductio ad absurdum argument, based on my observation above that money issuance must affect prices, or else printing money will create infinite purchasing power. Suppose the Bank of Japan prints yen and uses them to acquire foreign assets. If the yen did not depreciate as a result, and if there were no reciprocal demand for Japanese goods or assets (which would drive up domestic prices), what in principle would prevent the BOJ from acquiring infinite quantities of foreign assets, leaving foreigners nothing to hold but idle yen balances? Obviously this will not happen in equilibrium. One reason it will not happen is the principle of portfolio balance: Because yen balances are not perfect substitutes for all other types of real and financial assets, foreigners will not greatly increase their holdings of yen unless the yen depreciates, increasing the expected return (including the risk premium) on yen assets. It might be objected that the necessary interventions would be large. Although I doubt it, they might be; that is an empirical question. However, the larger the intervention that is required, the greater the associated increase in the BOJ's foreign reserves, which doesn't seem such a bad outcome.

In short, there is a strong presumption that vigorous intervention by the BOJ, together with appropriate announcements to influence market expectations, could drive down the value of the yen significantly. Further, there seems little reason not to try this strategy. The "worst" that could happen would be that the BOJ would greatly increase its holdings of reserve assets.

Money-Financed Transfers

Suppose that the yen-depreciation strategy is tried but fails to raise aggregate demand and prices sufficiently, perhaps because at some point Japan's trading partners do object to further falls in the yen. An alternative strategy, which does not rely at all on trade diversion, is money-financed transfers to domestic households—the real-life equivalent of that hoary thought experiment, the "helicopter drop" of newly printed money. I think most economists would agree that a large enough helicopter drop *must* raise the price level. Suppose it did not, so that the price level remained unchanged. Then the real wealth of the population would grow without bound, as they are flooded with gifts of money from the government—another variant of the arbitrage argument made above. Surely at some point the public would attempt to convert its increased real wealth into goods and services, spending that would increase aggregate demand and prices. Conversion of the public's money wealth into other assets would also be beneficial, if it raised the prices of other assets.

The only counterargument I can imagine is that the public might fear a future lump-sum tax on wealth equal to the per capita money transfer, inducing them to hold rather than spend the extra balances.[5] But the government has no incentive to take such an action in the future, and hence the public has no reason to expect it. The newly circulated cash bears no interest and thus has no budgetary implications for the government if prices remain unchanged. If instead prices rise, as we anticipate, the government will face higher nominal spending requirements but will also enjoy higher nominal tax receipts and a reduction in the real value of outstanding nominal government debt. To a first approximation, then, the helicopter drops will not erode the financial position of the government and thus will not induce a need for extraordinary future taxes.

Note that, in contrast, a helicopter drop of government bonds would not necessarily induce significant extra spending. Even if government bonds pay essentially zero interest (as they do today in Japan), if they are of finite maturity, then at some point the debt they represent must be refinanced, possibly at a positive interest rate. The usual Ricardian logic might then apply, with the public realizing that the "gift" of government debt they have received is also associated with higher future tax obligations. Money is in this sense special; it is not only a zero-interest liability, but also a perpetual liability. Money-financed transfers do have a resource cost, which is the inflation tax. But (1) this cost comes into play only as prices rise, which is the object the policy is trying to achieve, and (2) again, to a first order, the real cost is borne by holders of real balances, not the government.

Of course, the BOJ has no unilateral authority to rain money on the population. The policy being proposed—a money-financed tax cut—is a combination of fiscal and monetary measures. All this means is that some intragovernmental cooperation would be required. Indeed, the case for a tax cut now has already been made, independent of monetary considerations (Posen 1998). The willingness of the BOJ to purchase government securities equal to the cost of the tax cut would serve to reduce the net interest cost of the tax cut to the government, which could not hurt the tax cut's chance of passage. By the way, I do not think that such cooperation would in any way compromise the BOJ's newly won independence, as some have suggested. In financing a tax cut, the BOJ would be taking a voluntary action in pursuit of its legally mandated goal, the pursuit of price stability. Cooperation with the fiscal authorities in pursuit of a common goal is not the same as subservience.

Nonstandard Open-Market Operations

A number of observers have suggested that the BOJ expand its open-market operations to a wider range of assets, such as long-term govern-

5. Of course, this is not even a potential issue if money-financed government purchases are used instead of transfers. Ideally, these purchases would be complements to, rather than substitutes for, private consumption.

ment bonds or corporate bonds; and indeed, the BOJ has modest plans to purchase commercial paper, corporate bonds, and asset-backed securities under repurchase agreements, or to lend allowing these assets as collateral (Ueda 1999, 3). I am not so sure that this alternative is even needed, given the BOJ's other options, but I would like to make a few brief analytical points about them.

In thinking about nonstandard open-market operations, it is useful to separate those that have some fiscal component from those that do not. By a fiscal component I mean some implicit subsidy, such as would arise, for example, if the BOJ purchased nonperforming bank loans at face value (this is of course equivalent to a fiscal bailout of the banks, financed by the central bank). This sort of money-financed "gift" to the private sector would expand aggregate demand for the same reasons that any money-financed transfer does. Although such operations are perfectly sensible from the standpoint of economic theory, I doubt very much that we will see anything like this in Japan, if only because it is more straightforward for the Diet to vote subsidies or tax cuts directly. Nonstandard open-market operations with a fiscal component, even if legal, would be correctly viewed as an end run around the authority of the legislature, and so are better left in the realm of theoretical curiosities.

A nonstandard open-market operation without a fiscal component, in contrast, is the purchase of some asset by the central bank (e.g., long-term government bonds) at fair market value. The object of such purchases would be to raise asset prices, which in turn would stimulate spending (e.g., by raising collateral values). I think there is little doubt that such operations, if aggressively pursued, would indeed have the desired effect, for essentially the same reasons that purchases of foreign-currency assets would cause the yen to depreciate. To claim that nonstandard open-market purchases would have no effect is to claim that the central bank could acquire all of the real and financial assets in the economy with no effect on prices or yields. Of course, long before that would happen, imperfect substitutability between assets would assert itself, and the prices of assets being acquired would rise.

As I have indicated, I doubt that extensive nonstandard operations will be needed if the BOJ aggressively pursues reflation by other means. I hope, though, that the Japanese monetary authorities would not hesitate to use this approach, if for some reason it became the most convenient. It is disturbing that BOJ resistance to this idea has focused on largely extraneous issues, such as the possible effects of nonstandard operations on the Bank's balance sheet. For example, BOJ officials have pointed out that if the Bank purchased large quantities of long-term government bonds, and interest rates later rose, the Bank would suffer capital losses. This concern has led the BOJ to express reluctance to consider engaging in such operations in the first place. However, paper losses to the Bank's portfolio have no effect on its operating budget (which is approved by the Ministry of Finance) or on overall government finances, since the bank's losses are precisely offset by the fiscal authority's gains. Thus, to allow consideration of possible capital losses to block needed policy actions is misguided.

Needed: Rooseveltian Resolve

Franklin D. Roosevelt was elected president of the United States in 1932 with the mandate to get the country out of the Depression. In the end, his most effective actions were the same ones that Japan needs to take—namely, rehabilitation of the banking system and devaluation of the currency. But Roosevelt's specific policy actions were, I think, less important than his willingness to be aggressive and to experiment—in short, to do whatever it took to get the country moving again. Many of his policies did not work as intended, but in the end FDR deserves great credit for having the courage to abandon failed paradigms and to do what needed to be done.

Japan is not in a Great Depression by any means, but its economy has operated below potential for nearly a decade. Nor is it clear that recovery is imminent. Policy options exist that could greatly reduce these losses. Why isn't more happening? To this outsider, at least, Japanese monetary policy seems to be suffering from a self-induced paralysis. Most striking is the apparent unwillingness of the monetary authorities to experiment, to try anything that isn't absolutely guaranteed to work. Perhaps it's time for some Rooseveltian resolve in Japan.

References

Bernanke, Ben, and Mark Gertler. 1995. Inside the Black Box: The Credit Channel of Monetary Transmission. *Journal of Economic Perspectives* 9, no. 4 (Fall): 27-48.

Bernanke, Ben, and Mark Gertler. 1999. Monetary Policy and Asset Price Volatility. In *1999 Symposium: New Challenges for Monetary Policy*, 77-128. Kansas City: Federal Reserve Bank of Kansas City.

Bernanke, Ben S., Thomas Laubach, Frederic S. Mishkin, and Adam S. Posen. 1999. *Inflation Targeting: Lessons from the International Experience*. Princeton, NJ: Princeton University Press.

Blinder, Alan. 1999. Monetary Policy at the Zero Bound: Balancing the Risks. Paper presented at a Federal Reserve Bank of Boston conference on monetary policy in a low-inflation environment, Woodstock, VT (20 October).

Clouse, James, Dale Henderson, Athanasios Orphanides, David Small, and Peter Tinsley. 1999. Monetary Policy When the Short-term Interest Rate is Zero. Photocopy (October). Board of Governors of the Federal Reserve System.

Hoshi, Takeo, and Anil Kashyap. 2000. The Japanese Banking Crisis: Where Did It Come From and How Will It End? In *NBER Macroeconomics Annual*, vol. 14, eds. B. Bernanke and J. Rotemberg. Cambridge, MA: National Bureau of Economic Research.

Krugman, Paul. 1999. It's Baaack: Japan's Slump and the Return of the Liquidity Trap. *Brookings Papers on Economic Activity* 2: 137-205.

McCallum, Bennett. 1999. Theoretical Analysis Regarding a Zero Lower Bound on Nominal Interest Rates. Carnegie-Mellon University. Photocopy (September).

Meltzer, Allan. 1999. The Transmission Process. Paper prepared for a conference on the monetary transmission process: recent developments and lessons for Europe, sponsored by Deutsche Bundesbank, Frankfurt (25-27 March).

Okina, Kunio. 1999. *Monetary Policy under Zero Inflation—A Response to Criticisms and Questions Regarding Monetary Policy*. Discussion Paper no. 99-E-20. Tokyo: Institute for Monetary and Economic Studies, Bank of Japan.

Posen, Adam S. 1998. *Restoring Japan's Economic Growth*. Washington: Institute for International Economics.

Reifschneider, David, and John C. Williams. 1999. *Three Lessons for Monetary Policy in a Low Inflation Era*. Finance and Economics Discussion Series 1999, no. 44 (August). Washintgon: Board of Governors of the Federal Reserve System.

Svensson, Lars E. O. 1999. How Should Monetary Policy Be Conducted in an Era of Price Stability? In *1999 Symposium: New Challenges for Monetary Policy*, 77-128. Kanasas City: Federal Reserve Bank of Kansas City.

Ueda, Kazuo. 1999. Remarks presented at a Federal Reserve Bank of Boston conference on monetary policy in a low-inflation environment, Woodstock, VT (20 October).

8

US-Japanese Economic Policy Conflicts and Coordination during the 1990s

EISUKE SAKAKIBARA

World capitalism since the early 1990s has been experiencing a dramatic transformation because of the information and telecommunications revolutions and accelerating globalization. As a result, the economic interdependence of the world's countries—in particular, the relationship between the United States and Japan—has deepened significantly. Thus, US policy vis-à-vis Japan, whether overt pressure or benign neglect, has had conspicuous effects on the Japanese economy and political structure. There are various channels of influence for US policy toward Japan—political pressure, public relations campaigns, economic sanctions, and trade negotiations—but what characterized the 1990s was the importance of markets, especially the foreign exchange and equity markets, which transmitted US policy toward Japan.

We can perhaps subdivide the 1990s, or more precisely the Clinton years, into three periods. The first period was from January 1993, the month of the president's inauguration, to January 1995, when Robert Rubin became secretary of the Treasury. This period's Japan policy was heavily influenced by the US trade representative (USTR) and the US embassy in Tokyo, notably by USTR Mickey Kantor and by James Foster, counselor in charge of public relations at the US embassy. The period was characterized by trade frictions and aggressive US criticism of the Japanese old guard, the Liberal Democratic Party, and bureaucracy.

Eisuke Sakakibara is a professor at Keio University and former vice minister of finance for international affairs of Japan.

The second period lasted from January 1995 until September 1998. During these years, more emphasis was rightly placed on markets and coordination within markets rather than on political or trade confrontation. Rubin and his team took the reins of economic policy in the United States, while Japanese political turmoil calmed down somewhat. Toward the end of this period, Japan plunged into an unprecedented financial crisis, and the United States insisted on market solutions to the problem. In particular, the United States took the position that easy infusion of public money into the financial system was unwarranted.

It was not until the third period—between September 1998 and the present—during which the Asian financial crisis spread to Russia, Brazil, and finally Wall Street, that the US government started to take a more pragmatic, less ideological approach. In this period, coordination to avert a potential global crisis was fully implemented.

Viewed in this context and in these periods, we can see some substantial improvement in US-Japanese economic policy coordination during the 1990s as the United States restored its own confidence and as the crisis deepened in the late 1990s. Whether this will continue during the election year 2000 is as yet uncertain, but it is clear to almost everybody involved that the contentious trade negotiations of the early 1990s ended up serving, in the words of Bowman Cutter, then White House aide on economic policy, "neither US national interests nor Japanese interests." As Cutter later confided, however, open bickering between Japan and the United States in the mass media might somehow have worked to the advantage of certain politicians.

Trade Pressure and the Rising Yen: January 1993-95

It is often said that the Japanese economy was stagnant throughout the decade after 1992 following the bursting of the bubble, but this is incorrect. The economy did recover in fiscal 1995 and 1996. Real GDP growth was 3 percent in fiscal 1995, and 4.4 percent in fiscal 1996, the highest rate at that time among the Group of Seven countries.

Masaru Yoshitomi, managing director of the Asian Development Bank Institute, usefully divides the development of the Japanese economy during the 1992-98 period into three stages—recession caused by falling plant and equipment investment, from fiscal 1992 to 1994; recovery, from fiscal 1995 to 1996; and a surge in deflationary pressures resulting from the destabilization of the banking system, from fiscal 1997 to 1998.[1] If I might add to this classification of periods, fiscal 1999 will probably be remembered as the year that the subsequently long-lived recovery began.

---

1. Yoshitomi, Masaru. 1998. *Nihon Keizai no Shinjitsu* (in Japanese). Tokyo: Toyo Keizai.

These three periods describe the evolution of the Japanese economy, and correspond somewhat with changes in US economic policy toward Japan. This is no coincidence. Throughout these three periods, Japanese-US relations and foreign exchange and equity markets played a very important role.

The recession years 1992-94 in Japan were also the period of transition from the Bush to the Clinton administrations, and the first 2 years for Clinton's new team. At the time the new team took over, there was a strong legacy of the Bush-Armacost policy geared toward structurally changing the Japanese economy and political system. During the late 1980s and early 1990s, there was a persistent perception in the United States that the strength of the Japanese economy, which seemed at that time rather permanent, was derived from a somewhat closed hierarchical structure, often called Japan Inc.

At the top of this Japan Inc. hierarchy, it was perceived, big keiretsu companies—centering on banks, the bureaucracy (the Ministry of Finance in particular), and the ruling political party (the Liberal Democratic Party, or LDP)—skillfully ruled the country. Although too broad a generalization and inaccurate in many respects, this Japan Inc. theory was very popular not only among Americans but also among many Japanese, partly because of its simplicity and partly because conspiracy theories always appeal to those mystified by incomprehensible facts. US-Japanese negotiations on Japanese structural impediments thus became the focal point of the economic relationship between the two countries during the Bush administration. Implicit targets of the United States were, among others, the LDP and the Ministry of Finance as headquarters of Japan Inc.

This legacy of 1988-92 was inherited by the Clinton administration in its early years. An inclination toward populism, which was conspicuous in the early Clinton years, also contributed to contentious trade poiicy that centered on Japan's structural problems as related to its current account surplus. Key Clinton advisers included former election campaign staff members, such as White House spokesman George Stephanopoulos and USTR Mickey Kantor. Robert Rubin, who later became the US Treasury secretary, was then chairman of the National Economic Council, and the present Treasury secretary, Lawrence Summers, was then Treasury undersecretary for international affairs. During this first period, the populist group represented by Kantor and Stephanopoulos held more sway than the macroeconomists, who included Rubin and Summers.

In 1993, when the Japanese economy was still in recession caused by declines in plant and equipment investment, the Tokyo Stock Exchange showed some signs of an upturn. The April Nikkei average topped 20,000 points and was approaching 21,000 (see figure 8.1). However, under pressure from the tough US stand toward Japan, the dollar, which traded around ¥125-126 when Clinton first took office, depreciated rapidly

Figure 8.1 Nikkei stock average, 1993-94 (points)

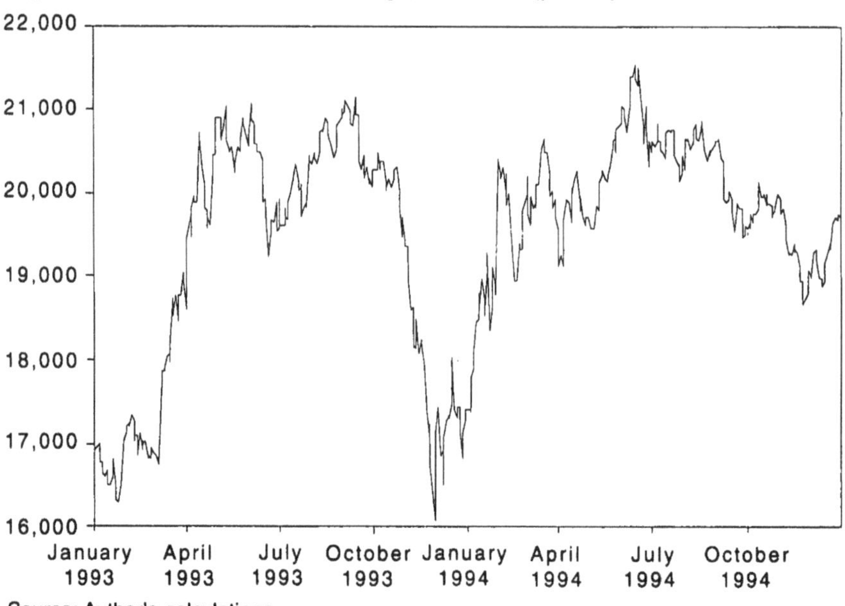

Source: Author's calculations.

against the yen. At the press conference following a summit with Prime Minister Kiichi Miyazawa on 16 April, Clinton said that a strong yen would effectively cut Japan's trade surplus. His comment triggered the dollar's fall toward 110 yen (see figure 8.2).

Rubin and Summers were understandably concerned about the rapidly depreciating dollar, because a weak dollar could lead to a rise in long-term interest rates and inflation, which they feared could delay the recovery of the US economy. The Japanese government intervened to buy US dollars in April 1993 for the first time since 1988. On 27 April, the US government also stepped in to buy the dollar. The joint US-Japanese intervention in the foreign exchange market continued, on and off, until June. However, the focus of the Japan-United States relationship continued to be trade problems, which reduced the effectiveness of these foreign exchange interventions.

During the 10 July Clinton-Miyazawa summit, a comprehensive agreement on a new Japanese-US trade framework was reached, which gave the impression to market players that Japan had promised to keep its current account surplus within 2 percent of its GDP, further boosting the strength of the Japanese currency, even though Japan flatly refused to comply with the US demand during the summit. On 20 July, Miyazawa said he would resign, following House of Representatives election results that ended 38 years of Liberal Democratic Party rule. On 6 August, seven former opposition parties and a parliamentary group joined an adminis-

Figure 8.2 Yen-dollar exchange rate (yen per dollar)

Source: Author's calculations.

tration led by Morihiro Hosokawa. While Japan-US relations were growing tense, the domestic political scene was becoming fluid.

On 17 August, the yen-dollar exchange rate closed at 101.2 yen, a gain of nearly 25 yen since the beginning of the year. The appreciating yen was basically brought to a standstill when Summers said on 19 August that a rapid appreciation of the yen was not desirable for the US economy, and Tokyo and Washington intervened in the market once more to strengthen the dollar. The sharp plunge in the dollar's value, however, severely hampered the pace of economic recovery in Japan. This was because the strong yen dampened the nation's business confidence, in addition to hurting exports.

The Clinton administration did not have well-defined trade and currency policies in its first year, because of the conflict between the populists and the macroeconomists, as highlighted in the book *The Agenda* by US journalist Bob Woodward.[2] Summers made his 19 August announcement alone, suggesting that he had perhaps taken the initiative to rally against the populists on the foreign exchange rate issue. Tokyo did not issue any statement, but Finance Minister Hirohisa Fujii said the next day that he welcomed the announcement.

2. New York: Simon & Schuster, 1994.

Japanese-US cooperation fell to pieces after the Hosokawa-Clinton summit on 11 February 1994 failed to reach a comprehensive trade agreement. I took part in the talks as senior deputy director general of the International Finance Bureau of the Finance Ministry. During the talks between Foreign Minister Tsutomu Hata and USTR Mickey Kantor on 10 February, before the Hosokawa-Clinton summit the next day, the US side demanded that Japan commit to numerical targets in certain trade areas, such as automobile exports to the United States, government procurement, and opening the domestic insurance market to more foreign competition. Japan refused the US demands on the grounds that numerical targets could lead to managed trade, which ran counter to the principle of free trade.

In preliminary meetings that were held on and off from around 5 February, US officials appeared unsure whether to seek numerical targets. In a 9 February meeting between Deputy Foreign Minister Koichiro Matsuura and White House aide Bowman Cutter, Cutter proposed easing the demand for numerical targets, but the US team did not adopt his proposal. The Treasury team, led by Summers, was not sure about setting numerical targets for US access to the Japanese insurance market, and was trying to reach a compromise agreement that would credit Japan's macroeconomic policies.

President Clinton, however, when he returned to the White House on 8 February from a stump tour, sought a clear-cut settlement to the bilateral trade dispute. The Treasury was strongly dissatisfied that Japan's ¥6 trillion tax-cut stimulus package announced 8 February was to last only 1 year. Consequently, Clinton decided in favor of the tougher policies toward Japan that were sought by officials close to Kantor. In his talks with Hata, Kantor apparently thought that he could convince Hata to accept numerical targets. Three Kantor-Hata talks took place, with the final session held in the early morning hours of 11 February. The talks eventually became a four-man meeting, also involving Cutter and Matsuura. Hata remained opposed to numerical targets.

At a press conference later the same day, Hosokawa said that instead of having an ambiguous agreement that could lead to misunderstanding in the future, "It's better to admit what Japan cannot afford to do." Such straightforwardness, he added, represented a "mature relationship" between the two countries. It was probably unprecedented that a Japanese prime minister had said "no" so bluntly in talks with a US president. Almost all of the Japanese negotiating team, including myself, felt happy about his remark, but Takakazu Kuriyama, the Japanese ambassador to the United States, appeared depressed following the prime minister's statement.

At first, Japanese business leaders and media credited Hosokawa for talking of a "mature" relationship with the United State. However, as the yen subsequently entered another round of appreciation, with the dollar falling to the ¥101 level on 15 February, the atmosphere changed. Critics said that Hosokawa's remark was absurd in light of failure to reach an accord at his summit with Clinton. They held that the failure of the summit was the cause of the yen's appreciation and declines in stock prices, despite the implementation of a large-scale pump-priming package. Hosokawa's Washington advisers, including myself, therefore came under fire. We returned from Washington feeling mystified as to whether we should have accepted the US demand for numerical targets, which the *Financial Times* had called unreasonable, simply for the sake of maintaining good relations with the United States. We were unhappy that populist US officials had used foreign exchange rates as leverage in trade negotiations.

The Background and Effects of Federal Reserve Tightening: February-April 1995

On 4 February 1995, one week before the Japan-United States summit, US Federal Reserve Chairman Alan Greenspan issued a rare statement announcing an imminent federal funds rate increase from 3 to 3.25 percent, the first belt-tightening monetary step in 5 years. This was a precautionary step taken to prevent the US economy from overheating after it was reported that the real GDP in the fourth quarter of 1993 grew at an annualized rate of 6.3 percent over the same period in 1992 (compared with 2.7 percent year-on-year growth in the third quarter of 1993). Right after the federal funds rate was raised, US Treasury Secretary Lloyd Bentsen and Treasury Undersecretary Lawrence Summers made it clear that the United States had no intention of guiding the yen higher. The breakdown of trade negations on 11 February led the dollar to plunge further, and the yield on benchmark 30-year Treasury bonds, which had leveled off after gradually increasing, rose again, exceeding the 6.5 percent mark. The Dow Jones industrial average on the New York Stock Exchange began to slide during the latter half of February and recorded its lowest level for 1994 at 3,593 points on 4 April.

Actually, there were stormy discussions within the Clinton administration over the need for tightening monetary policies by the Federal Reserve. About two weeks before the federal funds rate was raised, Greenspan, Clinton, and his administration's secretaries in charge of economic affairs gathered at the White House to discuss the issue. Greenspan argued for a modest interest rate increase as early as February to prevent the yield on 30-year Treasury bonds—which stood at 6.3 percent—from rising on fears of inflation. Clinton, who had a keen interest in the movement of long-term interest rates, was in favor of raising the key short-term rate if it was deemed necessary to lower the long-term rate. Bentsen and Rubin, then chairman of the National Economic Council, supported Greenspan, but Vice President Al Gore and Laura Tyson, chairwoman of the Council of Economic Advisers at the White House, were opposed to an immediate interest rate increase.

The Federal Reserve, which was nervous about the movement of long-term interest rates, raised the federal funds rate again by 0.25 percentage point on March 22. That sent long-term interest rates plummeting temporarily, but the Treasury bond yield soon rebounded and rose to surpass the 7 percent mark. The third hike of the year in the federal funds rate on April 18 was not sufficient to stop the rise of long-term interest rates; the Treasury bond yield rose above 7.4 percent, continuing the upward trend since Clinton's inauguration. Clinton was apparently irritated by the situation. But Bentsen told the president that it would take about a year to see the effects of interest rate hikes on the economy, and that it would be wise to cool the economy down immediately, rather than raising interest rates in 1995, just before the presidential election.

During 1994, the federal funds rate was raised further in May, August, and November, reaching 5.5 percent, which was 2.5 percentage points higher than the January level. Despite the increase in the short-term rate, the Treasury bond yield rose to 8.16 percent in early November. At the end of that year, the yield stood at 7.89 percent.

In theory, a 2.5 percentage point hike in the federal funds rate and a rise of about 2 percent in the yield on 30-year Treasury bonds should result in a stronger dollar and diminish inflationary pressures. But it had the opposite effect in 1994. On 1 November 1994, the dollar plunged against the yen to an exchange rate of ¥96.68, despite joint interventions by the Japanese and US monetary authorities to hold the dollar at the ¥100 level.

The anomalies in the exchange rate and in macroeconomics undoubtedly resulted from the fierce trade war between Japan and the United States. The "Framework Talks," which were suspended on 11 February, resumed on 24 May. Although some progress was made in the areas of government procurement and insurance by that autumn, major conflicts over the key areas of automobiles and automobile parts could not be resolved in 1994. Bickering over trade between Japan and the United States, which was intensively covered by the mass media, regrettably helped convince market players that the yen's surge would not be halted unless Japan's current account surplus was brought down.

Precautionary tight-money measures undertaken ahead of the 1996 US presidential election, including a steep rise in interest rates, together with overheated economies and rising interest rates in other member states of the Group of Seven industrial nations—particularly among the European members—became major factors that drastically changed the international flow of capital. Increasing demands for capital and tight-money policies adopted by the industrial powers pressed many investors to review their investment exposure in Mexico and other emerging economies.

Mexico's agreement to the North American Free Trade Agreement (NAFTA) in November 1993, and the implementation of NAFTA on 1 January 1994, boosted foreign investment in Mexico, and the fundamentals of the Mexican economy rapidly improved. Its real growth in GDP stood at 3.5 percent in 1994, easily surpassing the 0.6 percent registered the previous year. Consumer prices rose at a rate of 7.1 percent in 1994—the lowest in 10 years.

Reflecting its good economic performance, Mexico's imports increased, swelling its current account deficit to $29.5 billion in 1994 from $23.4 billion in 1993. But it had foreign exchange reserves of more than $25 billion, and if the inflow of capital had been about $30 billion—the same level as 1993—its current account would never have been in a critical state. Social unrest, however, caused by the assassination of presidential candidate Luis Donaldo Colosio on 23 March 1994, suddenly reduced capital inflows from abroad. The Mexican government was forced to shore up the peso, using $11 billion of its $28.3 billion foreign reserve funds.

The first wave of the crisis was mitigated by the provision of a short-term credit line of $6.75 billion by NAFTA members and an increase in interest rates. To stop capital outflow, peso-denominated debts worth $13 billion were swapped with US dollar-denominated short-term debts over the course of 8 months from March to October 1994. The second wave of the Mexican crisis hit the nation right after its new president, Ernesto Zedillo, took office on 1 December 1994. Triggered by political confusion in the state of Chiapas, where rebels and military troops clashed, capital flight spread even among Mexican residents, reducing the country's foreign reserves to $10.5 billion.

On 22 December 1994, Mexico adopted a floating exchange system, which saw the peso plunge by more than 40 percent in just over a month. Foreign reserves further shrank to $6 billion as of 22 December, and the county had accumulated $28 billion worth of dollar-denominated debts that were due in a few months. The situation was highly alarming. Mexico's economic fundamentals were relatively healthy, and its debts did not exceed its assets. But the shortage of foreign capital inflows saw Mexico on the verge of default and bankruptcy in early 1995.

The situation in Mexico was a new type of crisis that was triggered by rapid fluctuations in capital flows, resulting from changes in the capital market or from domestic political turmoil. This type of crisis was also seen in Asia in 1997 and 1998. Michel Camdessus, managing director of the International Monetary Fund, called it a crisis of the capital account balance, as opposed to the more traditional current account balance crisis. Confrontation between the US government and Congress stalled efforts to put together a bailout package for Mexico. But with an administrative order issued by President Clinton on 31 January 1995, which required no approval from Congress, a $52.8 billion bailout package, centering on loans from the International Monetary Fund and the United States, was finally announced, paving the way for the reconstruction of the Mexican economy.

The following day, 1 February 1995, the US Federal Reserve raised both the official discount rate and the federal funds rate by 0.5 points, to 5.25 and 6 percent, respectively, in a bid to halt the dollar's slide, which was the result mainly of financial unrest in Central and South American economies. Despite the efforts of the US government, the dollar continued to drop, keeping up inflationary pressures caused by the weaker dollar and the overheated economy.

Following Mexico, Argentina fell into a panic in the wake of the capital outflow, putting a number of Argentine financial institutions on the verge of bankruptcy. This only accelerated the dollar's slide. Argentina was able to avert the collapse of its financial system after the International Monetary Fund and others worked out a bailout package on 6 April 1995.

During this period, the dollar plunged against the yen and the German mark. On 3 March, the Japanese and US monetary authorities jointly intervened in the currency market, but this had little effect on the falling dollar. On 19 April, the yen-dollar exchange rate broke the ¥80 mark, reaching ¥79.75. The excessively strong yen during this period has often been referred to as a crisis for Japan, but it was also the biggest crisis during the first term of the Clinton administration, which used foreign exchange as a trade policy tool.

Looking back, it could be argued that the combination of contentious US trade policy toward Japan and precautionary tight monetary policy—which was at least partially responsible for having sent Mexico and Argentina deeper into crisis—had caused the dramatic decline of the US dollar from around ¥125 per dollar during the early part January of 1993 to ¥79.75 on 17 April 1995. As a result, prospects for a Japanese recovery that existed during 1993-94 were dashed as the strong yen canceled out the initially favorable signs of an upturn in domestic demand. Also, the loss of business confidence due to a too-strong yen, the so-called Yendaka syndrome, had had lingering negative effects on the economy. The Japanese recovery thus was delayed by as much as a year or a year and a half because the yen was too strong, which was the result, to a significant degree, of tough, populist, election-conscious US policies.

The Rise of the Dollar and Japanese Recovery: April 1995-December 1996

When Robert Rubin took over from Lloyd Bentsen as Treasury secretary in January 1995, the United States had undergone a major policy shift in its foreign exchange and trade policies. At the 10 January hearing of the US Senate Finance Committee, which approved the appointment of the new Treasury secretary, Rubin stated clearly that a strong dollar was in the best interest of the US economy. His support for a strong dollar formed the backbone of his macroeconomic policy right up until his resignation on 2 July 1999. The idea was to achieve sustained growth in the US economy by bringing down long-term interest rates and encouraging the flow of capital from abroad on the strength of a stronger dollar. These actions would reinvigorate Wall Street and curb inflationary pressure that would have built if import prices had risen due to a weak dollar. Rubin's position that a strong dollar was a good thing was also upheld by Federal Reserve Chairman Alan Greenspan and then-Deputy Treasury Secretary Lawrence Summers.

This position contrasted starkly with that of former USTR Mickey Kantor and a group of populists in and close to the White House, who throughout 1993-94 supported a weak dollar as a way of trimming the country's current account deficit with Japan. At the same hearing, Rubin also said, "We [the United States] should not use foreign exchange as an instrument of trade policy," adding that exchange rates would in the long run reflect underlying economic fundamentals. He also made clear his view that the fundamentals of the US economy were very strong and would remain so were the dollar to rise in value in the long run.

From that time onward, Rubin took every opportunity to reiterate that exchange rates should not be used as an instrument of trade policy. His remarks probably stemmed from his strong objection as a financial expert to the fact that exchange rates were greatly distorted in 1993 and 1994 by individuals who he believed knew little about financial and money market affairs but who were keen to cut the US current account deficit.

In the wake of the economic crises in Mexico and Argentina—set against the backdrop of a US weak-dollar policy—and Rubin's appointment, US macroeconomic policy shifted from approving of a weaker dollar for the sake of trimming current account deficits to one of promoting a stronger dollar, lower interest rates, and sustained, noninflationary economic growth. However, the shift in US currency policy failed to draw the market's attention in spring 1995, largely because the economic crises in the United States' backyard—Mexico and Argentina—were not yet over. Furthermore, the foreign exchange market was becoming volatile because of derivatives transactions, such as the "knockout" option. As a result, economic turmoil continued to build up.

Partly due to US concerns over the sharp drop in the value of the greenback, Japan and the United States made a coordinated effort to intervene in the market and buy dollars on 3 March and 3 April. However, the move failed to check the dollar's fall against the yen. Finance ministers of the Group of Seven major industrial nations then met in Washington on 25 April 1995, with Rubin chairing the discussion. The Group of Seven (G-7) finance ministers confirmed that the currency movement had "gone beyond levels justified by underlying economic fundamentals" and declared in a joint statement that "an orderly reversal of those movements is desirable." It was extraordinary for these G-7 ministers to refer to foreign exchange levels.

At about that time, the dollar began to experience a gradual rise against the yen and the German mark, although the market paid little attention to the G-7 joint statement, probably because it did not outline any concrete steps for G-7 nations to coordinate monetary and fiscal policies or market intervention efforts to prop up the dollar.

The prevailing view in the market, then, was represented by such economists as Richard Koo of Nomura Research Institute, who argued that as long as Japan continued to post large current account surpluses, the yen's rise would continue. He advocated viewing this instance of the Yendaka syndrome as an opportunity to quickly implement necessary structural reforms. There was an element of truth in this, but the rise of the yen—which even hit ¥80 against the dollar at one point—was undoubtedly excessive and unusual. It was also obvious that the yen's rise was caused by factors related to derivatives transactions, including "delta hedge" and knockout options, which many market players could not predict. Even leading international investor George Soros said that such transactions as knockout options should be regulated by financial authorities.

The joint statement issued by the G-7 finance ministers on 25 April 1995, calling for an "orderly reversal of currency movements," was gradually put into effect in the following months. On 31 May 1995, a group of 12 nations, including Japan, the United States, and a number of European states, coordinated foreign exchange interventions to buy US dollars. On 7 July, Japan and the United States bought dollars again, following a coordinated lowering of federal fund rates the previous day. Nevertheless, the market took these interventions for granted, and although they had some short-term effects they did not lead to a major change in market views. The marginal utility of orthodox intervention obviously declined as the market got more and more used to it. Moreover, the United States, which had carried out a series of interest rate hikes in 1994, had entered a phase of relaxed monetary policy in the wake of the Mexican and Argentine crises. If other factors had remained unchanged, the policy would have led to a weaker dollar.

There was an obvious need to do something different. Two ideas suggested themselves. One idea was to sever the strong link between Japanese-US current account imbalances and the yen-dollar exchange rate, and the other was to give the market, which had grown accustomed to intervention, a surprise of some sort. Theoretically, there was no problem with the first step. Because more than 90 percent of exchange deals are made on the basis of capital transactions, rather than goods transactions, if the direction of capital flow changed as a result of interest rate trends or anticipated exchange rates, it was possible—at least in theory—to promote the reversal of currency fluctuations. Yet institutional investors such as life insurance companies and trust banks, which have suffered major losses on a number of occasions in the past because of the yen's rise, were extremely reluctant to invest in dollar-denominated assets. The problem, therefore, was how to persuade Japanese institutional investors to act.

The point of the second step lay in making effective use of so-called push-up intervention, in which the authorities push up the market using huge funds on only a limited number of occasions. The market would be shocked into reacting to the surge of funds. The basic premise for conventional currency market intervention lay in the so-called smoothing operation, designed to smooth out excessive fluctuation in the currency market. On this premise, monetary authorities intervene in the market by carrying out small-scale yen-selling operations when the yen rises sharply, in a bid to prevent rapid fluctuation in the foreign exchange market. As long as the market is basically stable and deviations from exchange rate norms occur only briefly, this sort of market intervention can prove effective. Yet it seemed to me that in this "cybercapitalism" age, when huge amounts of information can travel around the world instantly and sizable amounts of money can be moved quickly, the market was not so stable.

In the cybercapitalism era, authorities, while watching market trends carefully, should intervene and send the market a message clear enough to change its perception by surprise. If the occasion demands, the authorities should also counter the market by force, at least temporarily. The authorities should push up the market to make it react, and continue to do so until the market accepts the authorities' viewpoint. This seems to me to be the principle of push-up intervention, as opposed to conventional smoothing intervention.

On the morning of 2 August 1995, Finance Minister Masayoshi Takemura announced at the ministry a package of emergency measures to counter the yen's rise, including ways to promote capital investment abroad by Japanese institutional investors and ways for government-run financial institutions to expand their loan-extending cooperation to foreign countries. Later the same day, the ministry intervened in the market in Tokyo. The yen, which momentarily stood at about ¥87 to the dollar, fell briefly to ¥90.1 to the dollar on 2 August. After confirming the reversal in currency movements in the Tokyo market, Japan and the United States jointly intervened in the New York market to push up the exchange rate reversal. We injected an unprecedented amount of funds into the market to push the rate above ¥90 per dollar. On 15 August, the yen fell briefly to ¥99.5 per dollar on overseas markets with coordinated intervention by Japan, the United States, and Germany.

With the continuation of joint efforts to achieve "an orderly reversal" of misaligned currency levels—including foreign exchange interventions in September 1995 and February 1996 by Japanese authorities—the yen gradually dropped against the dollar and closed at ¥116.21 in Tokyo on 30 December 1996. The Japanese economy also began to recover beginning in the fourth quarter of 1995 thanks to an easing of monetary policy, introduction of the ¥14 trillion pump-priming package, and efforts to redress the yen's hyperappreciation. Real GDP growth was at 6.8 percent in the first quarter of calender 1996, in comparison with the same period of the previous year. Relatively high growth rates of 4.4, 4.4, and 4.8 percent (at annual rates) were recorded during the second, third, and fourth quarters, respectively. The shift of US policy and the resultant joint, cooperative efforts by the two countries—along with Japanese policy to stimulate domestic demand—paid off, although belatedly, in the brief recovery of fiscal 1995 and 1996.

Crisis Coordination and Japanese Financial Reform: January 1997-October 1998

The Japanese recovery in fiscal 1995 and 1996 was short-lived. Although the contraction during April-June 1997 had been anticipated because of substantial withdrawal of fiscal stimulus, amounting to close to 2 percent of GDP, the government and most analysts thought the turnaround would occur, at the latest, between October and December 1997. The advent of the international financial crisis in Asia during the summer of 1997 and the bankruptcy of three major financial institutions in November 1997 plunged Japan into an unprecedented financial crisis. GDP growth in fiscal 1997 became −0.7 percent, sending the economy back to a severer recession than had occurred in the 1992-94 period. In October, net selling of Japanese stocks by foreigners amounted to ¥591.4 billion and ballooned to ¥754.5 billion in November.

In late November, the Japanese premium on interbank lending reached 1 percent, and Japanese banks faced difficulties in procuring funds in international markets. US and European banks also gradually reduced their credit lines to Japanese banks. On the other hand, interest rates for procurement of yen funds by foreigners dropped to near zero and were negative in some cases. From this period on, hedge funds and others borrowed yen funds that carried almost no costs and operated the so-called global carry trade, in which they bought the dollar or currencies pegged to the dollar and gained profit margins from investing using yen funds.

It was clear that Japan had entered a financial crisis and had become the target of speculation by hedge funds and other institutions. Thanks to the desperate efforts of the government and political parties following the financial crisis in November, the revised Deposit Insurance Law and a law on emergency measures to stabilize financial functions were passed on 16 February 1998. In addition, ¥30 trillion in funds, including ¥13 trillion for dealing with the collapse of financial institutions, was made available. However, distrust in Japan's financial systems and in Japan itself deepened rather than eased.

Foreign trading of Japanese stocks recovered temporarily due to the two new laws, but selling outweighed buying again in March 1998. "Japan selling" weakened the yen and caused anxiety, because the yen's further depreciation could have resulted in a currency free fall and the beakdown of the Japanese economy. Large-scale market interventions were conducted on 9 and 10 April, coinciding with the announcement of a ¥4 trillion tax cut that temporarily boosted the yen's value to above the ¥130 level against the dollar. However, its effects were not felt for long. When net selling of foreigners' holdings of Japanese stocks reached ¥507.8 billion in June, the yen's value fell to over ¥140 per dollar.

The government's effort to intervene could not strengthen the yen, and the last remaining option concerned a combination of drastic measures to rescue the financial system and concerted intervention with foreign authorities to reverse the trend and prevent the yen from falling further. However, due to the government's schedule at the time (which included the closing of the Diet session and the House of Councillors elections in July), it had been impossible to immediately implement new, unconventional policies. The only option available was to combine policy commitments after the upper house election with intervention. However, I was uncertain whether we could assemble a package before the election that would be approved both by then-Prime Minister Ryutaro Hashimoto and leaders of the Liberal Democratic Party and Western countries, especially the United States. Although I lacked confidence, I had no choice but to try. Washington demanded clear plans to dispose of banks' bad loans and additional stimulus measures. However, Tokyo could not immediately present practical measures in line with the request.

As a result of the negotiations, we agreed by the evening of 16 June that Hashimoto would release a statement in which he would indicate his intention to implement new policy measures but refrain from citing specific steps. Meanwhile, we arranged telephone discussions between Hashimoto and Bill Clinton, and Summers and then-Assistant Secretary of the Treasury Timothy Geithner eventually agreed to concerted intervention. However, Rubin and Greenspan at the time opposed such intervention.

Later, Rubin recalled that his decision concerning intervention was one of the most difficult judgments he had made as US Treasury secretary. Late in the evening of 16 June, Rubin clearly told Clinton during a meeting at the White House that intervention alone would be ineffective, and returned to Summers' office to continue negotiations.

The negotiations continued into the next day. We agreed to a visit by Summers to Japan and to hold an emergency currency meeting between deputy G-7 finance ministers and the Manila Framework Group—deputy finance ministers and central bank governors from the Asia-Pacific region—on 20 June. After that, Rubin finally agreed to concerted intervention on 17 June at 10:30 a.m. After the negotiations, telephone talks between Hashimoto and Clinton took place at noon on 17 June, and that day Japan and the United States began joint interventions in New York. The yen soared by nearly ¥6 to ¥137.60 against the dollar that day in foreign markets.

As suspected by Rubin and others, the effects of joint intervention did not last long. In August, the yen started to weaken, again, toward the high of ¥140 per dollar. Ironically, what saved Japan and, perhaps, the rest of Asia, including Hong Kong and Australia, was the Russian crisis of 17 August. Indeed, the crisis spread to Brazil and other Latin American countries and finally to Wall Street in late August and September. However, it was also true that this new round of the crisis seriously crippled hedge funds and others, forcing them to unwind their speculative positions in Asia. The yen-dollar rate, for example, came down from ¥146 per dollar on 17 August to ¥134 on 17 September. Crises in Hong Kong, Australia, and Malaysia had subsided somewhat.

In September 1998, the US position on Japanese banking issues shifted dramatically as well. Up to this point, the US Treasury was emphasizing the liquidation of insolvent banks and expeditious downsizing and restructuring of viable banks. Their position was that the infusion of public money had to be strongly conditional on liquidation and restructuring. However, in September, in the midst of suffering from the Long-Term Capital Management problem themselves, the US authorities dramatically changed their stance and demanded that the Japanese government increase to more than ¥13 trillion the public funds it had already committed to be injected into troubled but viable banks, and that the funds be infused as quickly as possible.

It was evident that Washington was worried about the danger that a collapse of the Japanese financial system would spread to New York and accelerate the meltdown of Wall Street and the global economy. This shift of US policy was a boon to the Japanese government, because US ambivalence about the infusion of public money had been a big factor in making Japanese public opinion largely antagonistic toward such infusion. The Japanese government, at least partially because of this shift in US policy on Japan, was able to pass the controversial bill to create ¥60 trillion credit lines of public funds on 16 October 1998. This shift in US policy toward Japan to quickly quell the Japanese financial crisis was a part of efforts by the G-7 countries to overcome the crisis of global capitalism that hit the world, including the United States, in the fall of 1998.

In retrospect, the three phases of US policy toward Japan were at least partially responsible for major developments in the Japanese economy during the corresponding years. The contentious trade policy of 1993-94 seemed to be an important factor in delaying Japanese recovery by as much as a year or a year and a half. Macroeconomic and foreign exchange cooperation starting in early 1995 helped the economy to recover in early 1996. The shift of US policy during the fall of 1998 finally helped to resolve the difficult political issue of infusion of public money into the financial system. Of course, Japanese domestic policies during the period were more important than US policy toward Japan. However, it still remains a solid fact that US policy plays an important and crucial role not only in the Japanese economy but also in the economies of the rest of the world.

9

Discussions of the Monetary Response

Bubbles, Liquidity Traps, and Monetary Policy

OLIVIER BLANCHARD

Monetary policy has been rather boring in most OECD countries since the mid-1980s. This is largely the price of (earlier) success: Inflation started low, fluctuations in demand were limited, and steady-as-you-go policy turned out to be all that was required. Not so in Japan, where the central bank has had to confront two of the toughest issues of monetary policy: how to react to asset bubbles and their aftermath, and more recently what to do when interest rates have already been reduced to zero. The essay by Jinushi, Kuroki, and Miyao, which focuses on the past, forces us to revisit the first issue. The essay by Bernanke, which focuses on current policy, forces us to think about the second. Let me take each one in turn.

Bubbles and Monetary Policy

How monetary policy should react to bubbles is clearly of more than historical interest. We now have one and a half experiments, the Japanese one, and the US one on the way up. What remains to be played out is the US one on the way down. It is an understatement that this may not be a bad time to assess the lessons from the Japanese full experiment.

Olivier Blanchard is professor and chairman, Department of Economics, Massachusetts Institute of Technology.

Let me start by making the world much simpler than it is. Assume that the central bank knows there is a bubble in the stock market, and that the price of stocks exceeds fundamentals. In other words, ignore the fact—a fact painfully clear in current discussions of the US stock market—that, no matter what the level of the stock market, things are never that clear, at least ex-ante. (Ex-post, I do not know of an economist who argues that the stock market increase in Japan in the late 1980s reflected fundamentals.) I shall return to this issue below. Assume also that bubbles eventually come to an end, and prices return to fundamentals, often abruptly.

The question is then: What should the central bank do? Let me go at it step by step.

In an important and influential paper, Bernanke and Gertler (1999) made the following argument: If the central bank is conducting the right monetary policy, then the existence of a bubble should not lead it to change the way it conducts policy. More specifically, they argued, if monetary policy is aimed at inflation targeting, such a policy will deliver the best outcome, bubble or no bubble.

The intuition underlying their argument is simple and powerful—and, indeed, reflects the attractiveness of inflation targeting as a monetary policy rule: Maintaining inflation, current and expected, at a constant level is in effect the same as maintaining output at its natural level. So, if the bubble leads to an increase in demand, and this in turn leads to an increase in output above its natural level, inflation will increase, leading the central bank to tighten policy—exactly what it should do under the circumstances. If instead the bubble leaves demand unaffected, then monetary policy will be unchanged—again, exactly what it should be under the circumstances.

This is an attractive answer. It is surely an attractive answer from the viewpoint of the central bank: Having to respond to bubbles is likely to be unpopular with financial investors. Much better to be able to say that the central bank only concentrates on inflation. It may also be the best first-pass answer: One can think of many worse policies, including perhaps that pursued in Japan in the late 1980s (again, more on this below). Yet, it may not be the best answer, for at least two reasons.

The first reason is composition effects. Suppose that the bubble affects some components of spending more than others. To be more concrete, suppose that the bubble leads to an increase in investment in publicly held firms, relative to the rest of aggregate spending. Is this a reasonable assumption? I think so. Let me elaborate a bit.

The question of what firms should do when they perceive that their stock is overvalued is a difficult one. (See Blanchard, Rhee, and Summers 1993 for a discussion and some empirical evidence.) One answer is that firms should issue shares and use the proceeds not for capital accumulation (which drives down the marginal profit rate) but rather to buy assets such as government bonds. However, such behavior by firms is likely to put the financial investors on edge, and prick the bubble. So firms may well increase investment beyond what is justified by fundamentals when there is a bubble. The empirical evidence suggests that this is indeed what typically happens.

This is only half of the argument. Even if investment goes up, consumption may go up as well. Consumers' wealth is higher, and it is reasonable for consumers to want to increase consumption. As I read it, the evidence is that the increase in the stock market in the United States in the 1990s indeed boosted consumption given income, but not quite by as much as traditional estimates of wealth effects might have suggested. So let me proceed on the assumption that investment is more affected by the bubble than the rest of spending. Indeed, for simplicity, let me assume that only investment is directly affected by the bubble. And to remove the ambiguity always present in words, let me use (very simple) algebra here. Let the equilibrium condition in the goods market be given by

$$y = i(r,b) + c(r). \tag{1}$$

The right-hand side gives the demand for goods, which is the sum of investment i, itself a function of the interest rate, r, and the bubble, b, and noninvestment (everything else, but call it consumption for simplicity), c, which is only a function of the interest rate r. It would change nothing but also add nothing to include output as a determinant of both i and c. The left-hand side is output. The equilibrium condition is that output equals demand.

In response to the bubble, the central bank can then pursue one of two policies (or a policy in between). It can target inflation or, equivalently, try to achieve constant output, constant y, by increasing the interest rate in the face of the bubble. But such a policy clearly comes with a change in the composition of output. Output, y, may be constant. But investment, i, is higher, and by implication consumption, c, is lower. In other words, on the way up, the bubble leads to excessive capital accumulation.

It can instead target investment, making sure that there is no excessive capital accumulation. This implies increasing the interest rate so i, not y, remains constant. This policy is clearly more aggressive than the first, and generates a recession: Investment is the same, but because of high interest rates consumption is lower, and so are demand and output.

Which strategy should the central bank pursue? The first strategy is the one recommended by Bernanke and Gertler (1999). It keeps output stable as the bubble grows. But it may imply a very unpleasant aftermath once the bubble has crashed—a lot of useless capital, serious collateral problems for firms, and thus a potentially low natural level of output for some time after the crash (the higher capital stock, and the collateral problems, work in opposite directions here).[1] The second strategy targeting investment avoids this problem. But it does so at the expense of tighter monetary policy and thus lower output as the bubble grows.

Admittedly, the choice facing the central bank is not pleasant. But this is not the point. The point is that the right strategy is likely to be somewhere in between the two pure strategies, that is, to tighten money more in the presence of a bubble than is implied by inflation targeting.

The reason the central bank faces an unpleasant choice is a very standard one: It has one instrument, namely r, in the presence of two targets, y and i. This characterization of the choice may be too stark, for at least two reasons.

First, there is at least one other instrument at the government's disposal: fiscal policy. Together, loose fiscal policy and tight money can achieve the desired outcome. The need for the combined use of the two instruments is a recurrent theme in macroeconomic textbooks, even if it has taken a back seat in current policy discussions.

Second, the discussion takes as given that the bubble b has a life of its own, independent of the stance of monetary policy. But this is surely wrong. Bubbles, by definition, are not based on fundamentals, but on animal spirits. And there are good reasons to believe that the stance of monetary policy can excite or dampen these spirits.

If Alan Greenspan stated that a reasonable level for the Dow Jones was 8,000, and that he was willing to move the interest rate so as to get there, few of us doubt the stock market would tumble down, even in the absence of any change in the interest rate. (This is not a recommendation to the Federal Reserve, for reasons to be discussed below.)

This suggests that his announcement of a policy that bubbles will be dealt with harshly might prevent the emergence of such bubbles in the first place. If this were truly the case, then the central bank, by announcing a differential response to inflation and to bubbles, could achieve both of its goals: an output level equal to the natural level and no bubble (and, by implication, no distortion). This is surely too optimistic a view. But it suggests that announcing that monetary policy will react to bubbles may have substantial benefits and few costs.

It is important to note at this point that the two arguments I have presented are not about "pricking bubbles" but about preventing their emergence. An analogy to inflation and inflation targeting is relevant here. Reducing inflation when it is high is difficult and painful. This is not what inflation targeting is about; inflation targeting is a way of avoiding high inflation in the first place. Similarly, pricking a large bubble is difficult—and surely much more uncertain than reducing inflation. This

1. A very nice discussion of what may happen in general, and of what happened in Japan after the crash, is given by Flemming (1999).

is why announcing today that the right value for the Dow Jones is 8,000 would be a highly dangerous move. Just as for inflation, this is not what is proposed here. What is proposed is a policy designed, if not to prevent bubbles, at least to prevent them from becoming too big.

This last argument, however, takes us back to the initial assumption—that bubbles are easily identifiable. In fact, bubbles are hard to identify, even when they have gone on for a while and appear very large. This is a fortiori true when they are younger and smaller. So how can the advice above be translated in a world where the central bank never knows for sure whether fundamentals or nonfundamentals are at work? Quite simply, I think it translates into an additional term in the Taylor rule.

Write the standard Taylor rule as

$$(r_i - r_n) = \alpha_\pi(\pi - \pi^*) + \alpha_y(y - y^*), \tag{2}$$

where r is the real interest rate, and r_n is the natural interest rate (the rate of interest consistent with output being at the natural level), π and π^* are actual and target inflation, and y and y^* are the actual and natural levels of output. The discussion above suggests introducing an additional term $\alpha(P/E) - (P/E)^*$, namely, the deviation of the price-earnings ratio from what can be called the natural price-earnings ratio, on the basis of expectations about the growth of earnings and the required rate of return on equity. Other things being equal, if the P/E ratio is too high, the central bank should increase the real interest rate; if it is too low, the bank should decrease the rate.

One natural objection at this point is that the central bank knows little about the "natural P/E ratio." The point is well taken, but it applies to at least two other components of the Taylor rule: How much does the central bank know about the natural interest rate, and about the natural level of output? The issue of having to know the right natural interest rate is typically finessed by replacing r_n by a constant in the specification of the rule. But this is not satisfactory. A rule aimed at the wrong natural rate could be very bad for the economy in the long run. And, in Europe or in Japan today, reasonable estimates of the natural level of output cover a wide range of output values. In other words, constructing an estimate of P/E^* based on the long-run warranted rate of growth of earnings and an estimate of the required rate of return on stocks is no different from constructing estimates of r_n^* or y^*. In this sense, the subliminal message sent by the apparent simplicity of the Taylor rule is misleading: Monetary policy is not so easy.

In much of this discussion, I obviously had the current stock market boom in the United States in mind. But, on the basis of this discussion, let me now return to Japan. Here, the essay by Jinushi, Kuroki, and Miyao delivers a clear message, and one that I very much believe. The arguments I have developed imply that monetary policy should have been tighter than implied by inflation targeting on the upside of the bubble, more expansionary on the downside. The evidence is that the opposite happened. Jinushi and colleagues show that there was a "delay in restraint" in 1987-88, and "insufficient restraint" in 1990, and then "delay in easing" from 1992-95. (This confirms the empirical results in Bernanke and Gertler 1999.) This will not come as a great surprise; Japanese monetary policy made the bubble and its aftermath worse than they could have been. Unfortunately, one cannot rule out the possibility that the outcome will turn out to be similar in the United States.

Liquidity Traps and Monetary Policy

Turning to current Japanese monetary policy, I find myself very much in agreement with the arguments presented by Bernanke in his essay for this volume. Even at zero short-term interest rates, there is plenty that monetary policy can and should do. Let me develop four points in turn.

One of the major macroeconomic issues in Japan is how much of the poor performance in the 1990s was the result of a decrease in the natural level of output (due to the poor state of financial intermediation, etc.), and how much to a deviation of output below this natural level.

I fully agree with Bernanke that the old method of looking at what is happening to inflation is still the right way to proceed, at least as a first pass. The Phillips curve wisdom remains largely true in modern treatments of the determination of prices, wages, and output: If output is above its natural level, then we are likely to see inflation increase. If it is below, inflation is likely to decrease. As inflation is slowly decreasing today in Japan, this strongly suggests that output is below its natural level.

One caveat is in order here. Part of the lore of macroeconomics is the story of how the increase in inflation in the 1970s changed the Phillips curve relation from one between the unemployment rate (or equivalently, and more relevant in the case of Japan, the output gap) and the level of the inflation rate to one between the unemployment rate and the change in the inflation rate. In Japan and elsewhere, we may now be seeing the same process in reverse. Low and fairly stable inflation may well be shifting the way people form expectations of inflation, and shifting the relation back to one between the output gap and the level of the inflation rate. Put another way, low inflation rather than declining inflation may in the current context be the signal that output is too low.

I also fully agree with the point first made by Krugman (1999), and developed by Bernanke, that, even with zero nominal interest rates, monetary policy can still affect long real rates, and thus aggregate demand and output.

Let me use a bit of algebra here. If we look at an economy in which nominal rates are approximately equal to zero, the expectations hypothesis implies that the T-year nominal interest rate (yield to maturity on a T-period coupon bond) is approximately equal to the unweighted average of current and future 1-year rates:

$$i_T \approx \frac{1}{T}\left[\sum_{1}^{T} i_{1t}^e\right], \quad (3)$$

where i_T is the T-year nominal rate, and i_1 is the 1-year nominal rate. By implication, the T-year real interest rate, r_T is given by

$$r_T \approx \frac{1}{T}\left[\sum_{1}^{T} i_{1t}^e - (\log p_T^e - \log P_0)\right], \quad (4)$$

where P_0 is the price level today, and p_T^e is the price level expected T years from now. This relation implies that, for a given sequence of expected nominal interest rates, an increase in p_T^e translates $1/T$ for 1 in a decrease in the long real rate today.

So suppose the central bank wants to decrease the 10-year real rate by, say, 200 basis points. All that is needed is for it to convince markets that the price level 10 years from now will be higher by 20 percent. Equivalently—if we take for granted that, eventually, changes in money translate into proportional changes in the price level—all that is needed is for it to convince markets that money growth will be cumulatively higher over the next 10 years by 20 percent.

How does it achieve this change in expectations? In this context, many economists have advocated the use of inflation targeting by the Bank of Japan. If initial expectations are that inflation is likely to run at 0 percent on average for the foreseeable future, the announcement that the Japanese central bank is targeting an inflation rate of 2 percent a year for the next 10 years should in principle be enough to decrease the long-term real rate today by 2 percent. In practice, however, financial markets tend to believe deeds more than words. Thus, an alternative strategy may be to increase the stock of high-powered money today by, say, 20 percent, and commit not to reverse the increase in the future. Given the initial increase, the commitment not to reverse may be more credible than just an inflation target.

This use of monetary policy has often been presented as rather exotic, perhaps too exotic to be relied on. Krugman's (1999) "responsible irresponsibility" presentation of the case as the need for the BOJ to engineer more inflation, while conceptually right, may have been counterproductive here. In fact, this use of monetary policy is far from exotic. Indeed, one can argue that monetary policy works mostly—entirely?—through its effects on expectations.

If, when the federal funds rate changed in the United States, financial markets did not expect this change to last for some time, the change would barely affect the term structure of interest rates. It is only because financial markets expect the change in the federal funds rate to last for some time—or even, as is typically the case these days in the United States, to signal further changes to come—that the term structure is so strongly affected by monetary policy. Expectations are crucial. The only thing specific to Japan today is that the emphasis is not on changes in future expected nominal interest rates, but on the expected future price level. This is not an essential difference.

A very similar argument applies to the effect of monetary policy on the current nominal—and by implication on the current real—exchange rate.

Again, let me start with some basic algebra. Assuming the interest parity condition holds, solving it forward gives

$$e = \left[\frac{(1 + i_T^*)^T}{(1 + i_T)^T}\right] e_T^e, \tag{5}$$

where i_T is the T-period domestic nominal interest rate, i_T^* is the T-period foreign nominal interest rate, e is the nominal exchange rate, and e_T^e is the nominal exchange rate expected to prevail T years from now. The nominal exchange rate today depends on the T-year domestic and foreign rates, and on the nominal exchange rate expected 10 years from now.

Much of the focus has been on the implied relation between domestic nominal interest rates and the nominal exchange rate. The traditional way to engineer a depreciation and thus to increase demand and output is to decrease the domestic interest rate, leading to an increase in e, and thus to depreciation today. This is the channel that is not available to Japan at this stage: The BOJ has decreased i_T roughly as far it can go.

This does not mean that monetary policy cannot affect the exchange rate. To see why, one needs to shift the focus to the relation between the exchange rate today and the exchange rate expected T years from now. Note the implication of the above relation: Given domestic and foreign interest rates, a change of x percent in the expected exchange rate T years from now will be reflected, no matter what the path of interest rates, and no matter what T is, in a change of x percent of the nominal exchange rate today.

If we believe that relative purchasing power parity holds in the long run (i.e., if we believe that, for T large enough, the nominal exchange rate eventually reflects changes in the price level), then all the central bank has to do is to convince markets that the price level will be higher than they anticipated. If it can convince markets that the price level 10 years from now will be 20 percent higher than they expected, then the yen will depreciate today by 20 percent. How does it do that? This leads us back to the previous discussion, and to the same answer: This is probably best achieved through a combination of inflation targeting and a current large increase in the stock of high-powered money.

There is one interesting difference between the long-term real rate and the exchange rate channels, however. In an economy without indexed bonds, the decrease in real interest rates will not be directly visible. But the decrease in the nominal exchange rate will. This will allow both the central bank and financial markets to assess the credibility of the new policy, and help them assess in the future.

One last point. I have a much less positive view of measures aimed at changing relative interest rates (say, rates on corporate bonds relative to government bonds) through changes in their relative supply. If done through open market operations, in which the central bank buys, say, commercial paper rather than government bonds, the amounts are likely to be much too small to make any significant difference. The ratio of high-powered money to GDP in Japan is about 12 percent. Thus even a change of 20 percent of high-powered money represents a change equal to only 2.4 percent of GDP. With a ratio of government bonds to GDP approaching 100 percent in Japan, whether the increase in money is used to buy short- or long-term government bonds is unlikely to make much difference to their relative equilibrium rates of return. To make a difference would imply either letting the central bank be very long in some securities and very short in others, or letting the money supply change by truly enormous magnitudes. Such a policy is neither desirable nor necessary.

References

Bernanke, B., and M. Gertler. 1999. Monetary Policy and Asset Volatility. In *Symposium Proceedings: New Challenges for Monetary Policy*, 77-128. Kansas City: Federal Reserve Bank of Kansas City.

Blanchard, O., C. Rhee, and L. Summers. 1993. The Stock Market, Profit and Investment. *Quarterly Journal of Economics* 108, no. 1: 115-36.

Flemming, J. 1999. Policy for a Post-Bubble Economy: Lessons from and for Japan. Photocopy. London: European Bank for Reconstruction and Development.

Krugman, Paul. 1999. It's Baaack: Japan's Slump and the Return of the Liquidity Trap. *Brookings Papers on Economic Activity* 2: 137-205. Washington: Brookings Institution.

The Political Economy of Deflationary Monetary Policy

ADAM S. POSEN

For the past 20 years, both academic and practical discussions of monetary policy mostly have been about how to keep central banks from allowing *too much* inflation. Modern theoretical approaches to monetary policy emphasize the time-inconsistency problem for central banks—because central banks get a short-term real output gain from surprise inflation, commitments to low inflation will not be believed by the public, and thus inflation expectations will rise. Recent empirical academic studies of central bank independence, exchange rate pegging, inflation targeting, and simulated "policy rules" all have stressed the importance of different central bank strategies and institutional arrangements in explaining cross-national variation in average inflation levels.

In the realm of practice, developing-country central banks have spent much of the past two decades in the IMF-advised pursuit of monetary stabilization, while central banks in the industrial democracies have been consolidating their long and costly victories over the relatively high inflation that began in the 1970s. In the end, stabilizing inflation expectations at low levels in the OECD countries proved a little easier than the theoretical literature might have led one to expect, but getting central banks to keep down inflation and inflation expectations was still seen as the hard part of monetary policy.

Then one comes to the Bank of Japan (BOJ) in the past decade. Suddenly, the problem is not keeping inflation from rising, but how to keep the price level from falling; suddenly, the responsible academic and practicing monetary economists are not criticizing a central bank for being too lax with regard to inflation, but for being too tough. And as the essays in this volume by Jinushi, Kuroki, and Miyao and by Bernanke make clear—as do a host of other recent publications, including Bernanke and Gertler (1999), Krugman (1999), Posen (1998b), and Svensson (1999)—the BOJ by all recognized standards has been too tough on inflation, and on the Japanese economy, during this period.

Adam S. Posen is a senior fellow at the Institute for International Economics.

Prices have been falling for 3 years, and are continuing to fall on most measures, while unemployment is rising, and both growth and the yen-dollar exchange rate have been allowed to languish at unfortunate levels (the first too low, and the second too high). This is the paradigmatic case for looser monetary policy, when growth is below potential, and labor and capital are underemployed, in part because prices are falling. Except for a couple of quarters in Switzerland in the 1980s and Canada in the 1990s, both of which met rapid responses by their central banks, no other industrial democracy has allowed deflation to occur since the Great Depression.

The interesting question is one of political economy: Why? Why is the BOJ pursuing this deflationary policy when everything would lead us to expect that a central bank would want to (at a minimum) stabilize the price level? Why is the BOJ able to get away with such a policy politically when the bulk of political economy research on monetary economics in the past 20 years has been about how difficult it is for central banks to oppose calls for inflation?

In their essays in this volume, Bernanke and Blanchard both make it quite clear that the BOJ, or for that matter any central bank, can create inflation if it wants to do so (an idea that history should have made an easy sell to objective observers). In their essay, Jinushi, Kuroki, and Miyao demonstrate that at one time the BOJ was reasonably typical of OECD central banks in its behavior, taking both output and inflation goals into account (if, to a salutary degree, a little above average in its opposition to inflation). In his essay, Shafer, to my mind, convincingly rebuts the claims in this volume of Sakakibara that Japanese monetary policy was determined by US mercantile and political pressures through the exchange rate.

So why is the BOJ refusing to reflate the Japanese economy, and in fact raising interest rates in the absence of inflationary pressures?[1] The officials of the BOJ have offered several reasons, as have the authors of the essays in this volume, and I will now review them. The existence of such a very large number of explanations for a clear and consistent policy strategy is itself an indicator that the actual motivation is not evident, and that the supposed reasons offered are not terribly convincing.

Economic Excuses

The first category of reasons to consider for the BOJ's willing acceptance of deflation is the purely economic, that is, reasons based on arguments that the BOJ is optimizing a reasonable objective function over macroeco-

1. On 11 August 2000, the BOJ's policy board voted to raise the overnight money market rate from 0 to 0.25 percent. This was the first time in 10 years that the BOJ raised interest rates.

nomic variables, but that external constraints limit it. A first reason is the BOJ's repeated claims that it is bound by its mandate for "price stability" to keep inflation at bay at (almost) all costs. As pointed out in Posen (1999), no postwar central bank has treated any similar mandate as literally binding them to a policy of zero-measured inflation.

In fact, the two arguably most successful central banks of the post-Bretton Woods era, the Deutsche Bundesbank and the Swiss National Bank, explicitly targeted 2 percent measured inflation as their long-term goal consistent with practical price stability, and flexibly altered this goal in the face of difficult shocks.[2] Certainly, as Jinushi, Kuroki, and Miyao demonstrate, in keeping with the earlier work of Ueda (1997) and Cargill, Hutchison, and Ito (1997), the Japanese economy had both better overall performance and—for all practical purposes—price stability when the BOJ took its mandate a little less literally.

The remaining economic explanations must rely on claims that something has changed in Japan during the past decade to justify the BOJ's policy stance. It is therefore worth stressing just how striking is the evidence of a large shift in Japanese central bank behavior, whatever the surrounding conditions. The results of Jinushi, Kuroki, and Miyao's research—that the BOJ became much more "conservative in the 1990s" (in the sense of Rogoff 1985), putting a far greater weight on inflation relative to output goals—are extremely robust. The authors use the two different methods that are standard in the literature for assessing a central bank's behavior: estimating a Taylor-rule central bank policy reaction function on output and inflation, testing for structural breaks in the relative weights on the goals[3]; analyzing narrative accounts from the central bank's own statements, and searching for the coincidence of shifts in the narrative with structural break(s) in the time-series behavior of monetary and macroeconomic aggregates. Both give clear indications of a shift toward counterinflationary conservatism in 1987. Bernanke and Gertler (2000) and Kuttner and Posen (2000), using similar but not identical methods, independently come up with the same break point in BOJ behavior, showing a shift toward greater conservatism.

Of course, such a large shift in central bank behavior itself influences the economy, however much it may be a reaction to prevailing economic conditions. In making monetary policy decisions, the placing of such a high relative weight on current inflation levels at the expense of real output predictably has led to greater output and exchange rate volatility

---

2. See Bernanke et al. (1999, chaps. 2-4), for an extended discussion of why central banks should not target zero inflation, and how the German and Swiss central banks anchored inflation expectations even with above-zero inflation targets.

3. I say two methods because I do not believe that there is any meaningful difference between the authors' first exercise of estimating a Taylor rule, strictly speaking, and their third of fitting a Svensson (1997) policy rule to time-series data.

in Japan, as well as to very sticky deflationary expectations.[4] It is this feedback of tight monetary policy upon the economy that gives the lie to the BOJ's claim that its motivation for the so-called zero interest rate policy (ZIRP) was that it wanted to reflate the economy, but could do no more.

The ZIRP was defined as keeping the nominal overnight money market rate at zero, starting in February 1999, until "deflationary concerns subside."[5] For more than a year, the BOJ contended that such a policy represented the limit of possibility for looser monetary policy, even if they wanted to go looser. This argument was formalized at length in the working paper by Okina (1999), which Bernanke addresses in his essay, and which was strongly promoted by the BOJ in interactions with English-speaking economists. It later gave way to alternative justifications for the lack of monetary policy response to deflation, which I discuss below.

The problem with this argument by the BOJ is not just its economic absurdity, including conflating real and nominal interest rates, ignoring all nonbank channels of monetary policy transmission (such as the exchange rate), and asserting completely inert inflation expectations in Japan—all of which Bernanke and Blanchard amply make clear. The problem is also that the monetary policy pursued was itself having a predictable (and publicly predicted) deflationary, destabilizing effect on the economy. Contrary to its self-portrayal, the BOJ's policy was not neutral or at its limit, and the Japanese economy was not going its own bad way despite monetary efforts. In fact, as mentioned above, the deflation and real volatility were exactly what any monetary economist would have predicted to be the result of pursuing tight monetary policy at zero or negative inflation in an advanced economy.

It is on this point that I believe Jinushi, Kuroki, and Miyao go astray. In their "Interpretations" section, they ascribe the current problems to both a structural shift in the Japanese Phillips curve and the aforementioned increase in BOJ conservatism. Because they believe that part of the deflationary problem is due to the economic situation itself, they give the BOJ a bit of an out. In their conclusions, this contributes to their skepticism about the wisdom of the BOJ adopting an inflation target under the present circumstances. Yet the worsening of the inflation-output trade-off at single-digit inflation levels is a well-known, well-established regularity. There is also good reason to believe that counterinflationary conservatism

4. Such a limiting case of central bank conservatism is what King (1997) has called the "Inflation Nutter," not expecting any real world central bank to approximate this strategy.

5. See, e.g., Yamaguchi (2000): "Then, in April 1999, the Bank decided to continue the zero interest rate policy until such time that it could be ascertained deflationary concern had been dispelled."

increases the sacrifice ratio of a rise in unemployment for a given drop in inflation.[6]

In short, the flattening of the Japanese Phillips curve in the late 1990s that Jinushi, Kuroki, and Miyao find, along with all the attendant ills of volatility and misery, are directly due to the BOJ—it was the BOJ that knowingly allowed inflation to go below 2 percent in the first place, that kept inflation there, and that had to have known it was increasing the real costs of trying to establish its counterinflationary credibility by keeping inflation there. It was not a condition that the BOJ policy board came upon, forcing a reoptimization, from which a tighter policy resulted ex machina.

Some Japanese observers, as well as the BOJ, have attributed part of recent Japanese deflation to structural shifts in the economy brought on by deregulation and recession-induced restructuring[7] (as opposed to just debt deflation, aggregate demand deficiency, and poor monetary policy, which would seem sufficient cause). Even if such salutary developments were to account for a significant portion of the ongoing deflation, which seems doubtful, they would be *increasing* price and wage flexibility in the Japanese economy, and therefore *steepening* the Japanese Phillips curve (i.e., reducing the sacrifice ratio). That could not bring about the structural shift in the other direction that Jinushi, Kuroki, and Miyao find in their econometric investigations, and that would justify a shift toward tighter policy.

A more sophisticated version of the BOJ-cannot-do-more-than-ZIRP argument emerged in 2000, when the bank found the claims of literal impossibility to loosen were met with incredulity by much of the economics profession (in part following the wide citation of the prepublication version of Bernanke's essay in this volume). This "practical impossibility" view asserted that, although the BOJ or any central bank of course can always engage in expansionary policy, no matter what the condition of the banking system or the level of nominal interest rates, actually to do so would be extremely risky.[8]

---

6. See Ball (1994), Debelle and Fischer (1994), Akerlof, Dickens, and Perry (1996), and Posen (1998a) for evidence and discussions of why this is the case.

7. BOJ Deputy Governor Yukata Yamaguchi (2000) states: "The current decline in the CPI is partly attributable to such structural changes as those in the distribution system in addition to the appreciation of the yen and the falling prices of consumer durables." As reported in July 2000, "consumer prices in Japan are currently falling at the fastest rate in the last decade. . . . Central bank policy board members argue that much of this is 'good deflation,' but they have yet to produce convincing evidence" (Stephanie Strom, "Convalescing, Japan Debates A Rate Rise," *New York Times*, 5 July 2000, A1).

8. In the words of BOJ board member Kazuo Ueda (1999), "Hence, suggestions have been made to go beyond traditional tools of operations. The list is very long: long-term government bonds, stocks, consumer durables, real estate, foreign exchanges [sic], and so on. . . . Whether central banks can systematically affect the prices of these assets is an old question to which no one has a satisfactory answer. . . . [O]utright purchases of nontraditional assets . . .

It is no doubt true that the BOJ at present would not be able to move inflation as predictably as in the precrisis era because its primary instrument (the nominal overnight interest rate) was at its lower bound, the normal bank channel of monetary transmission was disrupted by financial fragility, and the economy was in such bad shape. Indeed, the BOJ would have to rely on large open-market operations in the Japanese Government Bond (JGB) market and in the foreign exchange market (unsterilized), or on buying large amounts of nonstandard assets for central banks (e.g., private-sector obligations or real estate). And it would be difficult to predict what the necessary size and lags of such purchases would need to be to have the desired effect.

But so what? Just because a policy is difficult to implement precisely does not mean that it carries enormous risks beyond inexactitude, or that it cannot be the best of available alternatives. Remember, doing nothing is not a neutral option for the BOJ—by seemingly sitting tight at the supposed practical limit of ZIRP, the bank is actually choosing to impose deflation, financial uncertainty, and output volatility on the Japanese economy.

Monetary policy often has to be made when there is great uncertainty about the transmission mechanism, and all one can know with confidence is the direction in which one wants policy to move price and credit conditions. This certainly was the case repeatedly in the United States when, in the 1980s, the Federal Reserve had to cope with financial deregulation and the breakdown of stable monetary aggregate relationships and, in the 1990s, the Fed had to deal with structural change that was initially undetectable and always impossible to observe directly. Meanwhile, central bankers in emerging-market economies facing the ongoing conditions of thin markets, frequent shocks, threat of capital flight, forecasting difficulties, and continuous structural change are still required to make policy decisions on a regular basis.

As for the risks of the BOJ pursuing "nonstandard" operations, they cannot be specified because they are difficult to imagine on a purely economic basis. Bernanke, Blanchard, and Kashyap make clear in this volume that practical matters—such as the BOJ's balance sheet and capital position, the taboos on purchasing JGBs, the need to coordinate with the Ministry of Finance on foreign exchange intervention, and the potential for "beggar thy neighbor" effects from a yen devaluation—are all essentially trivial and can be dealt with if the BOJ has the will to do so. And these

generate various types of costs for the central bank and for the economy, some of which we may not be aware of and most of which are not explicitly dealt with in formal models economists use. These costs certainly ought to be weighed against possible benefits of the operations before any decision is made. I hope we will not be the one to make such a risky decision."

are the concerns that BOJ officials raise in discussions with monetary economists, including central bankers, around the world.

Yet the most senior officials at the Bank have engaged in nothing short of scaremongering to the general public and to markets that looser monetary policy could have disastrous consequences. In a December 1999 interview with the *Financial Times*, Masaru Hayami, governor of the BOJ, "warned that setting a target for inflation in an attempt to increase private demand was a dangerous policy that 'could cause uncontrollable inflation.' "[9] Later public statements by Hayami and by Deputy Governor Yamaguchi surrounding the interest rate hike of 10 August 2000 were a bit more restrained, but nonetheless forcefully asserted that a preemptive interest rate *increase* was all that stood between Japan and at least a partial repeat of the 1980s' asset price bubble, if not accelerating inflation:

> Officials from BOJ Governor Masaru Hayami on down began explaining that a slight increase in interest rates wouldn't amount to a monetary tightening. . . . They argued that if the BOJ didn't fine-tune interest rates preemptively, the central bank might be forced to sharply jack up interest rates if economic activity and prices shot up later.[10]

> We often hear the argument that monetary policy should be changed only when the risk of inflation becomes evident. . . . As a matter of fact, in the bubble period of the late 1980s, the conduct of monetary policy was based on this argument . . . what are the lessons learned from the experience of the late 1980s in today's context? . . . First, the policy change in response to a clear and present risk of inflation would inevitably be monetary tightening, and, moreover, cumulative interest rate hikes would probably be needed as was the case in 1989 and 1990. . . . Second, if the zero interest rate policy continues for a long period even after the economy clearly recovers, more economic agents will tend to conduct activities based on the expectation that current extremely low interest rates will be sustained indefinitely. This is what happened in the bubble period, leading to an enormous waste of resources which continues to inflict pain on us today.[11]

The characterization of the current economic situation presented to the Japanese public and financial markets by the BOJ's leadership is one in which any signs of recovery not offset by contractionary monetary policy would lead to spiraling price expectations.[12]

---

9. Quoted in "Japanese Business Turns Positive," *Financial Times*, 10 December 1999. http://www.ft.com.

10. Kenneth McCallum, "BOJ Watch: Some Analysts Expect Next Rate Hike in Jan-Mar," Dow Jones Newswires Column, 24 August 2000.

11. Yamaguchi (2000).

12. This claim comes despite Yamaguchi, e.g., admitting just two paragraphs earlier in the speech cited above that "the BoJ has recently stated that Japan's economy is coming to a stage where the condition for lifting the zero interest rate policy is being met. However, *since there are no inflationary risks* [emphasis added], some argue that the termination of the zero interest rate policy is unnecessary. . . ."

These assertions are directly contradicted by all the available econometric evidence on inflation dynamics, as well as the experience of preemptive monetary policy around the world. Several cross-national studies have demonstrated that inflation is a very inertial process at low (below 20 percent per year) levels, and only becomes more persistent as the rate of change in prices approaches zero.[13] In other words, there is no precedent for an advanced country to go from 3 years of deflation to an annual inflation rate even in the high single digits without an extended period of economic boom in between—and presumably, such a noticeable boom period would allow plenty of time for monetary policy to respond as required.

The idea of a speculative asset price boom in Japan within the foreseeable future is laughable, given the factors of debt and land overhang, the changing regulatory environment, and structural change discussed in the essays by Mikitani, Shimizu, and Kashyap in this volume. Who would buy, especially in an environment where the BOJ has led a loud chorus of Japanese government officials using their authority to bemoan the economy's purportedly declining potential growth rate and the vast overcapacity of capital waiting to be junked rather than used?[14] To argue with some merit that loose monetary policy contributed to the Japanese bubble of the late 1980s is not the same as proving that loose monetary policy is sufficient to generate an asset price boom irrespective of the recent past, current balance sheets, or perceived prospects.

This is why we have to look beyond the realm of economics for an explanation, let alone justification, of why the BOJ has pursued the policies it has in the past decade. On the economic arguments: The BOJ's ZIRP, and later increase in interest rates, do not constitute in any way a loose monetary policy, once real interest rates and credit conditions are considered; the BOJ has many options for how it could further loosen policy; the difficulties presented by these nonstandard open-market operations (in scale or in assets purchased) are not only surmountable, but not all that different from those confronting most of the world's central banks on a recurring basis; any structural changes contributing to deflation are either induced by the Bank's policy or are best accompanied by an expansive policy; and the risks of a policy-induced rise in inflation leading to spiraling inflation expectations or an asset price bubble are essentially zero in present-day Japan, which is beset by deflation and lack of confidence. Finally, as is nearly universally acknowledged by macroeconomists, the direct costs to the real economy of low positive rates of inflation are

13. See Dornbusch and Fischer (1993), Fuhrer (1995), and Sarel (1996) for examples of this evidence and summaries of the literature on the dynamics of inflation based on cross-national panels.

14. E.g., Hayami (2000) makes both of these claims in some detail.

small,[15] whereas the costs and risks from deflation are demonstrably much larger. This distance from accepted best practice for central banks is also why the BOJ's recent behavior stands out as so divergent from its past good practice in the 1970s and 1980s (in Jinushi, Kuroki, and Miyao's analysis), and from Bernanke's basic arbitrage logic of what works.

Political Explanations

By "political explanations," I mean those reasons that have to do with pressure on the BOJ to change its policy preferences from those considerations that could be satisfied by a standard utility-maximizing model of central bank behavior taking inflation, output, and observable macroeconomic constraints into account. These can be institutional factors, such as the relationship between the central bank and the finance ministry; they can be international factors, such as the pressures from the US government on Japanese policymakers to which Sakakibara gives great pride of place as an explanation for BOJ behavior; and they can be ideological factors, imposed on the ostensibly technocratic decisions of the central bank by its own leadership.

I will argue here that the pattern of policies pursued by the BOJ since the bubble, and especially its reluctance to loosen policy in recent years (as documented by Jinushi, Kuroki, and Miyao), are best explained by ideological factors. In this sense, I agree halfway with the assessment in Bernanke's title: Japanese monetary policies from 1992 to the present were "self-induced," but given their intent and their effect on the economy, they were hardly an instance of "paralysis."

In fact, since undertaking the ZIRP in February 1999, and perhaps since gaining independence from the Ministry of Finance in April 1998, the BOJ has taken great pains to give the public the impression that it has pursued an activist policy. Ueda (1999) characterized the ZIRP by saying: "This was already a very extreme monetary policy stance, and we had gone to the extreme using a traditional tool, i.e., the overnight rate. I must say that we needed a lot of courage to go to the zero rate." Yamaguchi (2000) took much the same line, declaring: "To avoid such a [deflationary] situation, in February 1999 the Bank adopted the zero interest rate policy, which was a drastic monetary easing measure." In describing the rate

---

15. Both Barro (1995) and Sarel (1996) find in their international datasets that the real GDP costs of inflation are statistically indistinguishable from zero at annual rates below 12 and 8 percent, respectively, and do not rise to any economically meaningful amount until at least 20 percent (about where inflation's persistence erodes and accelerating inflationary spirals become possible).

hike ending the ZIRP, Hayami was quoted as saying that the BOJ was engaging in "fine-tuning" the easy policy.[16]

The quotations above, when combined with the statements accompanying the interest rate increase about preemptively acting at the first signs of inflation (or even before), indicate that the Bank clearly wants to be seen as in charge of events rather than as just reacting. The desire to put the best light on the policies undertaken, and in times of low confidence to act as though in command, is certainly understandable on the part of a central bank, which always must concern itself with the credibility of its actions. Yet even if credibility for central banks is (to paraphrase Mervyn King) a matter of saying what one is going to do, and then doing what one says, it helps to be able to explain why one is doing what one is doing.

This need to explain the reasons for monetary policy decisions—in terms of ultimate goals, beliefs about the structure of the economy, and forecasts from current trends dependent on policy—is particularly important for independent central banks. Central banks can only remain independent over the long run if they have public support (Posen 1995), and public support requires a combination of competence, transparency, and accountability.

Since the BOJ gained independence in April 1998, its structure has built in a good amount of formal transparency. It publishes the minutes of its monthly monetary policy meetings (with only a one-meeting lag), recording the votes of its nine members and admitting their differences of opinion. Transparency of process alone, however, does not provide full transparency; an articulation of the central bank's goal, and enough information to track the bank's performance in meeting that goal over time, are also required.[17] Without a clearly defined goal, even if the goal is occasionally set aside (but with those instances explained), accountability is impaired. In the case of the BOJ, not only is there no standard to which to hold it accountable, there is no process by which the public can do so: no published inflation reports, no required testimony before the Diet, no direct role for elected officials in setting the BOJ's intermediate target.

In this context, attributing the BOJ's policy stance in recent years to a desire to assert its independence makes some sense. It also highlights just how far the BOJ is going beyond the practices of most other even newly independent central banks, and thus is reflecting its own beliefs about

16. See McCallum, "BOJ Watch." Since the inflation of the 1970s, most central banks have abjured the use of the term "fine-tuning" for fear that it gave the impression of excessive confidence and activism.

17. See the discussions of monetary transparency in Posen (1999) and Kuttner and Posen (2000).

independence rather than the behavior inherent to such banks. Independent central banks want to be seen as outside partisan control, and particularly as unwilling to subject policy to electoral demands; such banks will respond to what are believed to be unreasonable demands from the fiscal authority by publicizing their disapproval. In general, however, an independent central bank does not disagree with a policy proposal just because it comes from the government, does not set interest rates simply to demonstrate refusal of a government request, and does not provide less explanation to markets of its policy than do elected officials when it is in a public dispute with them.[18]

In the summer of 2000, the BOJ did all these things.[19] The supreme irony is that the BOJ behaved for the most part like an independent central bank from the mid-1970s to the mid-1990s, when it was formally under Ministry of Finance control—sufficiently so as to be an outlier in regressions of the relationship between independence and inflation (Walsh 1997), and to show no sign of engaging in political monetary cycles (Cargill, Hutchison, and Ito 1997)—meaning that it made its wishes known without engaging in open conflict with elected officials, as the "new" BOJ does. It will surprise no one that I therefore agree with Bernanke, my past coauthor on inflation targeting issues, in his assessment that "cooperation with the fiscal authorities in pursuit of a common goal is not the same as subservience." One need look no further than the US example of cooperation between the Alan Greenspan-led Federal Reserve and the Clinton administration to see the benefits that can be gained in so doing without loss of credibility.

In this light, it is clear that if part of the motivation for the BOJ's recent stance is a desire to assert its independence, it is doing so because of an idiosyncratic belief about what is necessary to take advantage of independence, not because independence requires it to take such actions. In fact, such obstreperousness by central banks, when unaccompanied by measures to enhance accountability, has occasionally backfired, with the result being diminished public support, and therefore diminished functional, if not legal, independence.

This is why I believe that Jinushi, Kuroki, and Miyao's claim that the BOJ would have made the same mistakes in the past decade if its strategy

---

18. See Bernanke et al. (1999) and Laubach and Posen (1997) for historical descriptions of the behavior of newly independent central banks (including that of the Reserve Bank of New Zealand, the Bank of Canada, the Bank of England, and the early history of the Bundesbank).

19. Hayami—in explaining the BOJ policy board's refusal to agree to a 1-month delay in voting in August 2000, requested by the Ministry of Finance in line with the new BOJ law—told reporters at a news conference: "It is precisely at such a time . . . that we must exercise our independence." See Bill Spindle, "Heard in Asia: Rate Rise Alone Is Unlikely to Spoil Japan's Recovery," *Asian Wall Street Journal*, 14 August 2000, 13.

had been one of "explicit inflation targeting" rather than "implicit" does not hold water. Perhaps deciding whether or not to prick the bubble would not have been made easier, but every decision since would have been improved. Simply put, if the BOJ had been required to state and justify an explicit, public, numerical goal for policy, its leadership would have had to admit that it was (and is) targeting zero measured inflation, and that it is doing so in pursuit of another goal rather than price stability per se—and such a policy would never have been allowed to stand. It would not have survived public scrutiny, whereas what Jinushi, Kuroki, and Miyao call the "implicit" framework for the BOJ has allowed an unjustifiable policy to be covered with smoke and mirrors.

Even better, had there been (as advocated by Bernanke et al. 1999) a strict division through an inflation target between goal dependence of the BOJ striving for the target set by elected officials, and an instrument of the BOJ setting policy as it chose to meet that target, there would have been full explanations of the reasons for the target, perhaps prompted by the central bank. In addition, there would have been an anchor for inflation expectations, which has been lacking due to the opaqueness of the BOJ's framework, and the absence of which has made any policy measures more risky.

So what ultimately is the motivation for the BOJ to pursue the policies it has in the past several years? The BOJ in general, and Governor Hayami in particular, want to impose sufficiently stringent credit and economic conditions on the Japanese economy so that inefficient businesses will have no choice but to shut down. The BOJ wants to use monetary policy to induce structural reforms. This was made evident by remarks by Governor Hayami after the ending of the ZIRP:

> Mr. Hayami also repeated his view that the zero interest rate policy was undermining structural reform in Japan and preventing the rise of promising high-tech industries. "If we retain zero interest rates indefinitely, these places will lose vitality . . . and it will end up being a minus for Japan's economic recovery."[20]

This was not a last-minute, individual rationalization, but a broadly held view at the bank:

> Yukata Yamaguchi, a career central bank official and member of the policy board, declared in a speech late last year that the many rate cuts the BOJ made in

20. Quoted in Spindle, "Heard in Asia." An alternative translation: "Explaining the Bank's move on Friday, Hayami said virtually free money was sapping Japan's economic dynamism. 'I think there may be a possibility this would work as a negative for the rebirth of the Japanese economy,' he said" (Jane Macartney, "Japan: Analysis - BOJ Crusader Hayami Draws Sword As Critics Circle," Reuters English News Service, 13 August 2000). The *Times of London* (12 August 2000, 21) put it thus: "[Hayami] said the 'free money' policy had encouraged irresponsible lending and provided companies with no incentive to embark on structural reform."

the 1990s "might have dampened the restructuring efforts at Japanese financial institutions." He warned that the central bank's easy-money experiment might result in a "Pyrrhic victory," where a deep recession is avoided but a true recovery can't be sustained, because too many bankers and businessmen put off painful restructuring. Mr. Hayami, who doesn't put it quite so bluntly in public, regularly warns of "moral hazards" in an economy where there's no real cost for borrowing heavily and delaying reform.[21]

It must be noted that in both Hayami (2000) and Yamaguchi (2000) there is slight backpedaling, whereby they say that while loose money induces moral hazard, the reduction of moral hazard alone is insufficient justification for lifting the ZIRP. Yet if raising interest rates cannot be justified on an economic basis alone, which it clearly cannot when zero measured inflation is what is being targeted in the face of a significant output gap, there must be some noneconomic basis behind this preference. It is clear that "creative destruction," invoked and praised repeatedly in Hayami's speeches, is the motivating ideology.

We have come a long way from the arguments about whether Japan is (or was) in a liquidity trap, and whether the BOJ could do anything about it, which was the primary subject of Bernanke's essay, and still is the main topic of discussion among academic monetary economists working on the Japanese situation. We have even gone beyond Jinushi, Kuroki, and Miyao's evidence that the BOJ is pursuing a demonstrably tighter monetary stance given economic conditions than it would have in the past, and doing so with predictably destabilizing effects on the real economy.

We are now into the realm of motivating faith. I will not rehash the arguments based on mainstream economics for why macroeconomic-policy-driven creative destruction is overrated,[22] because logic has little to do with faith. I will, however, point out three facts. First, there is no example of a central bank anywhere unilaterally inducing structural reform through its own tight monetary policy. Instead, an initiative from political authorities has always been required.

Second, there is little doubt that if an objective observer assessed the trade-off between, on the one hand, the costs and risks of a central bank keeping a debt-ridden economy in deflation and, on the other, the estimated benefits of the marginal increase in restructuring induced by tighter credit, the costs would significantly outweigh the benefits (especially given the lags before structural reform is felt relative to the compounded loss of wealth). Third, no Japanese citizen elected the BOJ to pursue this policy of promoting restructuring, and in fact no elected official delegated

21. Bill Spindle, "Hayami Sees Role as Enforcer—BOJ Chief Makes Case for Rate Rise to Force Firms to Restructure," *Asian Wall Street Journal*, 5 June 2000, 1. A similar self-definition was offered by Hayami in an interview done with *Business Week* the same month.

22. See the discussion in Posen (1998a, chap. 6).

this task to the BOJ or put the goal of "encouraging creative destruction" into its mandate.

Explaining why the BOJ has been able to sustain its self-appointment as "enforcer" is a matter of political science, not even political economy. What has been made clear for the political economy of monetary policy from these events in Japan, and from the essays in this book, is that neither benevolent welfare optimization nor institutional design is sufficient to explain policy choices by central banks. Ideas, sometimes economically misguided ones, also play a role.

References

Akerlof, George, William Dickens, and George Perry. 1996. The Macroeconomics of Low Inflation. *Brookings Papers on Economic Activity* 1: 1-59. Washington: Brookings Institution.

Ball, Laurence. 1994. What Determines the Sacrifice Ratio? In *Monetary Policy*, ed. N. Gregory Mankiw. Chicago: University of Chicago Press.

Barro, Robert. 1995. Inflation and Economic Growth. NBER Working Paper 5326. Cambridge, MA: National Bureau of Economic Research.

Bernanke, Ben S., and Mark Gertler. 1999. Monetary Policy and Asset Price Volatility. In *1999 Symposium: New Challenges for Monetary Policy*. Kansas City: Federal Reserve Bank of Kansas City.

Bernanke, Ben S., Thomas Laubach, Frederic S. Mishkin, and Adam S. Posen. 1999. *Inflation Targeting: Lessons from the International Experience*. Princeton, NJ: Princeton University Press.

Cargill, Thomas, Michael Hutchison, and Takatoshi Ito. 1997. *The Political Economy of Japanese Monetary Policy*. Cambridge, MA: MIT Press.

Debelle, Guy, and Stanley Fischer. 1994. How Independent Should a Central Bank Be? In *Goals, Guidelines, and Constraints Facing Monetary Policymakers*, ed. Jeffrey C. Fuhrer. Boston: Federal Reserve Bank of Boston.

Dornbusch, Rudiger, and Stanley Fischer. 1993. Moderate Inflation. *World Bank Economic Review* 7: 1-44. Washington: World Bank.

Fuhrer, Jeffrey C. 1995. The Persistence of Inflation and the Cost of Disinflation. *New England Economic Review*, January/February: 3-16.

Hayami, Masaru. 2000. Revitalization of Japan's Economy. Speech given at the Japanese Economic Research Center (29 May). http://www.boj.or.jp/en/press/koen053.htm.

King, Mervyn. 1997. Changes in UK Monetary Policy: Rules and Discretion in Practice. *Journal of Monetary Economics* 39: 81-87.

Krugman, Paul. 1999. It's Baaack: Japan's Slump and the Return of the Liquidity Trap. *Brookings Papers on Economic Activity* 2: 137-205. Washington: Brookings Institution.

Kuttner, Kenneth N., and Adam S. Posen. 2000. Inflation, Monetary Transparency, and G3 Exchange Rate Volatility. Working Paper 00-6 (July). Photocopy. Washington: Institute for International Economics.

Laubach, Thomas, and Adam S. Posen. 1997. Disciplined Discretion: Monetary Targeting in Germany and Switzerland. *Princeton Essays in International Finance* 206 (December).

Okina, Kunio. 1999. *Monetary Policy under Zero Inflation—A Response to Criticisms and Questions Regarding Monetary Policy*. Discussion Paper 99-E-20. Tokyo: Institute for International Monetary and Economic Studies, Bank of Japan.

Posen, Adam S. 1995. Declarations Are Not Enough: Financial-Sector Sources of Central Bank Independence. In *NBER Macroeconomics Annual*, ed. Ben S. Bernanke and Julio J. Rotemberg. Cambridge, MA: MIT Press.

Posen, Adam S. 1998a. Central Bank Independence and Disinflationary Credibility: A Missing Link? *Oxford Economic Papers* 50: 335-59.

Posen, Adam S. 1998b. *Restoring Japan's Economic Growth*. Washington: Institute for International Economics.

Posen, Adam S. 1999. No Monetary Masquerades for the ECB. In *The European Central Bank: How Accountable? How Decentralized?* ed. Ellen Meade. Washington: American Institute for Contemporary German Studies.

Rogoff, Kenneth. 1985. The Optimal Degree of Commitment to an Intermediate Monetary Target. *Quarterly Journal of Economics* 100, no. 4: 1169-89.

Sarel, Michael. 1996. Nonlinear Effects of Inflation on Economic Growth. *IMF Staff Papers* 43 (March): 199-215. Washington: International Monetary Fund.

Svensson, Lars E. O. 1997. Optimal Inflation Targets, "Conservative" Central Banks, and Linear Inflation Contracts. *American Economic Review* 87: 98-114.

Svensson, Lars E. O. 1999. How Should Monetary Policy Be Conducted in an Era of Price Stability? In *1999 Symposium: New Challenges for Monetary Policy*. Kansas City: Federal Reserve Bank of Kansas City.

Ueda, Kazuo. 1997. Japanese Monetary Policy, Rules or Discretion? A Reconsideration. In *Toward More Effective Monetary Policy*, ed. Iwao Kuroda. New York: St. Martin's Press.

Ueda, Kazuo. 1999. Remarks presented at a Federal Reserve Bank of Boston conference on monetary policy in a low-inflation environment. Woodstock, VT (20 October). http://www.boj.or.jp/en/press/koen043.htm.

Walsh, Carl. 1997. Inflation and Central Bank Independence: Is Japan Really an Outlier? Unpublished manuscript. Santa Cruz, CA: University of California.

Yamaguchi, Yukata. 2000. Thinking behind Current Monetary Policy. Remarks at the Japan National Press Club (4 August). http://www.boj.org.jp/en/press/koen058.htm.

The International Aspects of Japanese Monetary Policy

JEFFREY R. SHAFER

My friend and former counterpart, Eisuke Sakakibara, has given us an enlightening review of US-Japan economic and financial relations since President Clinton moved into the White House. It is enlightening because of the light it sheds on the mindset and worldview at the Ministry of Finance in Tokyo during the 1990s. From my vantage point, first at the US Treasury and subsequently in the private sector, the history of this period looks quite different. I will highlight the core elements of Sakakibara's view, then outline the case for an alternative view, and finally argue that Japan's economic recovery depends on its leaders recognizing more clearly that they are challenged much more by powerful fundamental forces than by US officials. There are some encouraging signs recently that this recognition is taking place.

Sakakibara seems to see Japan and the world as driven from Washington by means of symbolic actions: For him, the 1990s begin with President Clinton's inauguration. The major forces acting in his view seem to be the shifting personalities in the administration. Political pressures, public relations campaigns, threats of economic sanctions, and trade negotiations were the major market movers, in his view, and determined the course of entire economies. He gives little attention to what, in my view, were the fundamental actions in Washington that had a positive effect on the global economy—elimination of the US budget deficit; brilliant monetary policy; leadership in the completion of landmark trade agreements; and responses to threats to global financial stability emanating from Mexico, Asia, Russia, and Brazil that, if not perfect, nonetheless contained the damage to the global economy.

Even if I were to accept the position that ascribes overwhelming power to officials, my recollections would still lead me to a very different view of the process in Washington through which policy toward Japan was formulated and implemented from the one that Sakakibara has put for-

Jeffrey R. Shafer is managing director at Salomon Smith Barney, New York and former undersecretary for international affairs of the US Treasury.

ward. For example, I sensed no watershed in US international economic policy when Robert Rubin moved from the White House to the Treasury. Perhaps his more public role as Treasury secretary made those outside Washington more aware of his sound judgment and immense influence, but he and others of like mind shaped policy from the first days of the Clinton administration.

Sakakibara's vision of a battle in Washington between populists and macroeconomists is similarly unrecognizable to me, although it is understandable how the Clinton administration might be seen in this way from Tokyo. There were two objectives of administration economic policy toward Japan, both of which reflected vital US interests. The first objective was microeconomic: To achieve through negotiation the removal of Japanese impediments to imports and foreign investment, which created an unfair and unbalanced economic playing field in the global economy. There may initially have been some residue of old US views that saw Japan as threatening and as strengthened by its closed system. But by far the stronger motivation was the desire to further the development of a global economy with rules that would be seen and accepted as fair by all participants. Many of us also believed that the removal of impediments to the functioning of markets would serve to revitalize a Japanese economy that seemed incapable of sustained growth without threatening the stability of the global economy through the scale of its current account surpluses. The second objective was macroeconomic: To encourage and support sustained, domestic-demand-led growth in Japan and thereby contribute to a strong, stable global economy, on which the Clinton administration's strategy for the US economy critically depended.

Pursuit of the first of these objectives inherently involved tough negotiations, with all of their trappings, including the public relations efforts and confrontation that play such a prominent role in Sakakibara's history. The Japanese side gave as good as they got in this process. The second objective was, at times, pursued publicly, but was much more often a matter for private discussion to avoid giving a win-lose coloring to what was a win-win agenda. Thus, those of us with macroeconomic responsibilities in Washington may have been perceived in Tokyo as less confrontational than our trade colleagues. Occasional tactical conflicts between objectives undoubtedly reinforced this perception, but the reality was a strong consensus from the early days of the administration on the pursuit of both objectives, with a recognition across agencies that both objectives were important and that they were complementary in serving US interests.

Whatever the administration's goals with respect to economic relations with Japan, their pursuit had nowhere near the impact on the exchange rate or on the Japanese economy more broadly as did the fundamental economic forces that were at work. The difference in focus between concrete actions to improve fundamentals on the one hand and words and symbols on the other was an ongoing source of tension between Tokyo and Washington. If US pressure had been more successful in stimulating structural reforms or in encouraging growth policies, it would have had a stronger impact. There were some results on both fronts, but they were unfortunately gradual and, on the macroeconomic front, not sustained. Perhaps my greatest regret from my 4 years at the Treasury is that we failed in our quiet effort to dissuade the Japanese government from its mistaken tax increase of April 1997, which killed off the growth revival of 1996 that Sakakibara points to with justified pride. The result was disastrous for Japan. It also contributed to the Asian financial crisis later that year, when Japanese imports collapsed and distressed Japanese banks withdrew loans to other Asian countries.

Fundamentals account reasonably well for the major movements in exchange rates during the period. The dollar weakened against the yen in 1993 as the prospect of a decisive turnaround in the US budget deficit induced declining dollar interest rates. That such bullish news for the US economy should be bearish for the dollar was disconcerting to some reporters and commentators but no surprise to macroeconomists schooled in the Mundell-Fleming theory: Tightening fiscal policy and—to compensate for the aggregate demand effects—easing monetary conditions lead to a weakening of the currency in a floating exchange rate system. Europe was in recession in 1993, and interest rates fell sharply there, so dollar weakness was not evident against European currencies. In Japan, there was little further easing of interest rates, despite some slowing of growth, and the differential with the United States widened. This and a rising current account surplus in Japan were the fundamentals at work.

Yen appreciation was arrested during the winter of 1993-94 as markets responded strongly to preemptive Federal Reserve tightening, but resumed later in the year as the Fed eased off. In the first half of 1995, the Mexican debt crisis created expectations of weak North American economic activity and still lower US interest rates. At the same time, slow progress on both the structural and macroeconomic discussions with Japan meant that adjustment of the US-Japan trade imbalance, with the US budget deficit now shrinking, would require more exchange rate adjustment to compensate for the continued inflexibility and weak domestic demand.

These developments took the dollar-yen exchange rate to its record low in the spring of 1995. We at the Treasury were increasingly of the view that, although the direction was understandable in terms of fundamentals, the movement was extreme. We also looked ahead to Mexican stabilization and renewed strength in the US economy. It appeared to be one of those infrequent occasions when intervention could contribute to a durable correction. It did, although we will never know how much the intervention accelerated a turnaround that would almost certainly have come at some point.

From the late spring of 1995 until 1998, the dollar was strong against the yen. One fundamental force behind this is evident only with hindsight: The trend productivity growth rate of the US economy ratcheted up about 1 percentage point in the middle of the decade, bringing with it strong investment demand and attractive returns to those who placed capital in the United States. This put persistent upward pressure on the dollar. Once Japan slipped back into recession in 1997 and much of the rest of Asia found itself in crisis, the trend in the currency gained momentum.

Once again, a case could be made that the response of the dollar-yen rate to the fundamentals eventually became overdone. As this became clearer, the US authorities were willing to engage in cooperative action despite the absence of clear indications that fundamental trends were changing. (By this time, I was no longer on the Treasury team and therefore have no information concerning their specific thinking.) The yen did not respond at first, but began to recover when new fundamentals did emerge: a change of policy in Tokyo that brought meaningful fiscal stimulus, an effective response to the banking crisis, and a resumption of growth. The reduction of market liquidity following the Russian crises undoubtedly reinforced the turnaround for a time as investors covered exposures of all types, including short yen positions. But the stronger tone to the yen outlasted these technical conditions in the market.

Throughout virtually all of President Clinton's term, the relevant authorities favored a strong dollar and said so. Treasury Secretary Bentsen did make one on-the-run statement at the very beginning of his term that suggested he would welcome a lower dollar, a statement that I know he regretted. No subsequent statements or interviews succeeded in fully correcting the impression left then, because fundamental forces were pushing the yen upward and the dollar down. The trend was reversed sometime after Robert Rubin came to the Treasury and the fundamentals turned around. From time to time after the dollar turnaround, one continued to hear statements from others in Washington that earlier would have been interpreted as bearish for the dollar. But now markets ignored them. The record strongly suggests that the fundamentals drove the exchange rate and these exchange rate movements drove the perception of statements. It was not the statements or the sterilized intervention that created the durable movements in the markets.

It could hardly have been otherwise. An overwhelming body of empirical research suggests that the instrument available to a Treasury secretary—sterilized intervention—has a relatively small and short-lived effect on the market, except when it comes at a time of changing fundamentals. How, then, could what the Treasury says or is thought to believe have much impact when the actions it could take have so little effect? I would not argue that they have no effect, and I do not believe my former colleagues would either. That is why Treasury and Ministry of Finance officials are well advised to choose their words carefully in order to avoid unintended consequences in the markets. But the fundamentals are by far the most important determinant of exchange rates.

A focus on the fundamentals led the Clinton administration to put its energy into eliminating the budget deficit and reducing barriers to the export of US goods, services, and investment as keys to better US economic performance. The Federal Reserve was expected to conduct monetary policy so as to allow maximum growth consistent with low inflation, and it did so. The exchange rate, by and large, was seen as the by-product of these policies and of other forces beyond official control, including economic developments abroad.

By contrast, Sakakibara's review minimizes the role that Japan's own authorities could have played in getting the Japanese economy on track sooner and paints a picture of an economy driven by the exchange rate, which in turn was managed erratically by US officials. In fact, Japanese officials have gotten results when they have focused on fundamental policy actions, as they did in 1995 to get recovery going (only to be derailed by the U-turn of April 1997), or as they did again in 1999.

If Japanese officials keep their focus on what they can do to improve Japan's fundamentals on both the macroeconomic and structural fronts, the Japanese economy will become healthier and the global economy more stable. This strategy will also reduce pressures that move the exchange rate in a direction problematic from the standpoint of Japan's economic performance. In the end, however, the exchange rate will not always behave as one government might wish, because it reflects a range of fundamentals, including forces acting abroad. Although there are times when it is both in the interests of governments to intervene cooperatively and in their power to influence the market, which may have drifted from fundamentals, these times are infrequent. Policy strategies need to be resilient in the face of exchange rate movements, as well as other shocks. This could serve as a definition of sound policy fundamentals.

Index

About the Contributors

Ben S. Bernanke is chair of the department of economics and the Howard Harrison and Gabrielle Snyder Beck Professor of Economics and Public Affairs at the Woodrow Wilson School of Public and International Affairs, Princeton University. A macroeconomist with interests in business cycles and macroeconomic policy, he is coauthor of *Inflation Targeting: Lessons from the International Experience* and editor of *The NBER Macroeconomics Annual*. Bernanke's research has focused on monetary policy, the role of financial markets in economic fluctuations, and the economics of the Great Depression.

Olivier Blanchard is the chairman of the economics department and Class of 1941 Professor of Economics at the Massachusetts Institute of Technology. His primary field of interest is macroeconomics. He is member of the American Academy of Arts and Sciences, research associate at the National Bureau of Economic Research, member of the Brookings Panel on Economic Activity, and Membre du Conseil d'Analyse Economique aupres du Premier Ministre, Paris. He is also a fellow at the Econometric Society since 1985. Among his many publications are *Restoring Europe's Prosperity*, macroeconomic papers from the Centre for European Policy Studies, which he coauthored with Rudiger Dornbusch and Richard Layard; and *The Economics of Post-Communist Transition* (1998).

Benjamin M. Friedman is the William Joseph Maier Professor of Political Economy, and former chairman of the department of economics at Harvard University. He is the author of *Day of Reckoning: The Consequences of American Economic Policy Under Reagan and After*, which received the

George Eccles Prize, awarded annually by Columbia University for excellence in writing about economics. He also serves as director of the Private Export Funding Corporation, adviser to the Federal Reserve Bank of New York, and trustee of the Standish Investment Trust. He is also member of the Brookings Panel on Economic Activity and the Council on Foreign Relations.

Robert R. Glauber joined the John F. Kennedy School of Government at Harvard University as adjunct lecturer after serving as undersecretary of finance of the Treasury (1989-92). He was responsible for domestic policy, which included the regulatory overhaul and recapitalization of the savings and loan industry and proposals for reform of commercial banks to permit interstate branching and broader products. Prior to joining the Treasury, Glauber was professor of finance at the Harvard Business School and chairman of its Advanced Management Program. In 1987, he served as executive director of the commission appointed by President Reagan to study the October 1987 stock market crash. His research interests focus on the performance and regulation of financial institutions and markets and on corporate governance issues.

Toshiki Jinushi is professor at Kobe University, Japan. He graduated from Harvard University. His areas of specialization are American economic theory, especially US financial system and monetary policy, and macroeconomics.

Anil K. Kashyap is professor of economics at the Graduate School of Business, University of Chicago, since 1991. He also serves as coeditor of the *Journal of Business* and is also on the editorial board of the *Journal of the Japanese and International Economics*, the *Journal of Financial Intermediation*, and the *Journal of Risk Finance*. He is also a member of the University of Chicago's Center for East Asian Studies, a consultant for the research departments of the European Central Bank and the Federal Reserve Bank of Chicago. Under the auspices of the National Bureau of Economic Research, he serves as the head of a working group that studies the Japanese economy. Professor Kashyap has also served as a staff economist for the Board of Governors of the Federal Reserve System.

Yoshihiro Kuroki is professor in the department of economics, Osaka Prefecture University, Japan. He is member of the Research Group of International Comparative Financial Studies at Kobe University. He has written extensively on macroeconomics and monetary policy.

Ryoichi Mikitani is professor of economics at Kobe Gaikuin University, Japan, and author of several books in Japanese. His area of specialization is monetary economics. He was trained at Harvard University and is a frequent visitor to the United States. He is member of the Research Group of International Comparative Financial Studies at Kobe University. He is coauthor of *Japan's New Central Banking Law: A Critical Review* (published by The Center on Japanese Economy and Business at Columbia University). He coedited *Monetary Policy and Financial Liberalization* (1993).

Ryuzu Miyao is associate professor at the Research Institute for Economics & Business Administration of Kobe University, Japan, since April 1995. He completed a master's program in economics from Kobe University in March 1989 and a PhD program in economics from Harvard University in November 1994. His current research interests include macro and monetary economics in Pan-Pacific countries and applied time series econometrics. His PhD thesis was *Essays on Money and Output*, and the master's thesis was *Portfolio Behavior and the Term Structure of Interest Rates*. His papers have been published in *the Journal of Money, Credit, and Banking*, and the *Journal of Japanese and International Economics*, among other publications.

Adam S. Posen, senior fellow, is the author of *Restoring Japan's Economic Growth* (1998; Japanese translation, 1999), and a member of the Council on Foreign Relations Task Force on Japan. A monetary economist, he was on the research staff of the Federal Reserve Bank of New York (1994-97), and is the author of several publications on comparative monetary policymaking, inflation targeting and central bank independence.

Eisuke Sakakibara is professor at Kieo University, Japan, and former vice minister of finance for international affairs in Japan. He has worked as economist with the International Monetary Fund (1971-75). He also served as associate professor of economics at the Institute for Policy Science, Harvard University (1977-80), president of the Institute of Fiscal and Monetary Policy (1994), director of several Japanese government divisions including the Treasury Division, Government Debt Division, Coordination Division of Financial Bureau (1981-89), and director-general of the International Finance Bureau (1995). His work has been published in the American Economic Review, Journal of International Economics, and Foreign Affairs. He is the author of *Beyond Capitalism/The Japanese Model of Market Economics*.

Jeffrey R. Shafer is managing director and vice chairman of Salomon Brothers International Ltd since 1997. Prior to that, he had broad responsibility for international economic and financial issues at the US Treasury, first as assistant secretary and then as undersecretary for international affairs. He has focused on strengthening economic growth and financial stability in both developed and developing countries, fostering financial market development and liberalization, and strengthening multilateral development banks. Before joining the Treasury, he served in high-ranking positions at the Organization for Economic Cooperation and Development, the Federal Reserve System and the Council of Economic Advisers.

He holds degrees in economics from Princeton University (A.B.) and Yale University (MPhil and PhD).

Yoshinori Shimizu is dean of the School of Management at Hitotsubashi University, Japan, and member of the Committee for Advancement of Financial System and Services, Ministry of Finance, Japan. He is a frequent contributor to both English and Japanese journals.

Ingram Content Group UK Ltd.
Milton Keynes UK
UKHW012008280423
420963UK00001B/48